BUDGET JUSTICE

Budget Justice

ON BUILDING GRASSROOTS
POLITICS AND SOLIDARITIES

CELINA SU

PRINCETON UNIVERSITY PRESS

PRINCETON & OXFORD

Copyright © 2025 by Celina Su

Princeton University Press is committed to the protection of copyright and the intellectual property our authors entrust to us. Copyright promotes the progress and integrity of knowledge created by humans. By engaging with an authorized copy of this work, you are supporting creators and the global exchange of ideas. As this work is protected by copyright, any reproduction or distribution of it in any form for any purpose requires permission; permission requests should be sent to permissions@press.princeton.edu. Ingestion of any IP for any AI purposes is strictly prohibited.

Published by Princeton University Press
41 William Street, Princeton, New Jersey 08540
99 Banbury Road, Oxford OX2 6JX

press.princeton.edu

GPSR Authorized Representative: Easy Access System Europe - Mustamäe tee 50, 10621 Tallinn, Estonia, gpsr.requests@easproject.com

All Rights Reserved

Library of Congress Cataloging-in-Publication Data

Names: Su, Celina, 1977- author
Title: Budget justice: solidarities and politics from below / Celina Su.
Description: Princeton: Princeton University Press, 2025. | Includes bibliographical references and index.
Identifiers: LCCN 2024054097 (print) | LCCN 2024054098 (ebook) | ISBN 9780691251318 hardback | ISBN 9780691251455 ebook
Subjects: LCSH: Municipal government—Citizen participation | Municipal budgets—Citizen participation | City dwellers—Political activity | Social justice—Economic aspects | BISAC: POLITICAL SCIENCE / Public Policy / Economic Policy | SOCIAL SCIENCE / Activism & Social Justice
Classification: LCC JS78.S858 2025 (print) | LCC JS78 (ebook) | DDC 323/.042—dc23/eng/20250312
LC record available at https://lccn.loc.gov/2024054097
LC ebook record available at https://lccn.loc.gov/2024054098

British Library Cataloging-in-Publication Data is available

Editorial: Bridget Flannery-McCoy, Dave McBride, and Alena Chekanov
Production Editorial: Theresa Liu
Text Design: Carmina Alvarez
Jacket/Cover Design: Marina Drukman
Production: Erin Suydam
Publicity: James Schneider
Copyeditor: Cindy Milstein

Jacket image: frimages / iStock

This book has been composed in Arno

Printed in the United States of America

10 9 8 7 6 5 4 3 2 1

For Althea, Ellen, and Åstra,
who notice and, with loving care, tend the seedlings.

CONTENTS

Prologue: *Linchpins of Solidarities*   ix

Introduction: *Budgeting Justice*   1

PART I.
OPACITY ABETS AUSTERITY

1. Moral Documents   17

2. Flip the Gaze   26

3. Follow the Money   39

4. Austerity for Profit   51

5. A Right-to-the-City Budget   64

    INTERLUDE: *An Interview with Makani Themba*   72

PART II.
DEMOCRACY IS A DAILY PRACTICE

6. No Taxation without Participation   85

    INTERLUDE: *An Interview with Tarson Núñez*   94

7. An Invitation to Participatory Budgeting   106

8. Terms of Deliberation   118

viii CONTENTS

9. Actionable Knowledges   131

10. No Algorithms, No Shortcuts   144

PART III.
CITIZENS MAKE CITIES

11. Neighborly Citizenship   157

12. Inventive Solidarities   169

13. Budget Lines of Desire   181

    INTERLUDE: *An Interview with Marc Serra Solé*   194

14. Insurgent Budgeting   207

Epilogue   219

Acknowledgments   231

Notes   235

Index   265

PROLOGUE

Linchpins of Solidarities

I MOVED to the United States from Brazil in the late 1980s. Newly arrived in New York City and then moving around the Northeast, my father took computer programming classes at DeVry, as advertised with 1-800 numbers on Saturday afternoon network TV; he became a computer programmer. My mother had taken similar classes in Brazil and became a database systems analyst. Sometimes my parents had trouble finding full-time jobs, and I remember my father coming home with fingers riddled with pinpricks he got from folding button-down shirts at Macy's. As a teenager, I took on jobs tutoring for $4 an hour, babysitting for $3 an hour, working in a bookstore for $6.02 an hour, and delivering the free local newspaper and marveling at the $5 tip one household gave me before the winter holidays. If I thought about socioeconomic class at all, my focus was limited to my own family, and how I might contribute to alleviating the ever-present sense of financial precarity. I rarely thought about other households; when I did so, it was usually to envy the Joneses.

I thought I wanted to go into business. In college, I majored in economics and English. I went on to work as an economics research assistant at the Brookings Institution in Washington, DC, as my first full-time job. Princeton professor Alan Blinder and the founding director of the Congressional Budget Office, Alice Rivlin, were my first bosses. When I got into MIT for graduate school, I called my parents with the news. I remember my father stating, "You did OK"—as in, "Good job; you did all right"—for what felt like the first time in my life. In that moment, I could so easily be read as a model minority, as an embodiment of the American dream, as if I wore proper boots with nice, long bootstraps.

I moved to the United States from Brazil in the late 1980s; that part is true. But the rest of my story has many different versions. I moved just in time for the glory years of middle school, not knowing any English. I didn't recognize some of the new math notation and kept getting Ds. When I asked questions in class, I was told, "MYOB." I wondered what "myob" (which I mentally pronounced "miobe," as if it were a biological microbe) meant until I realized, years later, that it stood for "mind your own business." At home, meanwhile, I listened to my parents describe feeling humiliated in job interviews—not getting a turn to speak in a group interview with twentysomething-year-olds, or being denigrated for their accents. Eventually, my math grades improved, and I approached the school's vice principal and asked, probably in grammatically improper English, to switch classes. I was given a test to graph basic equations, something like $y = 2x$. A few weeks later, I was placed into advanced math, skipping two years of the pre-algebra coursework. I couldn't have done well on the qualifying exam, since I had no idea what letters were doing in math equations. I don't know what prompted the administration to suddenly label me an honors kid. My educational achievements were probably shaped as much by chance—and the vice principal's presumptions that my Chinese heritage said something about my math abilities—as they were by my own efforts, if not more so.

In high school, I simply went through the motions of being a student, without a calling or strong community to lend me a sense of mission. I remember a classmate skipping lunch junior year so that she could take an additional AP science class; I could not relate. Friends whose families had strong ethnic or religious networks filled me with envy. I was into fashion and sewed a different (sloppy, punk, "wannabe punk") outfit for each day of an entire grade. Rather than simply covet preppy clothes I could not afford, I made "weird" clothes. In college, I occasionally showed up to affinity group meetings—like ones for Asian Americans—but never felt quite at ease there. With a vague sense of political and class consciousness, I sympathized with, but was not actively involved in, student actions regarding sweatshop labor conditions.

Back in São Paulo, it had been my job during our Sunday trips to Eldorado Supermercado to check the price of our brand of powdered milk and report it to my parents. How many zeroes at the end? As I moved to the United States, the movie *Gung Ho*, about US factory workers learning about just-in-time assembly line protocols from Japanese managers, played in movie theaters; pundits feared a Japanese "takeover" after the Mitsubishi estate conglomerate took control of Rockefeller Center. I grew up hearing about political economic conditions being talked about as national cultures—first as Brazilian ineptitude with their economy, and then as American laziness and entitlement.

I moved to the United States from Brazil in the late 1980s, when I learned to respect authority, but also that official narratives could not always be trusted. Because I was not yet sixteen when my parents became naturalized citizens, I automatically became one as well, without documentation. According to some federal databases, I am a citizen; according to others, I am not. This felt apropos given that my father's documents misstate his birthplace, his birth country, and my mother's her birth date. While I was growing up in Brazil, it was my job to note not only the official Brazilian cruzeiro to US dollar currency exchange rate but also the real, "black market" one, and to report both of these to my parents. In my family, our official histories are mistaken and our real ones become apocryphal.

I internalized the adage that "a penny saved is a penny earned," but my numbers did not compute. When I managed to secure an additional scholarship during college, for instance, my school reduced its financial aid package by the same amount. Even my mother's job at IBM, which I had thought of as a bulwark of stable, staid corporate culture, felt precarious. Years before either of us heard of the "gig economy," IBM made her apply for temporary gigs within the company every few months. She hated competing against her colleagues instead of working *with* them. For everyone in my family, the long-standing formula for financial security felt increasingly difficult to follow.

Maybe I was a late bloomer, reliant on adolescent signifiers along with a taste in clothes, film, and music to stand in for my own analyses and politics. I had trouble envisioning practices of solidarity outside of art, through zine making and the like. I had received a lot of lessons about self-reliance and interpersonal kindness, and Republicans versus Democrats, but I had little exposure to unions, community organizing, worker cooperatives, coordinated mutual aid, or different forms of collective action. And maybe, too, I had inherited a distrust of institutional politics and desire for politics in another form.

———

During my year at the Brookings Institution, I researched what sorts of public policies might contribute to better cities, and this usually translated into analyzing which policies might bring governments so-called bang for their buck. I attended multiple academic conferences with titles like Does Money Matter? Still, public budgets and their justifications sometimes made little sense to me. No actual, well-heeled person I knew sent their kids to overcrowded, underfunded schools in low-tax school districts. I turned my research to questions of struggle and power.

A decade later, I had an opportunity to give a guest lecture in a class on education inequities and youth-led social movements, taught by critical social theorist and education researcher Jean Anyon. At the end, she asked me a question I return to now: "I was a red diaper baby. My family imbued me with these politics. How did *you* end up here?"

What location is "here"? A political position? A literal place? I had no easy answer for how I'd arrived. For a long time, I hated the messiness of my story, that there were multiple true, yet somehow unreliable, versions relating to my class mobility and politics.

It took me years to realize that the contradictions in my story were its point, not a distraction. They delimited what I thought of as politically possible, probable, and righteous. When told in racialized terms, for example, my story is sometimes a triumphant model minority one, reaping the benefits of honors math. At other times, I felt the brunt of the flip side of racial stereotypes, too—that Asian Americans are "demure and weak," "soft targets." This occasionally made me feel self-conscious when I tried to speak up for myself, as if I was going off script. I witnessed how all stereotypes, from "yellow fever" to "yellow peril," subject people to impossible scripts.

The contradictions taught me about myself, certainly, but also about the larger structures of statecraft and empire in which I'm embedded. I was familiar with the consequences of racist tropes on an individual level, yet I realized that I had not sufficiently thought about their consequences on a policy level. They showed me, in deeply personal ways, how race and class cannot be separated out as variables, and how they color not just my life but every social and economic institution around me as well. How did popular understandings of Asian Americans' deservingness shape food assistance, school funding, and parks planning, I wondered? What was the role of "Asian Americanness"—however characterized—in justifying current public policies, whether for or against supposed "welfare queens" or "anchor babies"?

The indispensable work of scholars on Asian American subject positions, experiences, and understandings demonstrates that such contradictions are not to be explained away, but instead made the center of analysis. Interdisciplinary scholar Lisa Lowe details how the "life conditions, choices, and expressions of Asian Americans have been significantly determined by the US state" through immigration policies, enfranchisements, and processes of citizenship.[1] Asian Americans have not failed to properly assimilate; rather, they have succeeded in playing their roles as the "foreigner within." Political scientist Claire Jean Kim likewise upends any notion of neat binaries or even a linear spectrum, with Asian Americans and Latine Americans "between" White and Black Americans.[2] In her racial triangulation theory, she traces how Asian Americans are portrayed as "superior" to Black Americans—and thus more deserving of some social benefits—along one axis, but also less American—and hence less deserving of others—along another axis.[3] Such work shows that simultaneous and selective foreignness and respectability, mocked accents and MATH hats (as worn and touted by Andrew Yang), are what render Asian Americans quintessentially American.

American "meritocracy" requires Asian Americans as moving targets to justify educational inequities and enshrine inequalities, as in the

Harvard admissions court case, to then be cast aside or stigmatized if anything goes awry, like when post-9/11 recovery funding disproportionately benefited Tribeca and largely excluded neighboring Chinatown.[4] It assumes that the children of Chinese immigrants who came to the United States as graduate students belong in the same category as the children of refugees who moved here after the US involvement in the Vietnam War. This harms Asian Americans, too, by masking and ignoring high rates of poverty (and suffering from post-traumatic stress syndrome) in some communities, and trivializing the role of US economic and foreign policies in fueling immigration. Long histories of anti-Asian, anti-Black, anti-Latine, and anti-Indigenous policies are erased.

I understood from my research that better public policies *need* mobilized publics. Anyone's question about the journey to my political "here" reminded me that deciphering the role of people *like* me in popular discourse—however construed—is essential to everyday citizens' contributions to democratic politics. That Asian Americans play critical roles as wedges in politics around school admissions, for instance, means that we can also be critical linchpins in solidarities.

———

It was in summer 2020 that I started thinking about "budget justice" as an especially helpful framing for conversations about racial justice, democracy, and political economy, not as separate issues, but as inextricably intertwined ones. I was struck by how a phrase that sounded technocratic and policy wonk-y became a rallying cry, written on so many of the placards I saw at Black Lives Matter protests against police brutality. In this context, the framing of budget justice emphasized how George Floyd's death implicated more than any single police officer, or the culture of any particular police department.

The desperation and fervor of this structural analysis took on special resonance during the COVID-19 pandemic, when my sense of time seemed to warp with everyone's typical routines suddenly placed in suspension. In particular, what environmental justice writer and activist

Rob Nixon calls "slow violence"—gradual and often invisible killings by facially neutral forces like "natural" disasters or epidemics—collided with typical, hypervisible "fast" violence—that of speeding bullets and punches in the gut.[5]

Especially during the first days, the *pan-* part of the pandemic (affecting virtually everyone, everywhere) felt profound. I felt like I and those around me could swap stories and compare notes in ways we ordinarily would not. Via Zoom class sessions, I got to peer into my City University of New York (CUNY) students' apartments in disarmingly intimate ways. I saw that most of my students did not have their own desk spaces, so that relatives in various states of dress walked behind them. Some students were caring for chronically ill parents or grandparents. When we had to decide between different protocols in class, these students begged their classmates to err on the side of caution and abide by the precautionary principle of "first do no harm," since they risked their loved ones' lives by attending class in person.

Patterns emerged. Nationally, the Navajo Nation reported more COVID-19 cases per capita than any US state.[6] The Diné (as the Navajo call themselves) people's ability to contain infections was affected by rates of underlying illnesses, a lack of electricity among a third of households, and at least for some, "the failure of the United States to live up to its treaty obligations to Native Nations."[7]

In cities, neighborhoods that suffered from police violence were also those that suffered the highest COVID-19 rates. I was aware of different New York City neighborhoods' poverty rates, but it was an entirely different experience to watch mediating factors—regarding how equipped each of us was to protect ourselves—play out over the course of mere days and weeks. The pandemic crystallized inequalities, or what epidemiologists call the social determinants of health. I thought of geographer Ruth Wilson Gilmore's definition of racism: "The state-sanctioned or extralegal production and exploitation of group-differentiated vulnerability to premature death."[8]

That spring, I heard ambulance sirens every few minutes; I saw multiple neighbors being carried out of their homes on stretchers. In Elmhurst, Queens, the hospital morgue could not keep up with the alarming death rate, so refrigerated trailer trucks stored the bodies of victims in the hospital parking lot. I realize now that I was simply bearing witness to slow violence in real time.

———

Then President Trump weaponized the fact that the COVID-19 virus was first identified in Wuhan, China, by nicknaming it the "China virus" and condoning the fact that a White House official called it "kung flu."[9] As the virus spread across the United States, Asian Americans reported a surge in racially motivated acts of violence. In response, some Asian American groups advocated for more policing and more punitive policies against individual perpetrators. A group called Asians Fighting Injustice, for example, worked to limit bail reform and lower thresholds of what constituted hate crimes. The March 16, 2021, shootings in Atlanta spas, where six of the eight victims were women of Asian descent, prompted Congress to pass the COVID-19 Hate Crimes Act with rare bipartisan support. In May 2021, with lightning speed, then President Joseph Biden signed it into law. The law provided grant money to law enforcement agencies nationwide.

But other Asian American groups, such as 18 Million Rising, questioned why policymakers were so focused on punishing individual perpetrators as their main response, especially when so many Americans were out in the streets protesting police-perpetrated violence as well. They asked policymakers to instead bolster programs that would protect vulnerable Asian Americans, such as those who currently work in massage parlors and are particularly at risk for exploitation and abuse.[10] They also pointed to histories of policies that made Asian American women vulnerable targets in the first place. (It is telling that even before the Chinese Exclusion Act, the Page Act of 1875 focused explicitly on Chinese women because they were foreigners associated with sex work, and as such, deemed by the American Medical Association to carry "distinct germs to which they were immune, but from which white [men] would die if exposed."[11] They were deemed simultaneously alluring, subservient, filthy, and repulsive.)

Around the country, Asian Americans grappled with questions of safety. My students of all racial and ethnic backgrounds, too, debated: If not more police, what might public safety look like? If harsher punishments did not necessarily make them feel safer, what would? The work of collective decision-making and building solidarities felt formidable, and they were scared and tired. I felt moved by their grapplings, even or especially when they resisted slogans and found no easy answers.

———

Amid the devastation and violence, the pandemic also created new, urgent possibilities for connection. Even in mandated physical isolation, with classes conducted over Zoom, I felt nourished by my students attending online classes alone together in their respective homes and extending care to each other in new ways. They became more sensitive to others' extenuating circumstances. Hearing about a classmate's inability to access essential services, they shared tips on how to get online groceries for grandparents; they offered to do three-way calling and provide language interpretation in talking to a city agency. Friends do these sorts of things for one another all the time. What struck me was that my students did not make these gestures privately right after class; they explicitly worked to make them routine, for everyone.

Outside school, my neighbors also quickly mobilized to help one another. Flyers on every block announced phone numbers to call or text if someone needed groceries. Community fridges popped up around the neighborhood. Online, people organized meetings, schedules, and databases of both volunteers and folks in need. Both impromptu Google forms and more established websites like mutualaid.nyc simply asked visitors to identify whether they needed help or could help, and connected them with the right people. Those who could not help in person but instead could offer other skills, like graphic design, did so.

Few of the mutual aid efforts I observed questioned whether those who requested help "deserved" it. When collectives did prioritize helping certain groups, their criteria were more likely to focus on vulnerability or need than merit. My neighbors were not so naive as to think that no one would take advantage of them. But they wanted to spend their energy extending care, as opposed to policing each other.

Many of the reservations I previously had regarding mutual aid and alternative institution building for not being political enough, for letting the state abdicate its responsibilities, softened. I did not suddenly think that all neighborhood activities were inherently political. But, in the face of state failure in helping communities navigate the pandemic, I came to better appreciate the political possibilities of cooperation in a way that meets the needs even of those typically deemed undeserving—those without jobs, those simply in need.

—————

I share these personal anecdotes not as data, but rather as glimpses into how I came to formulate the questions that animate this book. The messiness of my story—in my schooling, sense of socioeconomic mobility or immobility vis-à-vis personal and public budgets, and relationship to different forms of political organizing and expression—met the complexity of events since 2020 to prompt new examinations of the road to budget justice. It galvanized me to oppose austerity as default policy, to work to disrupt racial hierarchies embedded in public policies, and to enable all of us to become political members of our communities.

For this, I am convinced that we must democratize how budgets get made—by organizing everyday citizens and building coalitions. And attempts to salvage or nurture our democracy and its institutions must, in turn, address not only growing political polarization but also growing economic inequalities—moving beyond experiments promoting civil discourse, deliberation, or inclusion, to shift our political economy.

BUDGET JUSTICE

Introduction

BUDGETING JUSTICE

ON MAY 25, 2020, an African American man named George Floyd was murdered by a White police officer, Derek Chauvin. Chauvin knelt on Floyd's neck and back for over nine minutes, until Floyd could no longer breathe. That summer, twenty-six million people participated in protests against police brutality and aligned with Black Lives Matter, making them the largest movement in US history.[1] The protesters foregrounded the need for institutional reforms and demanded that cities nationwide divest from police.

To me, that summer demonstrated that organizing related to budgets could make a profound difference—putting pressure on governmental bodies, foundations, and even corporations to do something about issues of equity. Bureaucracies could codify inequalities, but institutions could also be made accountable. I especially appreciated the many conversations I observed over what rules neighbors wished to live by, what communities might want or need to invest in, and what communities want to divest from. I was surrounded, in other words, by struggles for budget justice: public budgets that give everyone, especially those from historically marginalized communities, resources and power to address their needs.

In the years since, responses have been woefully inadequate. Though Chauvin was found guilty of killing Floyd, the prosecution's case hardly mentioned race. Beyond his conviction, cities around the country issued apology statements for institutionalized racism—acknowledging the role of urban planners in disinvestment of Black communities—and formed commissions for racial justice. But the results have been disappointing. The Philadelphia commission on Pathways to Reform, Transformation, and Reconciliation, for instance, launched economic programs aimed at Black small business owners, not wageworkers, freelancers, and the unemployed.

These moves give companies and governments a semblance of righteous action, even as they leave intact the histories and structures that enable police violence. They fail to redistribute funds toward new visions of community safety, freedom, and spaces where all individuals can flourish.

Meanwhile, it is not a coincidence that people around the United States continued to experience a grave affordability crisis. Both city- and household-level budget crunches have only become more acute. Between an end of federal assistance from the American Recovery and Reinvestment Act, an economic downturn, and seemingly endless euphemistic "rightsizing" by corporate employers, US households are suffering.

After the pandemic, lower- and middle-income New Yorkers, disproportionately Black and Latine ones, left the city in droves. They could no longer afford to live in the city. But New York will not function properly without them. As sociologist Andrew Beveridge put it, "If you want a subway system, an office sector, a restaurant industry, you need these people."[2]

I myself questioned whether my family's financial anxieties were exceptional or widespread, until I read that New York lost at least one-third of its childcare workers from 2020 to 2023. Most of them are women of color and cannot afford to live in the city.[3] Further, City Comptroller Brad Lander released a report stating that, "From 2019 to 2024, the average cost of child care for infants and toddlers in family-based care grew a whopping 79% (to $18,200), and center-based care was up 43% (to $26,000)—while the growth in average hourly earnings was only 13%." It is no wonder that over the same time period, families with young children left the city in droves.[4]

So I looked up the hourly rates my family paid for my child's day care—caring, safe, home-based programs without frills like fancy facilities or a Montessori curriculum. We paid $14 an hour in 2020, or approximately $2,500 a month for care so that two parents could work full-time. My child then began to attend public school. But had she needed full-time childcare just three years later, we would be paying $20 an hour, or around $3,600 a month.

The federal government states that childcare is considered affordable when it costs less than 7 percent of a household's income. For $3,600 a month to be considered affordable, a family would need a household income of over $600,000.

The childcare affordability crisis is a nationwide one.[5] A 2024 national survey found that instead of the recommended 7 percent, families were spending an average of 24 percent of their income on childcare, and that 47 percent of families reported spending more than $18,000 on childcare the previous year.[6] How could they balance their family budgets? When Congress's Joint Finance Committee in 2023 refused to extend pandemic era funding, experts predicted the eventual closure of 70,000 childcare centers around the country, jeopardizing care for 3.2 million kids.[7]

What can be done? In New York, both the city mayor and state governor repeatedly rejected proposals to tax the wealthy, fearing that any tax hikes would prompt millionaires and billionaires to move elsewhere.[8] But an analysis from the nonpartisan Fiscal Policy Institute finds that the top 1 percent of New Yorkers (individuals earning incomes of more than $815,000 a year) have not left the city since the pandemic. In fact, they generally move at much lower rates than lower-income earners; further, when they do leave New York, they tend to move to other high-tax states.[9] The report suggests that raising taxes could help fund programs like universal childcare without scaring away millionaires, who after all can afford to live wherever they please.

These different dimensions of budget justice—policing and childcare, safety and affordability for everyone—are often parceled into separate conversations, but they are profoundly linked.

4 BUDGET JUSTICE

Budget justice requires a new sort of democracy that emphasizes three points of analysis and practice: first, budgets are moral documents that make explicit what communities choose to *divest from* and *invest in*; second, *direct democracy* must engage everyday constituents rather than elected representatives in a range of decision-making conversations and actions about collective needs; and third, in turn, city residents must themselves practice *new modes of citizenship* as neighbors as opposed to individual consumers or members of voting blocs. Together, these practices will help communities to imagine, articulate, and forward truly different public policies—not just bandages to make the status quo a bit more tolerable.

This book begins with what ails city budgets, but it ends up grappling with what it will take to nourish small *d* democracy, writ large. It is divided into three main parts, each focused on one of the three points of analysis and practice mentioned above. The short chapters here serve as stepping stones on a citizen's journey toward budget justice.

Throughout the book, I refer to citizens as residents who belong to the city polity via their daily activities there, regardless of what papers they do or do not hold. I do so despite some reservations, knowing that among some communities, like those of undocumented immigrants or some Indigenous nations in the territorial limits of the United States, the word *citizen* is fraught at best. After all, in common parlance, notions of legal citizenship—predicated on declarations of allegiance to a flag—reign supreme. That notion of citizenship refers to the passport one holds, dictating the official rights and responsibilities one has vis-à-vis a nation-state. Legal citizenship is also a typically exclusionary one, rendered concrete by borders and literal walls; policymakers talk about whether someone is a citizen or noncitizen, and whether one might be eligible to hold dual citizenship.

While I sometimes use "constituent" or "individual" as alternatives to the word *citizen*, I primarily use the term *citizen* in the rest of this book purposefully, to broaden popular definitions of citizenship. Indeed, the shared Greek etymological roots of city (*polis*) and citizen (*polites*) underscore how everyday residents have stakes in a political life.[10] These shared roots also point to the importance of grassroots politics writ large, as opposed to politics confined to the perches at the top—the presidency, Congress, mayoralty, and city council.

Though I mainly draw on my research on New York City, this book's driving questions apply to cities across the country—and indeed across the world. To compare notes on the triumphs and challenges of budget justice across cities, each of the book's three interludes consists of an interview I conducted with an activist and thinker in another city working toward budget justice: Jackson, Mississippi, in part I; Porto Alegre, Brazil, in part II; and Barcelona, Spain, in part III.

———

Policymakers usually make budget decisions behind closed doors. When elected officials do make public budgets transparent, they frequently present them as neutral documents and claim that "numbers don't lie." Budget numbers do, however, often obfuscate our everyday circumstances and needs. For example, without a sense of historical data or where exactly money is going, it is difficult to discern whether additional funds for a particular school benefit all the students, barely make up for the prior year's budget cuts, or add amenities for a small selection of honors students.

While public budgets are typically and intentionally portrayed as technical, neutral, dull, and impersonal, they are moral documents that reflect specific public values, theories of government, and judgments about what is right or wrong in response to common social challenges. The numbers in our public budget shape and reflect the literal bricks and mortar as well as figurative bread and butter of urban planning and services: where waste treatment plants are located, whether subway signal systems from the 1930s are properly maintained so that trains run on time, or whether food benefits for residents and licenses for street vendors can be processed in a timely way.

Focusing on the *budget* part of budget justice prompts communities to articulate divest-invest strategies that redirect money away from expenditures the community doesn't value and toward those it does. For instance, in summer 2020, protesters camped out in front of City Hall for more than a month, asking the New York mayor and city council to cut the police budget by $1 billion from a total budget of $88 billion, and instead invest in much-needed forms of community care: health care and social services, childcare and elderly care, and well-maintained streets, gardens, parks, and libraries. Although the police eventually cleared the encampment, the monthlong Occupy City Hall protests significantly shaped the 2021 fiscal year budget, with more than $865 million in cuts to the police department's operating expenses compared to the 2020 budget.[11] (Then Mayor Bill de Blasio acknowledged the protests' impact by including lower fringe benefits in his calculations, precisely so that he could claim $1 billion in cuts.) According to the city council, these savings then went in part to summer youth programming, family social services, and broadband access in public housing.[12]

Citizens also need new tools to meaningfully hold city politicians accountable. Articulating concrete visions for budget justice is especially challenging because of pervasive institutional opacity and obfuscation of public budgets and how they get decided. It should not be so hard for the average citizen to access, read, understand, and compare one city's budget with another's.

In part I, I consider some of the basic makings of budget injustice. I argue that budgets feel daunting and off-putting not because they are too technical; they are designed to be antidemocratic and discourage public accountability or dissent. Viewing budgets as moral documents reveals policymakers' austerity as a political choice rather than necessary sacrifice.

Budget justice requires communities to "flip the gaze," giving government budgets the sort of scrutiny usually reserved for personal finances. I also examine trends in municipal budgets, showing how the federal government has unduly punished cities with austerity measures—which they, in turn, pass on to their most vulnerable residents—for half a century.

I end part I with a call for a right-to-the-city budget, in two ways: citizens have the right to democratically decide what it looks like, and they have the right to a city that helps them to thrive.

But campaigns for budget justice are unlikely to be spearheaded by those already in power. Those most impacted by overpolicing, unaffordable housing, and underfunded schools must have the chance to inform and make budget decisions as well. Likewise, many of the participants in the 2020 protests against police brutality argue that voting is not enough; they claim that demographic or descriptive representation along with placing "Black faces in high places," as African American Studies scholar Keeanga-Yamahtta Taylor writes, have not addressed racial inequalities nor stopped the killing of Black people in the United States.

In part II of this book, I examine how everyday citizens might begin to combat budget opacity and inform how local public funds get spent. I contend that budget justice entails more than fighting voter suppression and fixing the electoral college.

I use the term *ecosystem of participation* partly to emphasize that democracies cannot live on any single set of institutions. Planting monocrops looks efficient, but it is not sustainable.[13] It fails to give both the land it uses and people it attempts to feed an adequate range of nutrients. Likewise, democratic politics need diversity to stay alive.

Instead of formal chambers of power, like Congress or city hall, this book takes a closer look at formations of grassroots politics taking place in quotidian library meeting rooms, church basements, and on the streets. Shifting the setting of my ecosystem analogy from a farm to a North American forest, I turn my attention away from the commonly photographed treetops of stately red oaks and toward the spaces below, with their wandering mosses and soft lichens brimming with algae, cyanobacteria, and fungi. There, hybrid, mutualistic, provisional assemblages and entanglements defy planning or scientific categorization.[14] The forest canopy giants may hog the sunlight and limelight, but in the understory, the plot thickens.

Integral to such grassroots politics is participatory budgeting (PB), a process by which residents, rather than elected officials, allocate public funds. Since it first began in Porto Alegre, Brazil, in 1989, PB has spread to over eleven thousand cities worldwide. In past cases of PB, diversity in participation by gender, income, and racial background contributed to the legitimacy as well as redistributive potential of the processes.[15] In the United States, PB has spread from a single local process in 2010 to over five hundred currently active district, city, or institutional processes.

8   BUDGET JUSTICE

New York's PB process, run by the city council and known as PBNYC, is the country's largest by far. Since 2012, New Yorkers have decided how to spend more than $250 million on almost a thousand projects through PBNYC. I draw on a decade of fieldwork on PBNYC to ground my ideals of budget justice, the limits and uses of the foundation laid thus far, and how communities might build on PB processes for budget justice.

I attended dozens of PB assemblies, usually held in school cafeterias and auditoriums in which residents gathered to discuss what they wanted to spend public funds on. At one assembly in East Harlem, a middle-aged White man from the Upper West Side walked across town to pitch new amenities for his daughter's school. As he listened to elderly Asian American, Latine, and Black neighbors talk about the need for laundry in their buildings and the neighborhood's largest concentration of public housing in the country, he changed his mind. He decided to withdraw his proposal for his daughter's school and instead help his neighbors advance *their* proposals.

Through exchanges such as these, communities around New York have used PB to articulate and reprioritize funding allocations. An analysis by social researchers Carolin Hagelskamp, Rebecca Silliman, Erin Godfrey, and David Schleifer shows that from 2009 to 2018, capital spending in districts with PB were markedly different from those without. Schools and public housing, for instance, received more funding, while parks and housing preservation received less.

Whereas electoral politics typically engage the "usual suspects"— higher-income, older constituents—PB engages traditionally marginalized constituents, including youths, formerly incarcerated people, and undocumented immigrants. Research coordinated by the Community Development Project shows that nearly one-quarter of people who voted in New York City's PB process were not eligible to do so in typical elections.[16] The first citywide rulebook dictated that anyone over sixteen who lives, works, attends school, or is the parent of a student in a district could participate in neighborhood assemblies and project vetting, and residents over eighteen, including undocumented immigrants, could vote on the allocations. Enthusiastic and strikingly fruitful youth participation in neighborhood assemblies then convinced adults to lower the PB voting age to sixteen and the participation age to fourteen in 2012. The voting age lowered again in subsequent years, now standing at eleven.

Social researchers Carolina Johnson, H. Jacob Carlson, and Sonya Reynolds found that PB participants were 8.4 percent more likely to vote than those who had not participated in the process; the effects are even greater for those who have lower probabilities of voting, such as low-income and Black voters.[17]

Indeed, participants repeatedly stated that the PB process allowed them to engage in discussions with neighbors they otherwise wouldn't have met—the proverbial "other" in deliberations. They emphasized PB's deliberative nature, along with its encouragement to exchange ideas and compromise. This differs from electoral politics, even for those already politically active. For many, the combination of working with others unlike themselves and working toward binding budgetary decisions gave the PB process a sense of impact lacking in their usual civic engagement.

Through PB, groups of residents and organizations that might usually lobby for funds independently instead joined forces and formed dynamic alliances. Participants spoke to how PB deliberations allowed them to stress more than one aspect of their lives and identities—as African Americans, grandparents, public housing residents, or artists—and highlight issues of intersectionality, their combinations of experiences along lines of race, gender, and other social axes. More than one interviewee stated that like the Upper West Side resident mentioned above, they ended up backing projects they would not have otherwise thought of, let alone supported.

When PB works well, both citizens and government workers have likely stepped out of their respective comfort zones, disrupted or even shifted long-standing assumptions, and shared decision-making power. But robust democratic processes are hard. Some researchers argue that PB has morphed from an empowering process into a politically innocuous (or worse, vacuous) set of procedures that reflect subtle domination by elites.[18] When PB is *not* implemented well, citizens often feel burned out and even more alienated than they did before. Meanwhile, the issues they attempted to address in the city budget remain intact.

10 BUDGET JUSTICE

Participatory democratic experiments like PB are especially difficult in a context of deep-seated inequalities. White residents report higher incomes than other residents, and they frequently have the connections to navigate bureaucratic regulations more easily. This shapes both the inequities that residents experience every day and power dynamics of their deliberations. Race continues to serve, as cultural theorist Stuart Hall put it, as a fundamental "medium in which class relations are experienced."[19]

Even if the entire New York City budget were subject to a participatory process, to what extent does PB truly begin to address New Yorkers' varied and complex needs?

The city government's budgeting becoming more transparent does not render it liberatory. The majority of winning PB projects in New York look like expenditures that city agencies would have implemented anyway, if they had greater funds: air conditioners, lights for neighborhood sports facilities, and curb extensions on dangerous street corners. Such "wins" feel like consolation prizes in a game of permanent, punishing austerity.

I examine how participants relate to the city bureaucrats, as well as *whose* proposals held sway. PB deliberations can perpetuate existing inequalities without attention to epistemic justice—actively questioning what bodies of knowledge are counted as expert, rational, and valuable. In PB, this concerns how city bureaucrats sideline local knowledge in favor of technical knowledge. For budget justice, someone with lived experience should be considered an expert on their own environments as much as someone who has crunched quantitative policy analyses or studied the law.

There are no shortcuts or algorithms for democracy. Unless the funds and scopes of projects are substantially expanded, PB remains the exception to how municipal budgeting usually works: a way for constituents to voice concerns, let off steam, and see some of their ideas come to fruition while most of the budget remains opaque and predetermined. Further, by focusing exclusively on the *invest* side of the equation, PB will remain incomplete. It thus risks propagating the myth that the problem is a scarcity of funds, as opposed to austerity as a policy.

These are not simply questions about institutional design but also power. On whose terms and to what ends is PB carried out? Can PB harness the sort of energy that feeds protests for social justice and channel it in newly generative ways?

Despite or because of its significant limitations, the most impressive and important impacts of New York's PB process have not been the winning projects themselves. Rather, they lie in PB's spillover effects and the changes prompted by the process itself. For example, some participants balked at putting discretionary PB funds toward school bathroom stalls so that seven-year-olds would not hold in their pee all day. Should that even be necessary? Enough complained so that a few years later, the city government quietly doubled its allocation for school bathrooms. Moreover, many groups sought and secured funds for *losing* PB projects elsewhere.

When PB's limits leave participants frustrated, indignant, and angry, the PB process also trains constituents to want, demand, and fight for more. PB can hence serve as a site for politicization.

In part III, I argue that PB is a necessary but necessarily insufficient part of larger struggles for budget justice—a node in an ecosystem of participation. In addition to elections and the government-initiated, *invited spaces* of participation (like PB) I will discuss earlier in the book, part III examines citizens' own, *invented spaces* too, like the mutual aid collectives that proliferated during the beginning of the COVID-19 pandemic.

The last part of this book follows part II both temporally and substantively; it builds on my analysis of PB in part II to reconsider its role as a crucial entry point in a larger ecosystem of participation. While PB remains the center of my analysis, the view widens tremendously.

Emerging practices of citizen engagement across multiple spaces in an ecosystem of participation form, in turn, the basis for a new *ecology of citizenship*. At the heart of this ecology of citizenship lie contestations over how citizens engage the government and one another, especially in contexts with deep social inequalities. Namely, when even participatory spaces like PB often implicitly employ citizen-consumer logics—in which citizens "choose" social expenditures from preset menus of limited options in a context of austerity—everyday residents must struggle to forward and enact new *citizen-neighbor* dynamics, valuing solidarity and cooperation in lieu of competition, making claims over public resources and public space, and insisting on abundance in lieu of scarcity.

When invited spaces like PB constrain or even demobilize grassroots action, invented spaces play pivotal roles in enabling communities to sustain mobilizations after protests and crises, imagine and develop new ways of organizing resources, translate demands into policy proposals, and mobilize power for participatory cogovernance. Because citizen-consumer approaches fuel budget injustice, solidarity economy initiatives—which focus on social benefits alongside the financial bottom line—are especially relevant invented spaces because they demonstrate alternative ways of organizing budgets and nurture alternative democratic practices of the citizen-neighbor.

Even in a limited PB process, citizens can sometimes take logics from invented spaces and sneak them into PB as an invited space. I call this *insurgent budgeting*. Residents then pursue and realize policies that governments would not have enacted otherwise. For example, when hate crimes rose after the 2016 election, residents voted to fund self-defense workshops by and for Bangladeshi and Muslim women. These projects, revolving around neighbors helping each other to keep one another safe, contrast more common community safety policies, such as hiring more police officers and outfitting them with more high-tech equipment.

Residents grounded their conversations with observations about actual incidents, accessed and shared stories and evidence about national patterns, and deliberated about what sorts of resources they appreciated, as well as why older Asian women tended to be disproportionate targets of physical violence. Along the way, their conversations touched on histories of anti-Black urban policies, anti-Asian xenophobia and the so-called War on Terror, and contradictory tropes about Asian Americans as both model minorities and "foreigners." PB thus provides opportunities for tough conversations on the intersection between policing and gentrification, the availability of health and employment services, and how community safety policies should be defined and implemented.

Residents then work *across* political spaces to pursue policies that governments would not have funded or enacted otherwise. Realizing budget justice requires that citizens themselves articulate the criteria they wish to live by, forwarding new logics of collective care and community control.

———

The contemporary goal of budget justice pays tribute to the idea of abolition democracy W.E.B. Du Bois examined in *Black Reconstruction in America* ninety years ago.[20] In recent decades, Black feminist, queer, Indigenous, critical race, and anticolonial scholarship have pinpointed just how systemic hierarchies persist in the afterlives of slavery and empire. As Harsha Walia writes, abolition democracy also demands the "imagining and generating of alternative institutions . . . prefiguring societies based on equity, mutual aid, and self-determination."[21] This project of world-building must be rooted in on-the-ground community organizing and radical democratic experiments.

Cities are the crucial, contested sites where austerity policies first hit the ground, where citizens gather to rise up in response, and from which entire communities might look across borders to ask, and learn from one another by answering: What is to be done? Can communities hold enough political power to hold sway after the next election? Will processes like PB exist, and will they be implemented in ways that hold public budgets accountable and center the needs of everyday residents? Will residents' lives feel less precarious? Will their life savings and livelihoods not be at the mercy of the next recession, epidemic, or wildfire or hurricane?

Communities can only achieve budget justice by combining seemingly disparate forms of resistance and care in strategic ways, with a clear eye on the long game. Protests and elections are not enough. Budget

14   BUDGET JUSTICE

justice requires collective reworkings of nodes in ecosystems of participation and ecologies of citizenship, in ways that help everyday residents
to understand what, precisely, is happening in their public budgets, and to
reimagine what policies should look like in response—harnessed and sustained through organized initiatives that accrue political power. In so
doing, communities conceptualize democracy not as a set of institutions, but rather a set of practices and situated solidarities.

PART I

Opacity Abets Austerity

1

Moral Documents

I CANNOT REMEMBER a time when political pundits did *not* issue warnings of a looming "fiscal cliff." In New York, the ever-present austerity talk meant that every budget cycle, students wondered whether tuition at the local public colleges would rise, and librarians wondered about their work hours and subscriptions budgets. At the same time, I could not easily guess what would get cut and why, nor whether budget cuts would put the city on sound financial footing. Worse, I couldn't easily find out.

Without democratic accountability, it becomes impossible to differentiate prudent budget cuts from austerity as policy, a one-size-fits-all approach for public budgets even when cost cutting might backfire and undermine effectiveness. When are budget cuts truly necessary? When are they smart moves, and when might they seriously undermine everyday residents' ability to live and thrive?

Such questions hit home in new ways in 2022, when my then four-year-old child entered New York City's public school system as a pre-kindergartener. I felt grateful that I didn't have to spend August running around to find the right school supplies for my child; the parent-teacher organization (PTO) took it on itself to buy supplies in bulk on behalf of the students' families.

Still, as the first day of school approached, there was an emergency. Instead of buying supplies, the school sent emails pleading with parents to attend rallies at city hall and voice opposition to more than $370 million in school budget cuts.

18 BUDGET JUSTICE

These huge numbers being bandied about felt overwhelming to me. I had read in the news that the city council had just passed a $101 billion budget. What did $370 million in cuts entail for the school system or my kid's school? I looked up the number of public schools in New York, 1,867, and calculated an average of $198,178 at each school. I still felt lost on what that meant for the average student or family in the city.

———

How did a $370 million cut to the New York City schools get written into the city budget? Again and again, existing democratic safeguards were sidestepped because of "exceptional" or "extenuating circumstances." First, the schools chancellor issued an "emergency declaration" to circumvent a vote on the education budget by the Panel for Education Policy, a board that mostly consists of mayoral appointees. Then, the New York City Council passed the mayor's budget. And instead of holding a forty-five-day public comment period on the proposed budget, the city allowed members to comment for four hours in one meeting after the city council budget approval.[1] After hearing from their constituents, more than a dozen city council members stated that they regretted approving the budget, especially its education cuts. They protested that the mayor had not been forthcoming with his budget plans; administrative officials countered that council members had failed to ask the right questions.[2]

Somehow, even the numbers themselves were up for debate. City administrators had announced about $215 million in cuts, whereas the city comptroller presented $373 million as the true number.[3] Some additional cuts to individual school budgets had not been apparent before because the funds would be going to other areas within the school system, and the city had not reported school-level numbers; the latter were put together and exposed by advocacy organizations and investigative reporters.[4]

The budget cuts were supposed to signal fiscal responsibility, but educators argued that keeping budgets steady would be wise, precisely so that administrators could strategically plan budget cuts in smarter

MORAL DOCUMENTS 19

ways. A lot of cuts would be difficult for principals to implement on such short notice; a class with, say, twenty-one students should have the same number of teachers as a class with twenty-five students. Brooklyn's Middle School 859, for example, was slated to have approximately 15 percent, or $825,000, less than it did the previous year. Several teachers were then announced as "excessed" over the summer, and the school eliminated leadership positions for teacher professional development, planned to increase class sizes from twenty-five to thirty-three, and cut back on arts, music, and enrichment offerings.[5]

The cuts felt especially devastating considering that the city reported higher-than-expected tax revenues and federal aid.[6] In the preceding summer, City Comptroller Brad Lander released a report stating the Department of Education still had more than $500 million in federal COVID-19 stimulus funds that had yet to be allocated, and that these funds could fully cover the $469 million in cuts from Fair Student Funding (NYC schools' main source of funding) that year.[7]

What else should stimulus funds be used for, if not to help students recover from the pandemic? City officials could have used stimulus funds to, for instance, shorten school bus delays for the roughly 150,000 students who rely on buses. School bus delays rose to the highest level in five years, averaging more than forty minutes.[8] Meanwhile, school principals and teachers argued for greater resources for each of their students, citing students' well-documented developmental delays along with their need for social-emotional learning and support—particularly for the more than 8,700 New York children who lost a parent or caregiver during the pandemic.[9]

I felt overwhelmed when I tried to read about budget cuts, and I'm a public policy scholar. The public budgets I looked at felt like dismaying, overly technical documents. When I approached colleagues whose research focused on public schools, they told me they were also too intimidated to wade into "the technical weeds of public budgets." If public budgets felt anxiety provoking for public policy professors, how could the lay public hold government accountable? I had to keep reminding myself that my lack of technical prowess was not the main problem here. Budget opacity was.

The process became, according to the city administration, one of "exception," so that the budget cuts could escape legislative debate as well as public scrutiny. Taking a closer look, I learned that such budget opacity was no state of exception.

Although the details vary, such opacity is not limited to the current mayor, nor to New York. The acronyms and bigger numbers just tell the New York version of how US city budgets work in general. This hit home when I watched the *How-To Guide for Making Sense of Your City's Budget* video from the nonprofit organization Strong Towns; the video spends over an hour poring over an annual budget for Asheville, North Carolina (population roughly ninety-four thousand). In minute fifty-three of the video, the two interlocutors talk about how impossible it is to compare the police budget to social services spending in a meaningful way.[10]

Around the country, even elected officials often have a difficult time deciphering and giving input regarding city budgets. In Chicago, an elected council member named Michele Smith spoke to how "the budget is very difficult to get your arms around"—and she is a former general counsel to a publicly traded company. To make matters worse, she received copies of the budget just one week before she was supposed to vote on it. This lack of oversight has consequences; according to a University of Chicago Center for Effective Government report, the result has been "a fiscal mess."[11]

In Fresno, California, the official budget adoption process is ostensibly more open than Chicago's; a recent one involved five public hearings and two city council meetings. But the mayor went so far as to brag that "a lot of sausage was being made in the back room," away from the public and city council. Just what was decided in the proverbial back room is not public because the budget subcommittee remained closed; even agendas, minutes, and attendance records remained unshared.[12] The Fresno mayor argues that the city is allowed to keep the budget subcommittee meeting closed because it is a temporary, ad hoc one . . . that seems to convene year after year.

Chicago's budget process is codified to lack accountability; Fresno's mayor uses rules of exception like New York City's did. From coast to coast and in between, the lesson remains: city budgets are prohibitively forbidding not because they are technical; they are designed to be antidemocratic, so as to prevent public accountability. They are not just confusing; they are impossible to understand.

———

I begin with a vignette about public schools because I have a personal and immediate stake in it, and because most people know something about schools—as parents, neighbors, or simply current or former students ourselves. But austerity permeates all domains of city policy, not just schools.

Taking my child to school on an October morning, I took note of just some of the ways in which our little corner of Brooklyn reflected larger city policies. As we reached the end of our block, I saw that the intersection boasted new, soft traffic poles (officially called flexible delineators) to effectively extend the curbs a bit, making the corner safer than it was a few months ago.

I pay attention to hurricane season in New York now. The week before, that entire intersection had flooded with a river more than a foot deep rushing down the street. But it seems that with climate change, "unprecedented" amounts of rainfall are unfortunately not outliers but instead precedents for a new normal. I live in a neighborhood with the word "heights" in its name; such neighborhoods should not flood so easily. Clearly, the city's sewage systems and rain catch basins are not ready.

Then, as I turned the street corner onto a commercial strip, I noted which storefronts were vacant and wondered why. Had the rents risen too quickly? The city has a lot of small business loan programs; which businesses were eligible, and what were the criteria?

The compost bin sitting next to the garbage cans was full, as usual. The status of the city's community composting kept changing because of budget cuts. The program was popular; the community garden on the block often refuses food scraps from neighbors only because it cannot turn them into compost quickly enough without attracting pests.

22 BUDGET JUSTICE

With this exercise in mind, traversing one block in approximately one minute, I reflected on how the departments of transportation, libraries, sanitation, environmental protection, small business services, and emergency management impact my everyday life. I am sure that there are many other agencies involved as well, processing paperwork to hand to human resources as a new hire, planning maintenance of infrastructure taken for granted by most residents (until disruptions occur), and so much other work that makes the city run. I am confident that a closer look into any of these policy domains would, like my brief look into public schools, yield stories about tortured attempts at strategic planning and daily work, amid political battles and relentless budget cuts.

Austerity permeates all levels of government, not just local ones, but the city level is where everyday citizens tend to feel it most. When federal tax "cuts" in 2001 and 2002 reduced tax burdens for upper-income households but *increased* them for middle-income taxpayers, the resulting inequalities and budget cuts fell on cities.[13] As economic geographer Jamie Peck puts it, "Cities are . . . where austerity bites"; they are home to many of the "preferred political targets of austerity programs—the 'undeserving' poor, minorities and marginalized populations, public-sector unions and 'bureaucratized' infrastructures," and the chronically undercounted unhoused or undocumented.[14]

———

Neoliberalism as a governing rationality—emphasizing cost cutting, privatization of services, and tax incentives for private contractors, across scenarios and conditions—should be distinguished from fiscal discipline and sound, evidence-based policymaking. In fact, a problem with austerity is that it has become a public policy of habit, leaving little room for careful, evidence-based consideration *or* democratic accountability. It places stress on cutting costs as a one-size-fits-all approach for public budgets even when doing so might backfire and undermine effectiveness.

Contrary to what some politicians argue, permanent austerity does not lead to a more efficient government. My undergraduate students at

Brooklyn College are used to news of budget cuts, but they wonder about what "amenities" could possibly be cut without undermining their learning. They do not expect fancy buildings or catering at public lectures, but they did start an Instagram account called @cuny_brokelyn_college to document flooded bathrooms, crumbling ceilings, inoperable water fountains, and broken elevators. By far the most common complaint I hear concerns the availability of classes they need in order to learn, graduate, and get jobs. Each semester, faculty are told to cut underenrolled classes well before registration ends, even though some students are scraping together money for tuition until the first day of class. When classes get canceled, students have trouble finding enough courses to fit their schedules (especially around full-time jobs) to qualify for financial aid, and they consequently take longer to graduate. Slashing budgets is supposed to increase efficiency, and to trim the proverbial fat around our budgets to make them stronger and leaner, but as my students sometimes observe, "It's not efficient if it doesn't work."[15]

This is not to argue that fat does not exist, yet nor is it ever present. Besides, the bloat may be elsewhere. Austerity cuts do not seem to automatically stem costly administrative reorganizations at the school, like $2 million contracts with Turnitin, an online plagiarism detection tool that according to an academic study, is "marginally more effective than a 10-word Google search" and violates faculty senate resolutions regarding data privacy.[16] At current rates, $1 million could pay for 143 courses taught by adjunct instructors. Instead of the university's fat and bloat, austerity aims for its muscle and bone.

Lander used a different metaphor in response to proposed budget cuts, stating that they were pennywise and pound foolish.[17] As he noted, "Half of our new nurses and a third of public-school teachers graduate from CUNY, which means underinvesting in our public colleges will shortchange our workforce—hindering us from securing our next generation of healthcare workers, educators, tech workers, public safety officers, and more."[18]

Public budgets are moral documents that reflect specific values and theories of how government should work. As historian Kim

Phillips-Fein writes, "All budgets tell stories about the future. They are ways of describing how money will be raised and what it will be used to accomplish, always written before the money is actually in hand. . . . [G]overnment budgets . . . outline a society's dreams and its constraints."[19]

Policymakers consistently claim to aim for the "public interest" and fight "special interests," but the political economy of US cities has consistently defined the public interest as growth driven—whether by train tracks in the nineteenth century, automobiles in the mid-twentieth century, "urban renewal" that became nicknamed "slum clearance" and "Negro removal" in the late twentieth century, or "creative class" gentrification at the beginning of the new millennium—with write-down subsidies, municipal bonds, and eminent domain that quantified certain types of development as valuable and worthy of investment, and other types as not. Public budgets that emphasize sustainability, equity, and rootedness among residents will look different from those that place value on short-term growth above all else.

Further, budgets not only reflect different sets of values but also collective moral judgments on social problems like poverty, inequality, and climate change. Along the way, budgets delineate implicit codes of appropriate conduct for residents, community groups, local governments, and others in their respective roles as part of a working city. Public budgets are, in a way, reflections of a public's moral compass.

Common sense tells us that our basic needs—like class sizes in keeping with federal norms—are nonnegotiable; plus decades of empirical academic output backs up common sense. It shows us that programs like subsidized childcare and smaller classes in early education, for instance, are associated with long-term benefits like greater educational achievement, lower crime rates, longer life expectancy, and lower rates of public assistance enrollment.[20]

But austerity measures take basic needs and tell the public that they are irresponsible luxuries. They attempt to render budgets and budget cuts as impersonal and inevitable. Budget regimes hide behind an opaque curtain of neoliberal tropes claiming that austerity cuts are not discriminatory, but rather simply what is needed to make public services more efficient.

MORAL DOCUMENTS 25

These tropes are so pervasive that economist Zoë Hitzig turns to poetry to examine their discursive effects. Does repeating them, again and again, make them sound normal? Hitzig writes, "More cross armed supervisors with first-aid kits strapped onto ankles, next to pistols. More puzzling over numbers like *truth*. . . . More budget cuts. More for your dollar? More for the Dollar. . . . More casual more indifference. Mere casualties. . . . More can't breathe."[21] "I can't breathe" were the last words uttered by Eric Garner as he was killed on July 17, 2014, on Staten Island by police officer Daniel Pantaleo.

Austerity cuts routinely hurt the most vulnerable—not coincidentally, disproportionately those from historically marginalized communities—the most. They save money in the short run, but not necessarily in the long one, especially when they cut preventive services to the bone, so that needs grow exponentially in the medium term. They often enlarge the state, particularly in the areas of administration and policing. And they ultimately help subvert local rule and sovereignty, doling out punishment and fear in response to individuals' inability to meet public needs.

2

Flip the Gaze

IN 2011, soon after he sent police to clear Occupy Wall Street protesters from Zuccotti Park, then mayor Michael Bloomberg bragged, "I have my own army in the NYPD [New York Police Department], which is the seventh biggest army in the world."[1] While this statement about the department's world ranking may be an exaggeration, the department does employ more people than the Federal Bureau of Investigation.

But such "army"-level policing did not translate into safer communities. Consider, for example, the NYPD's stop-and-frisk detainments (detaining, questioning, and searching individuals without any notion of "probable cause") at their peak, in 2011. Out of the 685,724 recorded detainments made that year, 91 percent of those stopped were persons of color, and nearly 90 percent were innocent, neither being arrested nor receiving any summons. A significant percentage of arrests and summonses were then dismissed because they could not be justified in court. In a survey of over 1,000 residents in one forty-block community in the Bronx, more than half the respondents were stopped four or more times, and more than half were asked to show identification just outside their apartments. Of those who did call the police for help, 16 percent reported that the police never came, and 59 percent reported that they arrived late.[2]

After a judge ruled stop-and-frisk unconstitutional in 2013, the NYPD lowered its use of such detainments. Yet they are still emblematic of larger and deeper issues with policing in New York. In 2023, a court-appointed monitor reported that 97 percent of stops made by the rebranded "neighborhood safety teams" were of Black or Hispanic people, and 24 percent were unconstitutional.[3] Besides, the ramifications of its widespread use in the early 2000s continue to reverberate. Federal monitors noted a lack of reform and even basic reporting of stop-and-frisk detainments by the police. The city also faced an ongoing lawsuit forwarded by plaintiffs whose stop-and-frisk-related arrests were later dismissed or thrown out of court, but whose biographical records and facial recognition data (illegally) remain in criminal record databases.

It is no wonder, then, that street protests and uprisings proliferated nationwide after the murders of Eric Garner, Michael Brown, Sandra Bland, George Floyd, and others, demanding not just body cameras, training, or incremental reforms, but budget justice and significant divestments from police too. Budgets must be recognized as sites of public study and contestation so that communities can better articulate priorities to meet their needs.

In 2022, more than two years after the protests calling for "budget justice" in honor of Floyd nationwide, a thirty-two-year-old certified public accountant named Kenneth Mejia won the election to become Los Angeles's city controller, despite running against an incumbent with a far bigger campaign chest.[4] He did so with the billboard pictured in Figure 1 on the next page, which he posted on Twitter (now X).[5]

In other words, Mejia won the election campaigning on a divest-invest formulation, and shockingly, by helping "Angelenos to know where their taxes are being spent!"[6]

Public budgets are ostensibly already public; in New York, for instance, the mayor along with the Office of Management and Budget release PDFs and Excel spreadsheets each year. With great fanfare, the city made many additional datasets public during the Bloomberg administration. But public reporting does not inherently lead to greater transparency, since it can make it even harder for the public to know when some crucial financial information remains missing or obscured. Besides, most constituents find the primary financial reports issued by governmental entities to be intimidating.[7] As mentioned earlier, I know I do.

FIGURE 1. Photo of campaign billboard for Kenneth Mejia.

One recent spring day, I tried to make sense of the preliminary budgets released by the mayor. There were eleven main documents released in January for the next fiscal year.[8] Which should I start with? I quickly learned to not pay attention to capital budget numbers that focused on building infrastructure, as those numbers were more likely to be equally applied across all divisions or determined years in advance. I also put aside Program to Eliminate the Gap (PEG) numbers. I had never heard of PEG before, and I learned that it was created after New York City's 1975 fiscal crisis.[9] Historically, PEG plans have included advocacy for state and federal aid, debt refinancing, or ideas for increased revenues; the latest PEGs seemed to solely consist of across-the-board cuts.

It was only in conversation with community organizers and public services advocacy groups (like those fighting for school funding) that I honed in on expense numbers. One important document was called *Expense Revenue Contract* and bafflingly looked like it came from a dot matrix printer. It was 530 pages long. I tried to read it, but my eyes kept glazing over. Still, every time I *did* manage to carefully examine a page, questions quickly arose.

It looked like every agency faced budget cuts. Figure 2, for example, features a page for the Office of Emergency Management.[10]

The agency function was helpfully printed at the top of the page; it is responsible for the "city's response to all emergency conditions and potential incidents." It was set to shift from a budget of over $30 million to less than $10 million, losing more than two-thirds of its staffing budget over the next year. I am not an expert on emergency preparedness, but given the limitations of the city's response to the pandemic as well as Hurricanes Sandy and Ida, and the immense uncertainty of "potential incidents," I wanted to know more information about how this money was set to be spent *before* these drastic cuts were made. That information was not there, and it was not easy for me to find.

When numbers did stick out, I again had no way to make sense of them or learn about what happened. Figure 3 features a snapshot of the budget page for the Department of Information Technology and Telecommunications.[11] The bottom of the page, focused on equipment and not staffing, stood out to me because of the severe cost overruns. In the previous fiscal year, the agency spent $50 million beyond its $251 million budget on technology services, and the Mayor's Office of Media and Entertainment spent almost double its $17 million budget. What was this about? I had heard that the mayor was trying to revitalize the city's nightlife as part of his development strategy and therefore held "flashy" news conferences. Was this related? Even a one-sentence explanation would have been helpful. Given these egregious cost overruns, how seriously should I take each year's cuts?

Figure 4 presents a final snapshot from this bewildering, seemingly endless document. It is the bottom half of the first page of the personnel budget for the NYPD.[12] I noticed that the department has a lot more personnel—and a lot more kinds of personnel—than other city agencies.

At first glance, it looked like the agency would experience some proposed budget cuts as well—even if, compared to other proposed numbers, a cut of $33,576 out of a budget of $205.5 million for housing police appears negligible. But then, there were shocking new numbers. There was a new line called "patrol," with a $1.7 *billion* budget—with no

```
===============================================================================================================
                                        DEPARTMENT OF EMERGENCY MANAGEMENT
            017                             AGENCY EXPENSE BUDGET SUMMARY
===============================================================================================================
AGENCY FUNCTION:
COORDINATE, MONITOR, AND PREPARE PLANS FOR THE CITY'S RESPONSE TO ALL EMERGENCY CONDITIONS AND POTENTIAL INCIDENTS; IMPLEMENT
TRAINING PROGRAMS FOR PUBLIC SAFETY AND HEALTH; MAKE RECOMMENDATIONS TO THE MAYOR; INCREASE PUBLIC AWARENESS OF THE APPROPRIATE
RESPONSES TO EMERGENCY CONDITIONS AND POTENTIAL INCIDENTS; OPERATE AN EMERGENCY OPERATIONS CENTER; COORDINATE WITH STATE, FEDERAL,
AND OTHER GOVERNMENTAL BODIES TO EFFECTUATE THE PURPOSES OF THE DEPARTMENT.
===============================================================================================================
```

		CURRENT MODIFIED BUDGET			PRELIMINARY BUDGET		
		------------------FOR FY 2023-------------			-------------FOR FY 2024-------------		
	ADOPTED	FULL-TIME		CHANGE FROM	FULL-TIME		CHANGE FROM
	BUDGET	BUDGETED		ADOPTED	BUDGETED		MODIFIED
UNITS OF APPROPRIATION	FOR FY 2023	POSITIONS	APPROPRIATION	(+/-)	POSITIONS	APPROPRIATION	(+/-)
001 -- PERSONAL SERVICES	$26,605,837	230	$30,704,297	$4,098,460 +	81	$9,700,852	$21,003,445 -

```
            |-----------------------------------------------------------------------------------------------|
            | RESPONSIBLE FOR COORDINATING, MONITORING, AND PREPARING PLANS FOR THE CITY'S RESPONSE TO ALL EMERGENCY |
            | CONDITIONS AND POTENTIAL INCIDENTS.                                                            |
            |-----------------------------------------------------------------------------------------------|
```

| SUB-TOTAL PERSONAL SERVICES | $26,605,837 | 230 | $30,704,297 | $4,098,460 + | 81 | $9,700,852 | $21,003,445 - |

FIGURE 2. Partial snapshot of New York City's *Expense Revenue Contract* for fiscal year 2023, for the Department of Emergency Management.

```
002 -- TECHNOLOGY SERVICES - OTPS        $251,121,362          $301,386,817    $50,265,455 +        $240,557,571    $60,829,246 -
       -------------------------------------------------------------------------------------------------------------------------
       | OTPS APPROPRIATION TO PURCHASE SUPPLIES, MATERIALS AND OTHER SERVICES TO SUPPORT THE OPERATIONS OF DOITT AND|
       | OTHER CITY AGENCIES. VOICE AND DATA COMMUNICATIONS CHARGES FOR ALL CITY AGENCIES ARE PAID THROUGH DOITT,     |
       | INCLUDING THOSE RELATED TO THE CITYNET SYSTEM, AND ARE CHARGED BACK TO THOSE AGENCIES THROUGH AN INTRA-CITY  |
       | BILLING PROCESS.                                                                                             |
       -------------------------------------------------------------------------------------------------------------------------

004 -- ADMIN/OPERATIONS OTPS              $49,961,208           $49,961,208                          $45,961,208     $4,000,000 -
       -------------------------------------------------------------------------------------------------------------------------
       | OTPS APPROPRIATION TO PURCHASE SUPPLIES, MATERIALS AND OTHER SERVICES REQUIRED TO SUPPORT EXECUTIVE AND      |
       | ADMINISTRATIVE OPERATIONS.                                                                                   |
       -------------------------------------------------------------------------------------------------------------------------

008 -- 911 TECHNICAL OPERATIONS - OT      $86,928,113           $90,836,452     $3,908,339 +        $100,262,455     $9,426,003 +
       -------------------------------------------------------------------------------------------------------------------------
       | OTPS APPROPRIATION TO PURCHASE SUPPLIES, MATERIALS AND OTHER SERVICES REQUIRED TO SUPPORT PROVIDING          |
       | TECHNICAL ADMINISTRATION AND OPERATION OF THE CITY'S EMERGENCY COMMUNICATIONS NETWORK AND FACILITIES, FOR    |
       | BOTH PUBLIC SERVICE ANSWERING CENTER 1 AND PUBLIC SERVICE ANSWERING CENTER 2.                                |
       -------------------------------------------------------------------------------------------------------------------------

010 -- MAYOR'S OFFICE OF MEDIA & ENT      $17,168,640           $30,570,937    $13,402,297 +         $16,018,106    $14,552,831 -
       -------------------------------------------------------------------------------------------------------------------------
       | OTPS APPROPRIATION TO PURCHASE SUPPLIES, MATERIALS AND OTHER SERVICES REQUIRED TO SUPPORT PROVIDING          |
       | ADMINISTRATION OF THE MAYOR'S OFFICE OF MEDIA AND ENTERTAINMENT (MOME), WHICH INCLUDES NYC MEDIA; THE OFFICE |
       | OF FILM, THEATRE, AND BROADCASTING; WORKFORCE, EDUCATIONAL, AND INDUSTRY INITIATIVES; THE OFFICE OF          |
       | NIGHTLIFE; AND THE PRESS CREDENTIALS UNIT.                                                                   |
       -------------------------------------------------------------------------------------------------------------------------
```

FIGURE 3. Partial snapshot of New York City's *Expense Revenue Contract* for fiscal year 2023, for the Department of Information Technology and Telecommunications.

```
009 -- HOUSING POLICE-PS            $205,525,361 2,391   $205,525,361            2,391  $205,491,785        $33,576 -
      |--------------------------------------------------------------------------------------------------------|
      | RESPONSIBLE FOR PROVIDING A SAFE AND SECURE ENVIRONMENT IN UNION WITH THE PUBLIC HOUSING COMMUNITY THROUGH |
      | THE IMPARTIAL ENFORCEMENT OF LAWS AND THE SENSITIVE DELIVERY OF POLICE SERVICE. IMPROVE THE QUALITY OF LIFE |
      | OF THE RESIDENTS OF PUBLIC HOUSING BY PROTECTING LIFE AND PROPERTY AND PROVIDING A SAFE ENVIRONMENT FREE OF |
      | FEAR.                                                                                                  |
      |--------------------------------------------------------------------------------------------------------|

010 -- PATROL - PS                                                     20,793 $1,748,366,258 $1,748,366,258 +
      |--------------------------------------------------------------------------------------------------------|
      | PROTECTS LIFE AND PROPERTY, REDUCES CRIME, AND IMPROVES THE QUALITY OF LIFE OF THE CITIZENS AND VISITORS OF |
      | THE CITY OF NEW YORK. DEPLOYS SUFFICIENT UNIFORMED MEMBERS OF THE SERVICE TO RESPOND TO EMERGENCIES,   |
      | MINIMIZE HARM, AND MAXIMIZE PUBLIC SAFETY.                                                             |
      |--------------------------------------------------------------------------------------------------------|

016 -- COMMUNICATIONS - PS                                              1,729  $109,770,481   $109,770,481 +
      |--------------------------------------------------------------------------------------------------------|
      | PROVIDES PROMPT SERVICE TO EMERGENCY CALLS FROM THE PUBLIC. DIRECTS AND CONTROLS EMERGENCY CALLS FROM THE |
      | PUBLIC FOR POLICE, FIRE, AND MEDICAL ASSISTANCE BY DISPATCHING APPROPRIATE RESOURCES IN A PROMPT, EFFECTIVE, |
      | AND EFFICIENT MANNER. FACILITATES COMMUNICATIONS WITH OTHER POLICE AGENCIES.                           |
      |--------------------------------------------------------------------------------------------------------|

020 -- INTELLIGENCE AND COUNTERTERRO                                    1,534  $219,516,137   $219,516,137 +
      |--------------------------------------------------------------------------------------------------------|
      | THE COUNTERTERRORISM BUREAU CONDUCTS COMPREHENSIVE REVIEWS OF POTENTIAL TERRORIST TARGETS IN NEW YORK CITY, |
      | AND, WORKING WITH FEDERAL, STATE, AND LOCAL AGENCIES, AND PRIVATE SECTOR ORGANIZATIONS. DEVELOPS PLANS FOR |
      | SECURITY MEASURES FOR THESE LOCATIONS. PROVIDES COUNTER TERRORISM TRAINING FOR FIRST RESPONDERS. THE   |
      | INTELLIGENCE BUREAU CONDUCTS PROFESSIONAL AND JUDICIOUS INTELLIGENCE-GATHERING. INTERACTS WITH ALL LAW |
      | ENFORCEMENT ORGANIZATIONS TO ENHANCE THE SAFETY OF THE CITIZENS OF NYC.                                |
      |--------------------------------------------------------------------------------------------------------|
```

FIGURE 4. Partial snapshot of New York City's *Expense Revenue Contract* for fiscal year 2023, for the NYPD.

further details and no disaggregation. There was a new line called "intelligence and counterterrorism," with a $219 million budget. These are not new programs. Where did these numbers come from, and could I at least compare the proposed numbers for the next year with that year's numbers? This document did not help me with that.

———

Even this cursory look at New York's public budget documents yielded more questions than answers. Indeed, investigative reporters have documented systematic and widespread obfuscation, especially by the NYPD. For instance, a 2022 report by the Surveillance Technology Oversight Project and Legal Aid Society found that between 2007 and 2019, the NYPD spent almost $3 billion on surveillance technologies—officially listed under the vague category of "special expenses."

In June 2020, partly in response to Black Lives Matter uprisings, the city council passed the Public Oversight of Surveillance Technology Act. It requires the NYPD to report on its expenditures on surveillance technologies. For example, a $400 million contract with Vexcel, a Microsoft subsidiary, likely concerns the NYPD's Domain Awareness System, which some claim is the largest surveillance system in the world (connected to eighteen thousand CCTV cameras, collecting two million license plate readings, fifty-four million 911 calls, fifteen million complaints, and other surveillance data). It uses controversial methods such as machine learning algorithms and historical police reports (that critics argue reflect and perpetuate racial bias) in its predictive policing program, and links its data to individuals, including undocumented immigrants.[13] It remains impossible to hold the Domain Awareness System accountable or even know whether the Vexcel contract concerns other efforts as well, however, because the NYPD continues to flout parts of the act, redacting large portions of what should be publicly available contracts.

One might think that perhaps medium-term capital planning—for infrastructural projects that are supposed to last at least five years—would be a bit more straightforward than the expense items I examined in the preceding paragraphs. After all, purchasing and installing air conditioners should be simpler than hiring, negotiating salaries and benefits for, and training new staff. Yet somehow, New York's capital budget, which runs over $10 billion each year, is similarly difficult to examine and only released piecemeal, again via online PDF documents that render number crunching unnecessarily hard. Further, only capital projects costing $25 million or more—roughly 3 percent of the city's projects— are reported on the capital projects dashboard. So when WeGov, a civic technology initiative, scrutinized capital infrastructural project data, it found that most projects were over budget and/or past their projected timelines.[14] This makes it difficult for financial experts (let along laypeople) to parse what money is going where, partly because cost overruns, delays, timelines, and revisions are not well marked.

Put together, these data slippages, splinterings, redactions, and outright omissions make it difficult for elected officials to plan new projects, since they often spend the bulk of their term-limited time wrapping up projects shaped and funded by their predecessors. It also makes it virtually impossible for communities and even elected officials to hold city agencies accountable for projects with life-and-death consequences— from elevator shaft repairs in public housing, to storm sewer and water main repairs that could have prevented flash floods, and the subsequent deaths of thirteen basement apartment residents in Queens during Hurricane Ida.

———

Indeed, it feels particularly perverse to shield public budgets from public scrutiny given how much surveillance and judgment citizens live under as individuals, and the significant impact that these projects have on day-to-day lives.

As with personal budgets, a focus on budget cuts as the sole answer to woes (through constant emphasis on frugality) obscures larger— tectonic, even—shifts in political economic structures. The social contract of what it means to work hard by the rules, and what citizens might expect in return, has fundamentally changed over the past few decades.

This is perhaps why, slowly, popular press articles on millennials shifted from treatises on spoiled "hipster culture" in the early aughts to explanations of the student debt crisis in the early 2020s. Student loan debt has increased by 2,807 percent since the 1970s, when four of the nine US Supreme Court justices ruling on President Biden's 2023 student loan forgiveness program attended college.[15] The loan forgiveness program remains controversial, but policy analyses detail how ballooning debt reflects a changing college landscape more than any individual student's academic performance or financial decisions.[16]

"Now that millennials aren't buying avocado toast and lattes, can they afford a home?" asks a National Public Radio *Marketplace* news story. The answer is so obvious, the question might be rhetorical. *OK, boomer,* a millennial might sarcastically retort. *Easy for you to talk about graduating from college and buying a starter home. What was your college tuition again?* When average wages and prices are adjusted for inflation, Generation Z earners (those born in the late 1990s and early 2000s) have 86 percent less purchasing power than baby boomers did in their twenties. Meanwhile, median home prices have doubled and public college tuitions tripled since the 1970s.[17]

But the analogy of personal and city budgets is far from perfect. Personal budgets are often already discussed as reflections of moral decisions—reflecting consumerism, impulse buying, and an inability to save. By extension, average citizens are used to the scrutiny. I myself took these conditions for granted, until I read how many other countries have simpler tax-filing systems. In Japan, their equivalent of the Internal Revenue Service sends each taxpayer a postcard with how much they earned last year, how much they owe, and how much was withheld. In Estonia, it takes the average person five minutes to pay taxes. Eight Organization for Economic Cooperation and Development countries prepare returns for most of their taxpayers. Meanwhile, US taxpayers spend hours tracking down numbers and filling out forms, only to report to the Internal Revenue Service figures it already

36   BUDGET JUSTICE

has. The burden of responsibility to crunch the numbers remains with taxpayers.

While many taxpayers live in fear of audits from the Internal Revenue Service (even when sincerely doing their best), public budgets continue to be kept hidden from, well, the public. They are discussed in technical terms and with clinical distance so that they can seem apolitical.

In order to achieve budget justice, then, the public needs to flip the gaze. "The gaze" is a phrase I borrow from critical theory here to connote one's awareness of looking and watching. Gazing is not a neutral act; those watching usually hold more power. In his famous BBC series *Ways of Seeing*, art historian John Berger spoke about the "male gaze" in Western art, which tends to represent women as models/muses in certain passive ways.

I do not wish to fetishize transparency, nor to uncritically call for it as some universal value. The public needs to fight for institutional transparency and accountability, and instead give individuals the right to privacy and automatic access to basic services, rather than casting them as passive viewers lacking the observational and mental faculties to critique public budgets.

If the public were to flip the gaze of scrutiny back onto local government, it would not necessarily choose cutting essential services as its default and virtually only line of action. Communities would then demand to see where the state currently gets its money, who is paying and who is not, and who benefits. City residents would compare notes with other cities to take a step back and gain perspective, and not take what politicians say for granted. They would be able to contextualize their lived experiences and examine them through the lens of political economy alongside personal responsibility. Communities could investigate how current conditions came to be.

Thus budget justice demands what sociologist Michel Foucault called "histories of the present"—of how neighborhoods, cities, and metropolitan areas got to their current circumstances in the first place, and the historical conditions on which current injustices still depend.[18] I am particularly interested in what aspects of US cities and city budgets seem normal now but were not always so. That means that residents need to have access to historical data and be able to access data from other cities as well. It feels impossible to judge whether the mayor's fears of looming "fiscal cliffs" have any merit in a year with a budget surplus, for instance, without a sense of how New York and other US cities fared after previous downturns (like the post-2007 Great Recession) and during the pandemic.

For example, it is no coincidence that historically redlined areas— that is, neighborhoods marked in red by the federal government in the 1930s to denote lower grades for mortgages, merely because of the presence of Black and/or immigrant residents in them—are now, almost a century later, the exact areas with fewer trees and more parking lots.[19] As outlined in historian Richard Rothstein's *The Color of Law* and architect Adam Paul Susaneck's project Segregation by Design, some previously thriving neighborhoods were severed in half, their social and economic pulse decimated, by highways built in the mid-twentieth century.[20] And formerly redlined neighborhoods have continued to receive fewer parks and more waste treatment plants.

This has life-and-death consequences. On hot summer days in Portland, Oregon, neighborhoods greenlined and graded A decades earlier are now an average of thirteen degrees cooler than nearby, previously redlined neighborhoods. Heat waves kill as many as twelve thousand people in the United States each year, and every degree counts. Each degree increase can increase the risk of death by 2.5 percent.[21]

Histories of the present document communities' experiences with racial capitalism, wherein social, economic, and racial inequalities are not unfortunate by-products or aberrations of capitalism; they are foundational to it and keep the gears of business chugging along. As such, markets rely on the differentiation of social groups (by race, nationality, clan, or something else), around which they produce financial rules and products to help economies grow.

This contrasts typical narratives on how markets should work. According to those narratives, cases of racial discrimination might require special attention and redress. In markets, there are naturally winners and losers, and society can choose to help the unfortunate "losers."

Specific historical examples helped me to better understand ideas of racial capitalism in the context of cities. I was surprised to learn, for instance, that mortgage debts did not lead to foreclosure when the colonists first brought their property laws and debt structures from England. Rather, borrowers were usually given extra time to pay their debts, even after default, or had to pay fines or serve time in jail. Indeed, in the 1600s, colonies like Massachusetts and Connecticut followed suit, working to keep colonial settlements as stable as possible. But as legal scholar K-Sue Park writes, once colonists began to enter into contracts with Indigenous buyers, they started to combine debt-based financing with the Doctrine of Discovery—the principle used by European powers to claim ownership of land they had "discovered"—to "toxic and alchemical effect." This then normalized land debt. Before 1730, debt was a factor in one-third of land sale requests; in the next decade, it rose to 74 percent. Foreclosure in the United States became so associated with Native Americans that for the next two centuries, "it would remain common for whites to protest oppressive creditors and their threats of eviction or foreclosure by dressing in Indian costume, and even darkening their skin."[22]

Whereas foreclosure is often described as an unfortunate consequence of unmanageable debt, this history traces the consequence as a starting point from which colonists invented a new financial instrument with alchemical effects, in order to expropriate land from specific groups of people. Markets and racialized categories would not have developed in the same way without each other.

Flipping the gaze and delineating histories of the present are crucial to showing that cities did not naturally evolve to be segregated and unequal. As poet and scholar Claire Schwartz writes, "The past is only the past because the present / needs somewhere to point its crooked finger."[23] But cities still suffer from the cumulative effects of complex but mutable policies. Again and again, regimes of budget injustice operate by obfuscating these facts and normalizing the status quo.

3

Follow the Money

CITY RESIDENTS CANNOT HOLD mayors accountable for public budgets without following the money—tracing where public funds come from and go. Meaningful budget transparency and histories of the present involve at least three immediate policy implications for public budgets: They must be legible, comparable, and widely disseminated.

When municipal budgets are examined together, they show that US cities have a raw deal in federalist governance. Cities were told that their financial troubles were entirely of their own fiscally irresponsible making. As punishment, they have been subjected to mandated austerity measures and declining federal assistance for half a century. But policing budgets have grown steadily over the same period, even when tax coffers were slim. Ultimately, following the money shows the public that budget injustice is not an accounting problem, but instead a political one.

––––––

First, public budgets must be accessible and legible. It is no accident that "traditional financial reports are lengthy, complex, and unintelligible to the average citizen."[1] These reports are designed to inform and benefit the financial analysts, investors, and crediting agencies that judge a city's financial loan worthiness. Diving into the relevant policy and academic literatures on "popular budget reports," I learned that the shortest public reports out there tend to omit the big picture of government finance, like bonds and recessions. And I encountered new acronyms that almost felt like misnomers, like CCRs (four-page citizen-centric reports) and PAFRs (Popular Annual Financial Reports).

In New York City, the city comptroller issues a PAFR each year; the one issued in 2022 covers the fiscal year ending in summer 2021. New York's more comprehensive financial report apparently won awards for over forty consecutive years. The PAFR helpfully provides a basic organizational chart of city government, numbers people could relate to (like per capita debt figures along with median apartment and office rents), the big aggregate citywide numbers I saw in the Office of Management and Budget reports, and some graphs of trends. Moreover, each graph has a button allowing users to download the relevant data, averting the need to dig up the data via a separate link and file (or staring at dot-matrix-printed PDFs).

The report also helpfully tells me to look at Checkbook NYC, an online tool that puts "day-to-day spending in the public domain." At a quick glance, the Checkbook NYC website seems to do exactly what its name implies. It lists recent recorded contracts with individual contractors, like the lines for individual transactions in my own checkbook (back when people wrote physical checks). I can search for individual contractors and even set alerts for myself. Checkbook NYC still has some glaring omissions; when I click on the "Spending tab," for instance, the second biggest vendor is "N/A (PRIVACY/SECURITY)," which has already received $2.08 billion in the fiscal year I checked out. But even the possibility of pointing to and indirectly naming what exactly is missing feels like a triumph. Especially helpful are the accompanying analyses available, which surface patterns amid these thousands of transactions.[2]

Still, I yearned for hints of context—like percentages alongside spending amounts, so that I could have a sense of the relative size of different budget numbers as part of New York City as a whole. And more fundamentally, it remains difficult for me to compare revenues with expenditures. The two halves of the equation were for some reason not listed together. In 2024, the Federation of Protestant Welfare Agencies drew on data from Checkbook NYC to launch the NYC Funds Tracker, which helpfully puts revenues and expenditures together.[3] But it largely focuses on specific social services agencies, without disaggregating data from the huge category that it labels "other agencies."

In a twenty-four-page *Budget Summary* for Los Angeles, I found a Sankey diagram—the sort of graph I usually associate with data visualizations of oil flows or media corporate mergers—of cash flows.[4] Revenues like parking fines and property taxes flowed from the left side of the page into fiscal coffers in the middle of the diagram, and expenditures like "community safety" and wastewater treatment flowed out, to the right side of the page. Seeing this diagram clarified my burning questions: *Where does public money come from? Where does it go? Where should it go?* These questions should not be impossible ones.

I noticed, too, that the proposed budget for Los Angeles was, like New York's, more than five hundred pages long, but it has information like performance measures to inform public opinions on the proposed budget numbers.[5] Thus Los Angelenos can decide whether the cost savings from fewer building inspectors is worth a projected longer wait time for a building inspection. I did not know that I wanted this basic information until I saw it.

I later learned that the New York administration does release performance measures in the *Mayor's Management Report*, as mandated by the City Charter, and that the city comptroller even developed a helpful online transparency tool.[6] Still, informed decisions on public budgets are only possible when agencies report on their daily operations. It's impossible, for example, to hold police officers accountable when officers' discipline records are not consistently available in public databases.[7] It is telling that nonprofit journalism outfits, like *ProPublica*, created their own databases of civilian complaints against New York police officers.[8] Divesting and investing is therefore not only about reallocating money *across* domains, but *within* city agencies and policy areas as well.

I know there will never be a perfect public budget report; it is understandably difficult to find the perfect balance between concision and complexity. Still, reports need to include at least some details, so that numbers are not aggregated into meaningless averages that hide deep inequalities between schools or departmental subdivisions, for example. And they need to eschew jargon for accessible language that foregrounds public accountability and enables a community's collective ability to inform budgets that meet its needs.

Members of the public shouldn't need to wade through piles of city reports, third-party analyses, and research from investigative journalists to get a sense of the main budget stories the mayor's office should have made legible and clear in the first place.

Further, the public will not be able to inform budgets as moral documents until citizens are able to compare them across cities, for more ideas as to what they should or should not look like.

There are comparative indexes and scorecards out there, often with titles like "best performing cities," "safe cities," and "livable cities." Like the popular budget reports discussed above, each needs to be assessed with a critical eye. While some of these indexes articulate explicit implications for policy, others are aimed at market investors and employment firms. Like college rankings, most "best cities" ones aim to encourage competition between the entities listed. For example, the popular "walk score" serves as a commercial walkability index that scores any address in the United States, Canada, and Australia; it also publishes rankings of walkable cities. While individual users have sometimes critiqued its accuracy and representation of lived as well as felt walkability, real estate brokers and investment firms love it as a reliable arbiter of property values and mortgage default risk.[9] Where should companies lease new offices or invest in real estate holdings? It is easy to research rankings to divest-invest for profit; it should not be so hard to divest-invest for well-being.

The Sankey diagram I mentioned above is a tantalizing model for the sort of the visualization I want for all city budgets, but it is not too helpful for me right now because, as it turns out, Los Angeles does not include its expenditures on schools in its city budget. The US federalist, extremely decentralized—some might even call it labyrinthian—system means that it is virtually impossible to compare how different US cities handle basic services like water or affordable housing. Fortunately, the Lincoln Institute of Land Policy has constructed the Fiscally Standardized Cities database of local government finances for over two hundred of the largest US cities.[10]

The Lincoln Institute's database reveals that nationwide, the country's recent history of disempowering cities is, not coincidentally, also a racialized one. Police budgets have grown even when city coffers were slim, and through what the *New York Times* Upshot columnists call "a steep nationwide decline in violent crime that began in the early 1990s."[11] Indeed, according to the Bureau of Justice Statistics, violent and property crimes fell 71 percent between 1993 and 2022.[12]

Ruth Wilson Gilmore notes that the usual explanation for the growth of police and prisons goes something like this: "crime went up; we cracked down; crime came down." By examining real-life statistics and budgets, Gilmore asserts that "the string of declarative statements more properly reads: 'crime went up; crime came down; we cracked down.' If the order is different, then so are the causes."[13]

While this increase in police spending has no good correlation with crime rates, it does have a strong, statistically significant correlation with a city's demographics by race. Economist Ellora Derenoncourt's work shows that police are the "only public investment to increase in metro areas with more black migration" after World War II.[14]

These continually growing police budgets, across cities, reflect what historian Destin Jenkins calls an "infrastructural investment in whiteness" from the New Deal into the post–World War II era, and what historian Elizabeth Hinton dubs a larger, decades-long shift from President Lyndon B. Johnson's War on Poverty to the War on Crime.[15] Police have become the default answer to how policymakers define community safety, achieving egregious "mission creep" and overreach through the policing as well as militarization of policy domains like domestic violence and school safety.

These budget increases have consequences. The database Mapping Police Violence documents that in 2023, police killed at least 1,247 people in the United States, more than in any year since 2013, the earliest year for which it has reliable data. An astounding 97 percent of major city police departments kill Black people at higher rates than they do White people; from 2013 to 2024, Chicago police killed Black people at a rate twenty-seven times higher than White people. Roughly 70 percent of police killings began as encounters like traffic stops and mental health checks, rather than alleged violent crimes. Nevertheless, less than 2 percent of police killings have resulted in criminal charges.[16]

Studying city budgets and performance metrics nationwide—and embedded in federal policy—is essential to efforts to illuminate how even the most austere conditions do not interfere with the accumulation of funding within carceral institutions like prisons and policing.

———

When placed side by side, municipal budgets tell the distinct story of US cities getting the short end of the stick in federalist governance. Articulating divest-invest formulations for city budgets will not go far without changes in city finance as well—and in turn, federal finance.

While the national government can run a deficit, ninety-nine of the hundred largest cities in the country are mandated to balance their budgets. Yet federal aid to cities has been declining for almost a century now, even as localities remain responsible for labor-intensive services like education. US cities have become an archipelago of unfunded mandates.

After World War II, the US government poured money into highway construction and suburban development. Urban planning scholar Peter Marcuse found that federal tax subsidies that promoted specific kinds of investments (like depreciation allowances that discouraged refurbishing older factories in the Northeast and encouraged building new facilities in the southwestern United States) came to "more than twice the total budget of the United States Department of Housing and Urban Development for each year, and almost three times the total federal expenditure on community and regional development for the whole country."[17] It was not the fault of northern cities—and especially their inhabitants—that their cities became the Rust Belt, and technology companies flocked to the Sunbelt.

But even as the federal government abandoned (especially midwestern and northern) cities, it increasingly blamed them for their own misery. And certainly, many were easy targets, as municipal budgets deserved critique and desperately needed reform.

New York, for example, had been taking on risky forms of debt by the 1950s. As Phillips-Fein explains, "Especially striking was New York's increased use of short-term debt instruments known as tax-anticipation notes, revenue-anticipation notes, and bond-anticipation notes (or TANs, RANs, and BANs)." Unlike typical, safe bonds that take a long time to mature, TANs, RANs, and BANs were a dangerous, desperate measure. They were short-term loans that often matured after just a year, garnishing anticipated revenues like taxes collected. During John Lindsay's tenure as mayor from 1966 to 1973, the volume of such risky notes had quadrupled to a fifth of the city budget.

By the 1970s, the situation had become untenable. In 1974, the city's outstanding debts stood at $13.5 billion—$3 billion more than its revenues that year.[18] Lindsay's successor, Abraham Beame, suggested pushing some budget items into the subsequent year to make it look like the city had fewer costs to cover. And still, the city was hundreds of millions of dollars short of balancing its budget.

In 1975, the state passed the Financial Emergency Act of the City of New York, establishing an Emergency Financial Control Board filled with a council of just seven people, the majority of them appointed by the governor, to fulfill an "explicit mission of undercutting the fiscal authority of democratically elected politicians." Three years after the board's inception, the word *emergency* was removed from its name, and its charter was extended for another three decades. The fact that decision-making power was granted to a small group of largely unelected "people at the top of the city . . . whose interests were very different from those of New Yorkers . . . most affected by the cuts" seemed extraordinary at first. "But in the crisis, the unthinkable became real."[19] And in the aftermath, the exceptional became routine.

The board demanded drastic cuts to basic services along with the closures of entire hospitals and college campuses. National figures, too, insisted that the city's problems lay purely in overspending. President

46   BUDGET JUSTICE

Gerald Ford, for example, cited in a speech that New York City's worker salaries were "'the highest in the United States,' even though his own budget office had just released a report saying this wasn't so."[20]

National discourse on New York's fiscal crisis rarely contextualized its woes. Cities across the country were also, for instance, reeling from a recession. More pointedly, speeches like Ford's studiously avoided discussions regarding the loss of manufacturing jobs, rising unemployment, African Americans' Great Migration north and rising immigration flows, and a slew of postwar federal subsidies that built the American dream of white picket fences, homeownership, highways, and year-round sun—setting the stage for White flight from cities and suburban expansion—for people outside New York. State and federal policies thus starved the city of income tax revenues even as New York continued to serve as the backbone of remaining industry and economic activity.

National politicians held up New York as a paragon of profligacy so that the creation of the Emergency Financial Control Board appeared inevitable. This sounded a warning to other cities that they, too, better rein in their social services expenditures.

Hence 1975 became a turning point not just for New York but also "the country as a whole. . . . Throughout the country, at every level of government, public budgets suffer even as private fortunes grow . . . accompanied by the constant sense that any hope for a better society, any notion of collective action, must be a pipe dream—irresponsible, impossible to afford."[21]

Divisions of financial burdens between cities, states, and the federal government have worsened in the decades since. In the late 1970s, federal funds still constituted an average of around 15 percent of municipal revenue. In 1986, the Reagan administration eliminated the country's largest federal, no-strings-attached grant program, the 1972 State and Local Fiscal Assistance Act. In so doing, it also cut off billions of dollars to cities and local jurisdictions, so that such funds fell to and have hovered at around 6 percent of total municipal revenue since 1987.[22]

Even as it has given ever-lower amounts of aid to local governments, the federal government has kept for itself the most powerful sources of revenue, including personal income taxes, payroll taxes for Social

Security, and corporate income taxes. States also collect income taxes and impose sales taxes. Cities, by contrast, largely finance their expenditures through less powerful sources of revenue, including property taxes, permit fees, user fees, and municipal bonds.

In a vicious cycle, fiscal crises continue to be blamed on cities even when they were not a result of local spending, resulting in further, mandated retrenchment. It is with such logics that state officials in Flint, Michigan, switched the city's water supply to the lead-prone Flint River because it would cut costs. When General Motors tried to use the Flint River's water supply in its factories, the water was so corrosive that the company successfully got permission to use water from the Detroit River instead. Yet human beings were told to drink and bathe in water deemed too toxic for car parts. One study suggested that local fetal death rates increased by 58 percent after the city began to use water from the Flint River.[23]

Geographer Laura Pulido's analysis of environmental racism in Flint notes that some tests found lead levels ten thousand times over the federal legal limit. Miguel Del Toral of the Environmental Protection Agency was "pivotal in uncovering the scope and gravity of the poisoning" as well as "its deliberate nature." Remarkably, the city of Flint claimed that it was "optimizing anti-corrosive measures" when in fact it had "no measures in place," and adding an agent to keep the water safe would have cost merely $100 a day. As Pulido also remarks, "The situation in Flint is of concern to all of us, not only because of its tragic nature, but because . . . it is a testing ground for new forms of neoliberal practice that will become increasingly common."[24]

In a vicious feedback loop, politicians use austerity arguments to fend off public demands for accountability, crying that they are in crisis mode. And then, whether through "routine" budget opacity or criminal obfuscation (as in the case of the Flint water contamination cover-up), policymakers hide the inhumane and sometimes crisis-level consequences of their local austerity measures from the public eye. Budget opacity obscures the ways in which austerity is anti-Black, anti-Latine, anti-Asian, and anti–working class, hurting the life chances of everyone reliant on public goods like public schools and potable tap water.

The fiscal bind in which cities find themselves is a shared one—one that demands not competition but instead coordinated advocacy. Following the money thus has the potential of illuminating their difficult circumstances, harnessing popular support for antiausterity measures, and placing political pressure on the national government to do its share in pursuing equity and addressing budget justice.

———

Following the money allows the public to cast a wary eye on austerity, but it does not imply wanton largesse.

For example, one audit highlighted how Intensive Mobile Treatment teams for New Yorkers with severe mental health challenges lacked coordination between hospitals, the department of mental health, and the department of corrections. Patients were repeatedly released from hospitals, or rearrested without the treatment plans they needed to not harm themselves or others. Giving these agencies greater resources, but without changing their synergistic effects, would fail to keep New Yorkers safe.[25]

Transparency is pivotal to identifying and addressing the mismanagement of funds. That way, budgets can help the government to better manage expenditures—and earn the public trust again—rather than justify across-the-board cuts.

Following the money entails not only actuarial studies when gross mismanagement happens, but also routine accountability so that mismanagement is less likely to happen in the first place. In San Francisco, for instance, a faulty payroll system and inadequate staff training worsened a fiscal crisis in the city's school system.[26] In the second half of 2022, the district saved $1.1 million by understaffing its schools, so that it could use that money to fix EMPowerSF, a $13.7 million system that failed to properly pay school district employees for its first year of operations; the district's response then involved an $8.8 million contract with a consulting firm to fix EMPowerSF's mistakes and get teachers paid.[27] Two years later, the district voted to switch payroll systems, and the *Fiscal Health Risk Analysis* report noted that the district would likely continue to face fiscal crises unless it could better track its expenses and performance.[28] I was shocked to learn that in a major city like San Francisco, the analysis team found that "only one or two individuals know how to generate reports that all personnel in the [education] budget or accounting divisions should be able to run. . . . Because the errors have been pervasive for years and exist in a large system, tracing the errors is an enormous task that has not been undertaken."[29] Staff shared that they sometimes caught mistakes in the millions of dollars, but did not have the capacity for systematic oversight.

No city can afford such costly mistakes, often brought to light only through special reports and audits written after crises have already unraveled.

Finance researchers have found that fiscal transparency leads to an *increase* in government spending.[30] It breaks cities out of the vicious cycle of low public trust, leading to fewer taxes collected, leading to poor services, leading to low public trust, and so on. When taxpayers see that their taxes can make a meaningful and positive difference in their city, they willingly pay higher taxes.

———

Given New York City's history of eyebrow-raising accounting methods and high debt-to-income ratios before the 1970s' fiscal crisis, there is no question that city governments should practice financial responsibility. The public should expect public budgets to be carefully spent.

A remaining challenge lies in ensuring that specific austerity measures are not attempts to score political points under the guise of financial responsibility. Doing so is especially difficult because policymakers so routinely talk of fiscal crises stripped of context. As poet Rae Armantrout puts it, "Hit the refresh button / and this is what you get, / money pretending / that its hands are tied . . . money admonishes, / 'shut up and play.'"[31]

Rather than working with constituents to grapple with public budgets, politicians sometimes unleash austerity to make it look like that they are doing *something* to address a fiscal crisis, even when budget cuts do little to balance budgets, and worse, unleash suffering along the way.

Sometimes, policymakers render this explicit. Phillips-Fein writes of one instance in 1975, when a new and powerful public entity, the Municipal Assistance Corporation (created to sell bonds for New York City), pressured then Mayor Abraham Beame to introduce tuition at CUNY. Beame balked. He knew that CUNY was treasured as the "poor man's Harvard" largely because it was free. Beame also "objected that the money tuition would raise—about $32 million—would only be a drop in the bucket of what the city needed, while the poor and working-class population that the university served would find the fees a real burden." The Municipal Assistance Corporation board chair replied that it was the symbolism that mattered.[32]

Such moves are often not only financially ineffectual, but also fundamentally undemocratic, or even antidemocratic. Before the Municipal Assistance Corporation board's conversation with the mayor, a Chase Manhattan Bank executive, David Grossman, had already made tuition at CUNY likely, if not inevitable, when he promised it at a meeting with Federal Reserve officials—without first consulting city policymakers. Meanwhile, those suffering the consequences of budget cuts and new tuition fees protested the decisions; one demonstration at the mayor's residence attracted more than a thousand students, the majority of them African American.[33] But the students had no chance to help inform where sacrifices could be made and where they could not.

Such fiscal fundamentalism is only more entrenched today, so much so that it arguably abides by what psychologist Abraham Maslow calls the "law of the instrument." Maslow wrote that "if the only tool you have is a hammer, it is tempting to treat everything as if it were a nail."[34] If the only tool policymakers recognize is neoliberal austerity, they see every horizon as a fiscal cliff and every public budget as largesse. Some are, and some are not. Budget justice demands that policymakers focus on sound policy, based on evidence and public input, rather than scoring political points. It demands something other than an austerity hammer. It demands a more precise surgeon's—or more democratic bandleader's—touch.

4

Austerity for Profit

SINCE THE FISCAL crisis of the 1970s, New York's financial position and investment landscape has changed dramatically, but the refrain of neoliberal austerity has not. As such, neoliberalism is related to what Nobel Prize–winning economist Joseph Stiglitz calls fiscal fundamentalism, confusing means (such as cutting costs or lowering inflation rates) with ends (such as fiscal discipline or a robust economy).

In discussing national economies, Stiglitz points out the illogic of the International Monetary Fund's (IMF) fiscal fundamentalism in the 1990s; he notes one instance when the IMF suspended aid to Ethiopia, arguing that the country should not spend donor funds on, say, schools or health clinics. Instead, Ethiopia was supposed to put the aid money in reserves and only spend what it had *outside* the aid, potentially flouting both its needs and donors' explicit wishes.[1] The IMF had agreed with Ethiopia's leaders that its finances were pretty stable otherwise. It was as if, when Ethiopia's house needed repairs after a storm and it finally got extra funds for a new roof, it was told to pad its rainy-day fund rather than repair its house. The arrangement benefited Ethiopia's creditors, not Ethiopia, even though the IMF is an intergovernmental organization beholden to its member nations.

This sort of parasitic governance traverses scales and locales. Local entities like cities are likewise robbed of sovereignty in dealing with their respective national governments. They are forced to implement austerity measures that do not work. But why? Here I briefly examine examples in which austerity measures ultimately benefit certain agencies or political actors—such as policing agencies, real estate developers, and private services contractors like education testing companies.

————

New York consistently spends more on policing than the Departments of Health, Homeless Services, Housing Preservation and Development, and Youth and Community Development combined.[2] The bulk of the city government's overtime spending goes to uniformed officers in the NYPD; in its 2023 fiscal year, for instance, the police department's overtime costs were estimated at around $740 million, exceeding its $374 million overtime budget by 98 percent.[3] Yet the NYPD and Department of Corrections did not face the same proposed budget cuts as universal 3–K programs, K–12 schools, CUNY, and public libraries.

Because many social programs are known to prevent or address crime, such moves do not arguably make New York safer. For instance, New York City's preschool programs for three-year-olds (3–K) have been lauded as a national model, and early childhood education is a bargain in the long run.[4] It yields returns of as much as $16 for every $1 invested in the form of less crime and fewer social services needed in the future.[5] Likewise, participants in mental health courts, which divert formerly incarcerated people into treatment and coordinate care, report significantly lower recidivism rates, as compared to those with mental illness who go through the regular courts.[6] Yet, while early childhood care and mental health courts appear on perennial budget chopping blocks, the NYPD also regularly appears on the news to announce new technologies, like two robotic dogs that cost approximately $750,000—making two new dogs worth a year of preschool for approximately fifty-eight three-year-olds.[7]

In cities with smaller tax coffers, austerity and carceral policies are even more tightly coupled. As political scientist Naomi Murakawa writes, "Organized abandonment means that financially strapped cities rely on policing to contain austerity's carnage."[8] In some cases, city budgets are put on receivership and subject to so-called consent degrees, losing any semblance of self-determination.

Gilmore links the sort of organized abandonment facilitated by austerity policies to the concept of an antistate state—a consolidation of state power premised on government being, as former US president Ronald Reagan intoned, "not the solution to our problem; government is the problem."[9]

Compared to cities like New York, less wealthy US ones can be even more vulnerable to being trapped into low-tax, low-service, low-democracy, high-police conditions. In Ferguson, Missouri (the working-class, predominantly African American town where Michael Brown was killed on August 9, 2014, by police officer Darren Wilson), austerity pressures led to a model of municipal financing that American studies scholar Jackie Wang calls governmental "extraction and looting," and social policy scholars Joshua Page and Joe Soss dub "criminal justice as revenue racket."[10] In 2014, court fines and fees added up to $2.63 million and the second-largest source of the town's revenues. In a town with a population of roughly 21,000, the Ferguson municipal court issued arrest warrants for 32,975 nonviolent offenses that year, most of them driving related.

To reveal the essence of Ferguson's policies, legal scholar, writer, and prison reform activist Reginald Dwayne Betts redacted text from a lawsuit against the city; the resulting poem reads in part, "The City of Ferguson / devastated the City's poor / trapping them / in debts extortion and cruel jailings . . . grotesque dangerous and inhumane conditions a Kafkaesque journey / a lawless and labyrinthine scheme of / perpetual debt."[11] As Betts suggests, this budget injustice was not a discrete set of civil rights violations but instead baked into the town's political economy. A true accounting of how Ferguson ended up intensely segregated, poor, and overpoliced in a formerly White suburban community would not focus solely on the roles of individual racist real estate brokers or families participating in White flight. Rather, a true accounting would revolve around long histories of budget policies such as tax subsidies, government-backed mortgages, and financial products conditioned on the exclusion of Black people.

Austerity as policy is a sleight of hand that politicians use to justify real estate growth as the only acceptable vision of economic development. This is the city-level version of nation-states obsessed with GDP growth above all else. Long-term sustainability, policies to address long-standing and widening inequalities, and democratic accountability become de-emphasized, or even disregarded. In the case of New York, this has translated into more jail proposals and multimillion-dollar luxury condos, with fewer affordable apartments or preschool programs along the way.

When he first became mayor of New York City, Bloomberg made statements against "corporate welfare" and canceled stadium deals made by his predecessor, Rudolph Giuliani. "Given the lack of housing, given the lack of school space, given the deficit in the operating budget—it is just not practical this year to go and to build new stadiums," he said.[12] Yet by the time Bloomberg left office, his administration had authorized three stadium deals (for the Mets, Yankees, and Nets), with billions of dollars in public subsidies, and used eminent domain powers to displace hundreds of businesses and private homes.[13] Somehow, too, the new Yankee Stadium and Barclays Center were exempt from typical land use laws, like special permits for venues with more than twenty-five hundred seats.[14] In 2022, Mayor Eric Adams also announced a deal for a new soccer stadium in Queens for the New York City Football Club.

Bloomberg and Adams are hardly alone in pursuing stadiums as economic development—even though, on pure economic terms, these projects tend to have a poor track record. Economist J. C. Bradbury, who coconducted a comprehensive review of more than 130 studies on the economic impact of sports teams and stadiums, wrote, "Unfortunately, I am not aware of any stadium that has produced a positive return on investment to its host municipality."[15] Despite this, cities across the country continue to pursue such projects. In 2022, New York State and Erie County representatives agreed to give the Buffalo Bills $850 million in public money, the largest taxpayer contribution ever for a National Football League stadium. Just one year later, Nashville surpassed Buffalo's record, offering the Titans Stadium a $1.2 billion public subsidy.[16] The list goes on.

Nor are stadiums a new move in cities' austerity-for-profit tool kit. Phillips-Fein examines how during New York's 1970s' fiscal crisis, "the city helped subsidize an expansive renovation of Yankee Stadium even as the neighborhoods around it burned." Alongside "hardship" tax reductions to other business interests, such subsidies "further diminished the amount that could be raised from local revenues."[17]

Beyond stadiums, Bloomberg's pursuit of megaprojects and tourism is also reflected in his failed bid to host the 2012 Olympics. Although New York lost out to London, the Bloomberg administration used the Olympic bid campaign to expedite megaprojects like Hudson Yards luxury shopping center and Bushwick Inlet Park, without the sort of public input that typically accompanies major rezonings. Hudson Yards was promoted as self-financing, but developers received $5.6 billion in public subsidies and funds.[18]

The Atlantic Yards project in Brooklyn, first announced in 2003, was especially controversial. The $6 billion plan to redevelop twenty-two acres displaced more than four hundred families, with a contract awarded to developer Forest City Ratner without a competitive bid or oversight development corporation.[19] The developers promised a new arena, open space, commercial development, and 2,250 affordable apartments. Two decades later, the plan's rail yard remains undeveloped and more than 800 promised apartment units remain unbuilt.[20] Meanwhile, the public has paid dearly for the project. Forest City Ratner says that it received $305 million in public subsidies; according to one *New York Post* article, the subsidies amounted to $2 billion.[21]

Urban planning policies that largely benefit investors, in place of average New Yorkers, are not limited to special projects. In fact, even tax subsidies originally created to facilitate moderate-income housing developments have instead largely gone to high-end ones. This was not surprising in the 1970s, when the city was in a panic and desperate for investment. But as historian Benjamin Holtzman writes, "Even as the crisis of abandonment of the 1970s transformed fully into a crisis of affordability in the 1980s, the Koch [mayoral] administration ensured that both tax incentives and bonus amenities remained principal development strategies."[22]

56   BUDGET JUSTICE

These programs were misused on such a regular basis—mostly subsidizing developments that would have taken place anyway—that when the city tried to deny a tax exemption to Donald Trump because his Trump Tower development was not replacing an "underutilized" site, the city lost the case in the courts. Even as Ed Koch complained about the court decision, questioning why "some of the most expensive and luxurious accommodations . . . in the world . . . [got] a tax break," the city's "arguments," Holtzman states, "were undermined by the entire administrative history of the program."[23] Trump's shenanigans were a distillation, not an aberration, of the weaponization of "affordable" housing incentives.

Besides, Koch never attempted reforms like limiting tax abatements to neighborhoods in need of development, limiting eligibility to not-for-profit developers, or requiring contributions to an affordable housing fund. In fact, a report at the time found that one-quarter of the total value of exemptions went to buildings on the Upper East Side, "the wealthiest urban residential area in the nation."[24]

Municipal governments remain obsessed with raising property values and competing for global investments. Reflecting what geographer Sam Stein calls "the real estate state," in which real estate investors have "inordinate influence" over all cities, even affordable housing initiatives often fail to move the needle toward budget justice.[25] Former mayor de Blasio's reliance on market approaches and mandatory inclusionary housing zoning policies, for instance, resulted in few apartments for low-income households.[26] In January 2020, just before the pandemic, eighty thousand people slept in shelters or on the streets, while half of the luxury condo units on the market in the previous five years remained unsold. The average price for a newly listed condo in 2019 was $3.77 million.[27]

Houses and apartments are no longer, first and foremost, places to live; they are places to invest. By 2014, a full 54 percent of all luxury real estate in the city (worth $5 million or more) was purchased by foreign shell companies, in which the investor's identity can remain anonymous. Nor is this a phenomenon specific to New York; the corresponding numbers were 51 percent in Los Angeles and 37 percent in Miami.[28]

And absentee owners are not sticking to the high end of the market. According to one study by the New York budget office, one-quarter of apartments in the city are not used as primary residences.[29] Another study found that from 2020 to 2022, the percentage of homes sold to absentee owners increased in 228 of 307 zip codes in the United States, from Austin, Texas, to Charlotte, North Carolina.[30]

Rather than trickling down benefits, extreme tourist- and investor-focused policies lead to ill distribution and displacement. In many cases, even "successful" tourism campaigns benefit one neighborhood at the expense of others, or hurt the locals they are supposed to employ and benefit in the first place. For example, the underregulated growth of Airbnb in many cities led to crowding out of housing for long-term residents and the closing of essential businesses, like dry cleaners and grocery stores, which cater to locals and not tourists.[31] One analysis not only concludes that Airbnb has resulted in significant displacement and a "large concentrated loss of rental housing" in New York City, but also that a considerable percentage of what appears to be newly constructed housing actually consists of new unlicensed hotels.[32]

Whether the project at hand is a stadium or small high-end condo building, crucial questions remain. Are these developments worth their public subsidies? Do they improve the city's tax base? And even when they do, are they benefiting the city as a whole, helping to alleviate poverty or improve housing affordability, or are they exacerbating inequalities in ways that newly fuel budget injustice? Given the cost-of-living crisis in so many cities in the United States and around the world, do such projects further promote cities as playgrounds for the very, *very* rich? What grand vision of the city do they contribute to?

The urban development policy similarities across New York's Republican and Democratic mayoral administrations—and other mayoral administrations across the country—occur against a backdrop of fiscal fundamentalism as a bipartisan condition.

To realize budget justice, city residents must ask political questions attendant to the economic and social ones above. Given their track records, why do so many policymakers pursue high-end or large-scale tourism developments as their lodestar, if not sole, projects? How might

58 BUDGET JUSTICE

they reorient cities to help all residents thrive? Budget opacity and discourses of austerity are two of the primary attendant conditions that maintain this status quo.

———

It is also instructive to follow the money in the policy domain I opened part I with: schools. Decisions about where money goes reflect the racialization of current budget regimes, lack of care about actually saving money, and reliance on neoliberal tropes to maintain state reach. These choices are ultimately not about efficiency or balancing budgets but instead about hoarding power, subverting local rule and sovereignty, and doling out punishment and fear.

In US public education, 90 percent of funding comes from state and local revenue streams—in particular, notoriously volatile sales and income taxes (at the state level), and unequal property taxes (at the local level). This is a deeply regressive system in which schools not located near high-priced residential and commercial properties become trapped in a vicious cycle of underfunding, and unsurprisingly, poor educational outcomes. Moreover, it stands in stark contrast to school systems in other industrialized nations, where more equitable funding is coordinated at the national level. Yet legislation like the 2001 No Child Left Behind Act and 2015 Every Student Succeeds Act attempted to remedy these inequalities not by equalizing resources, but rather by "incentivizing" struggling schools to do better. Education scholars Michelle Fine and Jessica Ruglis describe this dynamic as "the circuits and consequences of dispossession," taking the right to a meaningful public education away from students and their families.[33]

One might expect an idealized market approach—emphasizing competition, grit, and efficiency—to operate like a reality TV competition. By stressing market principles in government policy, it might give competing preschool programs or elementary schools decent start-up funds, eliminate most contestants, and reward efficient schools that use funds wisely. In other words, a market approach in public budgets is supposed to encourage investment, attract businesses and wealthier residents who then pay taxes and pad public coffers, and reward cost-effective provisions of public services.

But existing legislation operates with the even more cutthroat and perverse logic that only punitive measures—withholding funds for books and school materials, or threatening teachers with job loss if their students' scores on high-stakes tests fail to improve—will prompt schools serving lower-income student populations to muster the will and "efficiency" to succeed. It withholds the equivalent of even start-up materials *until* student test scores improve. In many contexts, it virtually guarantees failure.

At the same time, the government closes surprisingly few schools nationwide. Instead, the administrators, teachers, and students at these schools live under constant fear and "mere" threat of closure.

This is because "actually existing neoliberalism" entails not state retrenchment exactly, but rather what geographers Neil Brenner and Nik Theodore characterize as the "dramatic intensification of coercive, disciplinary forms of state intervention."[34] The neoliberalization of public schools is about more than privatization and corporate profits, replacing traditional public schools with charter schools or school vouchers under the guise of "school choice." It is about controlling how schools operate, as opposed to closing them.

The restructuring of US education since No Child Left Behind thus signals what sociologist Erin Michaels calls a "central power shift, an upward redistribution of state power." Echoing the fiscal fundamentalism of the IMF's structural adjustment programs (the official term for its loan programs, with so many strings attached), current federal education policies produce what Michaels dubs "structurally adjusted schools."[35] Rather than receiving grants and mentorship on effective leadership and teaching, schools marked at risk must formulate "reform" plans focused on high-stakes testing and safety.

Everything at these schools becomes organized around "security." They must narrow curricula, use public funds to purchase testing and testing preparation services from certain state-approved private corporations, retrofit buildings with additional security doors, install metal detectors, purchase student-tracking software and surveillance

60 BUDGET JUSTICE

technologies, hire *non*teaching security staff, and add police patrols.[36] Some students describe being actively encouraged to drop out of school, lest their scores lower the school average or place their funding at risk. Students learning English, or exhibiting emotional or special needs, learn to recognize themselves not as eager students with untapped potential, but instead as drags on the system.[37]

In New York City, teachers and staff are supposed to call on guidance counselors, school nurses, and other mentors and clinically trained staff to help students suffering from emotional distress. But the nonprofit journalism outfits THE CITY and *ProPublica* found that schools call on safety agents and police officers in such situations—not once in a while, but routinely. Between 2017 and 2019, New York schools called for police to deal with children in distress an average of thirty-four hundred times a year. In more than a thousand incidents, students were handcuffed while they waited for an ambulance and medical help to arrive. Some children were four or five years old; some mistakenly thought they were being arrested and became terrified of school; and some accrued thousands of dollars in bills for these ambulance trips. Again, these violent state interventions are not evenly distributed across racial groups: Black children constitute less than a quarter of the student body, but constituted 59 percent of those handcuffed in child-in-crisis interventions.[38]

What some call the school-to-prison pipeline could thus also be labeled a school-*as*-prison laboratory.[39] Such schools disproportionately serve Black and Brown communities nationwide. Statistical analyses show that less qualified teachers, fewer capital resources, high-stakes standardized testing (especially mandated for high school diplomas), and more surveillance technologies all correlate with higher proportions of low-income and nonwhite students. By contrast, affluent, majority White districts can afford to flout state and federal requirements for funding, and in some districts in New York State, as many as half the students opt out of taking high-stakes exams.

As educational theorist Michael Apple argues, austerity "reforms" fail to improve schools or save money; rather, they represent a process of "massive recentralization and . . . de-democratization," further enabling the subjugation of students of color as inferior or outsiders, never full citizens.[40]

———

Cities face a real money crunch. This compels many elected officials to enact austerity measures and turn toward real estate developers for investments or carceral agencies for fines, even when they have awful effects. It is no wonder that communities are searching for new ways to again render public budgets as truly public.

Sometimes this involves using existing urban planning processes and tools—such as payments in lieu of taxes (PILOTs)—for public benefit. Scholars have critiqued PILOTs because some cities have used them not only on special occasions (like when selling public land to nonprofits such as hospitals) but also as a general incentive for downtown development—in effect assuring developers that they would pay less in PILOTs than they would in taxes.[41] But PILOTs can be used to resist austerity too. In the past decade, Baltimore, Providence, New Haven, and other cities have negotiated PILOT agreements with local tax-exempt universities, medical centers, and other nonprofit institutions that own large swaths of land. In Baltimore, residents explicitly asked for new ways for these institutions to invest in community wealth rather than private wealth.[42]

In New York, private universities like Columbia and NYU became locally known as real estate empires as much as educational institutions. Their property holdings have grown considerably over the past few decades, so that Columbia can now boast of being the city's largest private landowner by the number of addresses.[43] Its portfolio is such that its students wryly note that the university's century-old fight song lyrics can be read literally: "Oh, who owns New York? . . . Why, we own New York!"[44] In 2023, Columbia and NYU saved $327 million on property taxes.[45] Lawmakers have introduced legislation to eliminate property tax breaks for Columbia and NYU; the funds would then go to the city's public university.

62   BUDGET JUSTICE

In addition to using existing institutional tools in new ways, there are growing movements for new tools and institutions that benefit many rather than the few, and for long-term benefits rather than short-term profits.

Public banks, for instance, could underwrite municipal bonds or fund housing developments, but do so at lower rates than commercial banks—profitable enough to keep operations going, without squeezing every financial drop from the city. North Dakota created one in 1919 when private banks made loans to the agricultural sector difficult.[46] Since the 2007 financial crisis and ensuing Great Recession, many more US states have expressed interest. As of 2023, twenty-eight states have passed legislation to create public banks, and bills in several additional states are likely to pass.[47]

Whereas commercial banks can charge expensive fees and make high-risk decisions, public banks aim to establish affordable, low-risk, community-driven loans to emphasize less sexy but essential projects like infrastructural maintenance, stabilizing communities in times of economic crisis, and funding worker cooperatives that have solid business plans—even when, unlike the sort featured on shows like *Shark Tank*, those plans do not involve market conquest.[48] And in lieu of scaling up or wide, public banks work to deepen their investments in specific localities, focusing on projects such as affordable housing.

Public banks contrast antidemocratic existing models of local economic development. In 2017, when Amazon invited cities to submit proposals for its second headquarters, it expressly encouraged "special incentive legislation" and made the final twenty cities sign nondisclosure agreements on their bids—forbidding them from reporting even the size of their public utilities discounts. Amazon argued that those discounts amounted to trade secrets; even some local politicians were kept in the dark about the incentives offered.[49] Unlike Amazon's shenanigans or the sorts of special authorities that oversee many stadiums around the country, public bank operations must be transparent and accountable to the cities they seek to transform.

And in the end, the projects mayors keep trying to attract ironically thrive not with tax subsidies, but rather with tax-financed infrastructure like public transit and people—and their ineffable, density-associated dynamism, creativity, and innovation. This is why Amazon ultimately located its second headquarters in the Washington, DC, area, where marketing professor Scott Galloway guessed it would go in the first place.[50]

———

Given that austerity, carcerality, and institutional opacity go hand in hand in hand (if only the monster of budget injustice had fewer hands), formulations of what the public chooses to *divest from* and *invest in* will be essential steps toward achieving budget justice—but they will not be enough on their own. Again and again, different sides of the public budget equation—revenues and expenditures, costs and benefits, economic development and austerity—fail to add up and make sense.

Public banks and justice-oriented uses of tax increment financing and PILOTs like the ones I referenced will not appear on their own; they come about when the public fights hard for them. No amount of transparency, number crunching, or well-designed, colorful data visualizations of government expenditures will be enough without a struggle for democratic power. Even if policymakers were to emphasize budgets as moral documents and lay bare the values embedded in them, communities will not be able to secure the budgets they want and need without redemocratizing cities as well.

Budget justice demands what sociologist Henri Lefebvre articulated as a right to the city—not only to access opportunities for "the good life," but help make the decisions that make it so. The ends of budget justice will not be achieved without a change in means.

5

A Right-to-the-City Budget

PERHAPS IT IS IMPOSSIBLE to crunch numbers out of a fiscal crisis because the ultimate problem is not just that of scarcity of funds per se but a dearth of democracy too. I take a break from the ins and outs of New York's budget to dream: What if cities were made for the people who literally build and make them, rather than those who can afford to live in them? What if these two categories of people were not so distinct? Construction workers, sanitation workers, teachers, delivery workers, nannies . . . all of the characters in Richard Scarry's children's classic *What Do People Do All Day?*, for instance, could then afford to live in the city without being housing cost burdened (paying more than 30 percent of their income on housing). According to a recent report by the Harvard Joint Center for Housing Studies, roughly one-third of all US households and half of renters are cost burdened.[1] And according to the Community Service Society, a third of New York City renters were *severely* rent burdened in 2021, meaning that they put more than half of their income toward housing.[2]

Besides, people do not just passively reside in a city, or consume food, services, housing, and transport. The construction workers who help to literally build the city and the cooks who make certain restaurants "authentic," for example, have a right to live in and comake the city. With such a right, they might not only repair and build new water mains or cook hundreds of lunches each day, but also inform what sorts of water infrastructure and restaurants go into which neighborhoods.

In children's books, cities already function in just ways. In real life, austerity politics and governmental opacity render large swaths of cities underserved or unaffordable. Communities must demand not just greater governmental transparency but more democratic ways to engage policy, too.

Everyday residents should have a right-to-the-city budget. I use this phrase in two ways. First, citizens should be able to shape what city budgets look like; they have a right to them. These rights are not necessarily legal, constitutional ones. Nor can they be encoded into technical laws mandating, say, a certain public review period before a city budget is passed.

Second, public budgets should nurture a right to the city writ large. Here, I draw inspiration from ideas of a right to the city—not only to traverse and inhabit the city, but to shape its future in the image of the people who inhabit it and make it great.

———

Both scholars and activists have taken inspiration from the notion of a right to the city, and they sometimes forward different interpretations of what it means. Even intergovernmental institutions like the United Nations have used the framing, advocating that governments not only upgrade housing conditions but give residents the tools to improve their own lives and built environments too.[3] In the United States, Right to the City is the name of a national coalition of more than ninety community-based organizations that emerged in response to mass displacement due to gentrification. It focuses on housing justice and renters' rights.[4]

Other campaigns have interpreted the framing more broadly; a European network of Solidarity Cities works to forward more inclusive policies of belonging than their respective national governments do. In Berlin, one movement is advocating for a health care card that ensures access for everyone, including those lacking legal status.[5] Likewise, many cities in the United States enact policies as part of the Sanctuary Cities movement, refusing to cooperate with national immigration laws

66   BUDGET JUSTICE

that punish residents solely because of their paperwork status when in everyday life, they are very much part of their local communities. Cities from San Francisco to South Bend, from Little Rock to New York, have enacted municipal identification cards as one way to codify otherwise unauthorized or undocumented immigrants as members of their local communities, with a right to the city.

In the Global South, urban dwellers draw on right-to-the-city framings to demand less precarious living and housing conditions "in response to neoliberal dispossession and inequality." Anthropologist James Holston argues that this latter formulation "constitutes a new conceptual frame for right to the city, emerging from the South and differing from that originally articulated by Henri Lefebvre and developed by many others. . . . [T]hose who make the city have a claim to it—what I call a contributor right."[6]

Indeed, while the right-to-the-city framing is perhaps most associated with Lefebvre, many contend that the original framing is a limited one.[7] "Feminist scholars," for instance, "have long argued that the [historical] right to the city framework neglects . . . gendered relations."[8] Further, political scientist Lester Spence notes that "while black radical organizers and intellectuals have long thought about the city as a specific space of black possibility and black subjugation . . . refract[ing] that concept through the work of Henri Lefebvre . . . ignores the work of organizers like James Boggs [based in Detroit], but more broadly if we take a figure like Boggs (who was an autodidact) as the center, it ignores the critical role people outside the university take in knowledge production."[9]

———

This book takes inspiration from the broader interpretations of the right to the city, including significant contributions from the Global South and those outside the academy. Namely, a right to the city entails not only the *what* of the budget—such as, say, affordable housing—but also *how* the budget is constructed in the first place. It signifies, in some ways, a right to democratic politics. I use the word *citizen* as it is discussed in right-to-the-city discourse—almost a city-zen, a denizen of a city.

"The right to the city is," as geographer David Harvey asserts, "far more than individual liberty to access urban resources: it is a right to change ourselves by changing the city. It is, moreover, a common rather than an individual right since this transformation inevitably depends upon the exercise of a collective power to reshape the processes of urbanization."[10]

In the context of budget justice, a right to the city entails *radical democratic governance*, in which policymaking is participatory, deliberative, and equitable, alongside active and substantive citizenship, in which citizens' practices can forward new policies instead of only choosing among existing ones, and in so doing, enact new solidarities.[11] Both radical democratic governance and substantive citizenship are essential to resisting hegemonic, largely neoliberal models of what cities and citizens should look like.

———

The sort of right-to-the-city budget I discuss here is not exclusive to cities, but cities—with their entrenched inequalities and fierce contestations for power—provide an especially fertile ground for it. Indeed, in the past few decades, city residents around the world have rebelled in the face of economic disaster and demanded what could be called budget justice. Between the Great Recession of 2007 and Black Lives Matters uprisings of 2020, protesters occupied urban public spaces to protest policy responses to the financial meltdown (like bank bailouts and the privatization of water utilities), growing personal debt, and the cost of living and education in cities, including Athens, Reykjavík, São Paulo, Caracas, Hong Kong, Santiago, Tunis, Cairo, Paris, and Madrid.[12] Not coincidentally, many of the protests also emerged from racially marginalized communities—sometimes from the literal peripheries of global cities. Some of the protests became inextricably tied to the specific neighborhoods or spaces in which they took place, such as Occupy Wall

Street and Zuccotti Park in New York, Tahrir Square in Cairo, Taksim Square in Istanbul, and Puerta del Sol square in Madrid.

Two points about these protests stick out to me. First, they stood for both economic and political rights. The Arab Spring, for instance, catalyzed when Tarek el-Tayeb Mohamed Bouazizi, a Tunisian French street vendor, self-immolated in response to governmental harassment and the confiscation of his wares. Before he set himself on fire, he shouted, "How do you expect me to make a living?" Although global newspaper coverage primarily portrayed the Arab Spring protests as prodemocracy ones against military rule, questions of livelihood remained paramount.

Second, many of the protests not only rejected existing regimes, whether dictators or political parties; they practiced and experimented with entirely new modes of social organization and political participation. In Madrid, decisions regarding the movement's tactics were decided by consensus, and assemblies that started at the Puerta del Sol square expanded to neighborhoods around the city. In fostering worker cooperatives, community gardens, and police-free zones around the country, these protests also enacted a sort of social life that deviated from that of both the market (which would suggest that organizers should have used the occasion to make a financial killing, as they might at a music festival) and typical politics (which would suggest that organizers should have focused on specific political messages, or specific campaigns for or against specific policies and parties).

It is no coincidence, then, that scholars have examined participatory democratic innovations and modes of citizen mobilizations as an urban phenomenon, and some use the term *urban citizenship* for what I call substantive citizenship.[13] Political theorist Hannah Arendt writes that the density of cities and "living together of people" are "indeed the most important material prerequisite for power."[14] This involves not only people rubbing shoulders in everyday life, whether on the subway or in local playgrounds while watching their children, but beginning to collectively deliberate community needs, priorities, and solutions as well.

As earlier chapters assert, cities are crucial testing grounds for austerity measures. Phillips-Fein shows how New York's pivotal and excruciating budget cuts in the 1970s were only possible because they were made in deeply undemocratic ways, "without the full participation of the people of the city itself. At the same time . . . to this day, few other places in the United States offer as many possibilities for common, public life."[15] Cities, then, also remain critical and fertile grounds for new economic policies centered on community wealth.

Still, facilitating a right to the city remains especially challenging because of what political theorist Iris Marion Young calls a "politics of difference" in cities—a way for city residents to live with others unlike themselves, without either forcibly assimilating nor actively "othering" them. Young writes that this politics of difference in city life operates "as an alternative to both the ideal of [monolithic or unified] community and the liberal individualism it criticizes as asocial. . . . In the city persons and groups interact within spaces and institutions they all experience themselves as belonging to, but without those interactions dissolving into unity or commonness."[16]

This sort of city life (and by extension, urban governance and citizenship) thrives on surprise, delight, friction, and frisson. Cities are exciting precisely because they "provide important public spaces—streets, parks, and plazas—where people stand and sit together, interact and mingle, or simply witness one another, without becoming unified in a community of 'shared final ends.'"[17] Everyday life in cities accrues meaning partly by stumbling on a film shoot and seeing a familiar street differently, listening to a busker singing one's favorite song in an unexpected style while waiting for the subway to arrive, encountering (and becoming suddenly superstitious, thus avoiding) chalk-drawn bubbles on the sidewalk marked "bad luck" by a local artist, or watching two people with different cultural heritages than one's own on what is clearly their first date. Some urban planners dub cities "serendipity engines," places where the unplanned happens, and people's encounters and entanglements with others sometimes prompt them to think in new ways.[18] Economists, too, study cities as

70 BUDGET JUSTICE

spaces of innovation—in everything from biotechnology to playwriting—through "agglomeration."[19]

Moreover, such moments reflect negotiations between different urban dwellers on how each resident can make their distinctive mark in the city. Both newly arrived immigrants and fifth-generation citizens of different racial backgrounds exist in abundance in New York, but generally speaking, their communities receive different levels of public help. Who can afford to live in the city, and in what neighborhoods? Whose spoken languages are reflected on subway walls? In close quarters, contestations over space and resources become ubiquitous, and heartrending inequalities are put on conspicuous public display. I, for one, cannot help but notice the number of people sleeping on the streets on my way to work each morning. When subway infrastructure is underfunded, commuters and visitors alike become trapped on overcrowded subways and suffer through seemingly interminable delays. The diversity and density of city residents attempting to share the commons distill a prerogative of the right to the city: any struggle for reclaiming the city must do so for everyone.[20]

While the scale and density of cities may help researchers and activists to more easily recognize democratic experimentation or mobilization in cities, their lessons apply to suburban and rural areas as well. The phrase *right to the city* is pithy and useful, but this right should not be exclusive to cities. Questions of budget justice and a right to the *town, forest,* or *place* are as poignant in the village of East Palestine, Ohio (the site of a 2023 toxic train derailment), or areas of Illinois, Iowa, North Dakota, and South Dakota hosting the Dakota Access oil pipeline. In small towns as well as big cities, residents sometimes engage in the sort of "citizen science" and substantive citizenship dramatized in films like *Erin Brockovich.*

Even in places without large-scale disasters or infrastructural projects, questions of how to raise public funds and use them remain paramount. Lack of broadband access is a dire issue in many rural areas; during the pandemic, one-quarter of those in rural areas and one-third of those living on tribal lands lacked internet and could not access telehealth visits.[21] And questions of state funding and police fines have shaped

Ferguson, Missouri (as noted earlier, with a population of about 21,000) as indelibly as Saint Louis (with a metro population of some 2.8 million).

———

Planning and urbanism scholars Alexandre Apsan Frediani, Barbara Lipietz, and Julian Walker characterize Lefebvre's notion of the right to the city as "an ethos rather than a recipe."[22] Because it becomes substantiated through practice, and because it is characterized by difference and unpredictability rather than sameness, it cannot be codified or reduced into a legal amendment. It becomes imperative to recognize different ways of claims making as well as knowing, in order to nurture new forms of governance and citizenship.

In part II, I turn to how communities might begin to contest the logics and practices that undergird status quo budget politics, so as to make budgets more publicly accessible as well as meaningful. I argue that budget justice requires a model of participatory democratic governance besides liberal representative democracy. In other words, a right to the city requires more than elections in which individual registered voters walk into a booth and cast secret ballots, or municipal identity cards that enable new arrivals to vote and participate in status quo institutions. It requires radical democratic practices and a new model of urban governance.

INTERLUDE

An Interview with Makani Themba

Jackson's Budget Needs Base Building with Rigor and Heart

HOW MIGHT CITIES begin to break out of the vicious cycle of mutually reinforcing austerity and opacity? For years I have admired efforts by the people of Jackson, Mississippi, to render it "the most radical city on the planet."[1] In a state known for anti-Black racism, this majority Black city forwarded the visionary three-pronged Jackson–Kush plan in 2012: people's assemblies to democratize local governance; a broad-based solidarity economy, anchored by worker cooperatives and other democratically self-managed enterprises, through the network Cooperation Jackson; and an independent Black political party.[2] While Jacksonians have yet to realize the third prong of this plan, they did elect a radical Black lawyer and organizer named Chokwe Lumumba as mayor in 2013. Although Lumumba passed away eight months later, his son, Chokwe Antar Lumumba, was elected mayor in 2017 and reelected in 2021.

At first glance, budget justice seems downright impossible in Jackson. Its water infrastructure, as but one notable example, has been in crisis for over a decade, leaving its tap water unsafe or simply unavailable for long periods of time—after storms, winter freezes, or waterline breaks. And after a $90 million contract with the technology conglomerate Siemens left the city's water billing system in shambles (failing to send any water bills to many residents, and then sending other residents $8,000 bills), Jackson was unable to collect funds to repair its water infrastructure. According to the Environmental Protection Agency, the city issued around three hundred boil-water notices from 2020 to 2022.[3]

These awful conditions were not created in a vacuum. As with public education, the US water system is quite fragmented. There are 153,000 public water systems in the country, and federal funding for local systems has plummeted by 77 percent since the 1977 passage of the Clean Water Act.[4]

Further, within Mississippi, state politicians routinely undermine Jackson's sovereignty. After the state legislature repeatedly rejected city requests for emergency aid, Mayor Lumumba forwarded the 2020 Jackson Water Bill, which would have provided residents relief for faulty water bills, written off water bill debts, and repaired the city's bond status, so that Jackson could fund repairs by issuing municipal bonds. Although the bill had unanimous support in the legislature, it was vetoed by Governor Tate Reeves.[5] In 2023, the state senate passed a bill to place Jackson's water system under state control, and the state house tried to pass a legislative bill that would dictate what Jackson sales tax revenues could and could not be spent on—even though Jacksonians imposed a 1 percent tax on themselves.[6] Meanwhile, federal funds that could have gone to Jackson, like $1.8 billion received under the American Rescue Plan Act, remained under state control.

But in 2022, grassroots mobilizations and international attention managed to help Jackson to secure a $600 million agreement between the Environmental Protection Agency, Justice Department, city, and state—through a third-party manager.[7]

Jackson's struggles make its hard-earned wins more poignant. As Reverend William Barber II, an activist and cochair of the Poor People's Campaign, notes, the city "is not an isolated battle. In some ways, Jackson may become a launching pad for more movements across the country, wherever this problem exists."[8] I particularly appreciate the Jackson–Kush plan's analysis of political and economic powers as irrevocably intertwined, as well as its commitment to making the politics of budgets more democratic.

I sat down over Zoom to speak with Makani Themba, a thinker and longtime community organizer focused on social policy, social justice, and narrative strategy. She is chief strategist at Higher Ground Change Strategies in Jackson. I was particularly excited to speak with her because of her work with Jackson People's Assembly, and her articles and case studies on race, class, media, policy, and public health.[9]

I wanted to learn more about Jackson's people assemblies, which felt like grounded and radical experiments in democracy at the heart of the city's larger struggles for budget justice. In these people's assemblies, Jacksonians come together to share ideas about the city in which they would like to live. The assemblies were modeled, as Themba writes, on "best practices from the growing participatory budget movement with resident leaders working with MXGM [Malcolm X Grassroots Movement] organizers to develop the process."[10] From the beginning, the assemblies have focused on developing policy initiatives around priorities identified in assemblies, such as economic development, food security, and health. Themba speaks about how these assemblies tackle both independent, "self-determination" projects like garden cooperatives and attempts to "reform" municipal policies, and how they have evolved over time.

This interview has been edited and condensed for clarity and concision.

CELINA SU: *How did you get into the work you're doing now?*

MAKANI THEMBA: I had an activist parent. I grew up in the sixties in Harlem and New York City generally, so that was a hotbed of activism. It was normalized for me, [that] this is what you do when things don't work—you fight. I'm grateful for that knowing. I have been involved in some aspect of organizing from a young age. I was a student activist; I helped found the statewide alliance of Black students in California and then moved from there into activist jobs. My first job out of college was at the Southern Christian Leadership Conference.

My arc to Jackson started with my activism in Los Angeles in the seventies and eighties. I connected with, became really bonded with, and have so much respect for the folk of the Republic of New Africa [a Black nationalist organization founded in 1968, of which Lumumba was a prominent member]. That's how I got my name. They've been organizing here for a long time, and so I made a decision. By 2013, I decided to leave an organization I founded and was director of. I then started leaning toward moving here; I did that in 2016.

Originally when I made the decision to move here, Chokwe Lumumba was still on this side. When he made his transition, I decided to still come. I wanted to support the work here. I've been involved for a long time here, even before I lived here. I had helped support starting the people's assemblies.

I've had some of my relationships with some of the folks who are on the ground here organizing since I was in high school, so the roots were deep for me, even though I'm not a Southerner. I've been around the South. My work continues to take me all around the country. Right before I moved to Jackson, I was living in Detroit, the Bay Area, and DC, simultaneously. And so Jackson was the first place in more than a decade where I ended up living in one place at a time. It wasn't a huge adjustment; it also afforded me community and a much more affordable living.

CS: *I'm curious how the Jackson residents come together and talk about budgets as moral documents, and thorny issues like how Jackson could address infrastructure, for instance.*

MT: I want to make it clear that this is not some utopian thing, that the vast majority of Jackson residents are not involved in people's assemblies. And we [still] have a group of city council people who push messages like, "We don't have the money," or "Everything needs to be about police," or all the things that you hear everywhere else. They are currently the majority; hopefully, that will change at one point. Those [council members] don't really attend people's assemblies.

We get somewhere between 100, 150 people at each assembly, sometimes more, depending on what [the topic at hand] is. But it is a growing and diverse group of folks, classwise, otherwise. It leans toward working-class [participants], which is great. What the people's assemblies first did was have some training on participatory budgeting. We worked with a group who came and did a couple of trainings, [and] we have a lot of city officials who attend them to listen, including the mayor. So people come. That helps because there's a direct bridge.

The assemblies are a space in which we try creative ways of engaging folks, especially in small groups. The budget piece was a part of that. We spent a good amount of time helping people understand the language, what the process is, how it works.

And we were fortunate—the chief operating officer for the city at the time made up a *Monopoly*-type game that he brought to the people's assemblies for people to play and practice budgeting. And so it was this great popular education thing. He even made [fake] money and all the [city budget categories]. People got to figure it out, and he also explained what things got set aside—that the state requires the city to do, [such as mandated] salaries. So people got into it and understood, but not in a way like, "You can't touch that," more like, "These are the kinds of decisions that we make as a city around the budget."

It was interesting to watch people be so engaged around all of these tools that were available to us, which I think may not be available for other folks. [This built] a different kind of relationship. Then you had kids involved in the conversation; they had their own little session at the same time in the same room. I felt like the conversations that people had were much more substantive and informed because they were grounded. They actually understood what the budget was. They got to play with the budget, literally, learning and synthesizing information. The quality of interaction around [the budget] was really important.

CS: *You have noted that Jackson's situation reflects a "states' rights ideology rooted in the history of White power. So states get the money, and they make decisions about where the money goes."*[11]

Were there common sentiments regarding these challenges, because you can't tax income and don't get much state aid?

MT: Absolutely, people are clear about that. That's why there was a whole set of work protesting the governor's mansion, every week—Moral Mondays—that was anchored by the Mississippi Poor People's Campaign. So there was a way where people tried to channel that energy and pressure, both mediawise and organizingwise.

The other thing we did that I thought was pretty amazing was generate a lot of media about the water situation in Jackson. We worked hard to do that, together. There was the city part, but also media helped put it on the national agenda. The way we're framing it also created conditions to have support from the Congressional Black Caucus, which then figured out a way to move money to Jackson. That wouldn't have to go to the state. That was like $800 million altogether. Which was huge. That had never happened before. But that also created a kind of a backlash by the state government to punish us; the capital corridor issued HB1020, which attempts to try to take over the system, and this independent third-party water manager [too].

Other issues bubbled up. Folks are concerned with public safety, and there's been some interesting work around alternatives to policing and credible messengers that have come out of people's assemblies. One of the things that came out of a people's assembly on safety was a whole group of folks who were formerly incarcerated, who were like, "You know, the real issue is jobs." They came up with a proposal, [which] then ended up being picked up by the city to hire more folk. Some other projects, like creating this contract, and collectives of folks who have come out of prison, came out of the assemblies— organizing and problem-solving, that's what's great about those forums.

CS: *How did you decide to focus on particular emphases and forms of activism, like the Jackson People's Assembly?*

MT: All of my life, I have alternated between local and national work. [When] I get sick of national [work], I do local [work]. And now I get to do both things; I move around.

But it was actually [author and social activist] Grace Lee Boggs. It was at homecoming at Highlander [Research and Education Center, formerly Highlander Folk School, Tennessee, which was famously attended by Rosa Parks before the Montgomery bus boycott]; I'd been on the board for a while. My brother, who is close to her, was going to be in a conversation with her as part of a program, and so I got to hang out.[12] And she gave me this whole lecture about how I was out of balance and needed to do more local work, which I know is her shtick. But also, it was what I needed to hear at that moment. It just was forming in my mind that Jackson would be that place for me to bring what I know with people I trust, and who already know me, as I didn't want to be that person to just drop in a place. I wanted to be in a place where I had relationships and political family. That is really it—my need to be connected to community again, in that way.

CS: *And why the people's assembly?*

MT: I was a part of the founding, but there's people who really did the work on the ground. I was supporting and helping people think about it. I believe in people's assemblies. My sense has been for a long time that we are as movements, as progressive movements, as left[ist] movements, whatever you want to call it, deficient in base building. I know few people have anything like a mass organization.

I've been thinking a lot about forms that reflect more mass organizing and also forms of governance. I was really interested in what was happening in Brazil with MST, and how they were building, and they continue to influence so many folks worldwide. [MST refers to the Movimento dos Trabalhadores Rurais Sem Terra in Brazil, with more than a million members, living in a majority of the country's twenty-six states.] And in the [United] States, you had Community Coalition [a grassroots organizing institution based in Los Angeles], which I got to work with. They had started a kind of a cell/block approach, doing these house meetings where people were connected to local leaders by block—very old-school, Chicago style, or like what I grew up with in New York but more around elections. This was around issues and a culture of how people came together.

cs: *What do you mean by "culture" here?*

mt: [It is] not this transactional thing where [organizers say], "We're going to have this action; come to this meeting. Let's plan this action. Let's do this thing." It was, "We're neighbors. How are you doing? I haven't seen you in three days. Are you sick? Do you need something?" So how do we build a culture of connection? [We were working toward] a culture of care versus a transactional organizing culture, even though these folks were very much trained organizers in the old-school [style], and definitely had rigor in terms of saying, "You need to make this many calls, you need to have this many contacts, you need to . . ." They refer to it at CoCo [Community Coalition, mentioned above] as the art and science of organizing. I wrote a book called *Making Policy, Making Change,* in which they're one of the case studies, to [highlight] this hybrid relationship.

People's assemblies felt like that for me, a vehicle to build that kind of hybrid—with rigor *and* relationships, a culture of care. And Jackson was a place where that could happen, because there were so many conditions that really lent [themselves] to building that kind of institutional base. In the beginning, it was a little wonky because the folks who were doing the organizing had the rigor, but not the heart. And so it started off . . . in 2006, maybe 2007. They were relying on junior organizers . . . [who] weren't developed with that kind of care. And they weren't southern people. They were from Los Angeles, from the Bay Area, from New York; they had other great talents and skills, but that wasn't their thing.

80 BUDGET JUSTICE

At that point, the people's assemblies were in Chokwe's council district, the second ward, and the people who got involved were those connected to him because he was the one who was operating with the heart, and the folks who had been there awhile.

And so [the dynamic] shifted. Rakia, his daughter, came down, and more people who were rooted in the work. Halima Olufemi, a native Jacksonian who I was hoping was going to lead that organizing anyway. Brooke Floyd, who's another longtime Jackson person who leads them. I think the shift to that more feminine approach, that heart, more integrated approach, [with] people who were really from there, who knew folk, who had those relationships. Brooke was a teacher. She also worked a long time in the homeless shelter. She knows *everybody* from every walk of life, and that makes a difference. And Halima, similarly, I think she's third-, fourth-generation Jacksonian. That rootedness allowed the people's assemblies in this period to be more of what I think everybody hoped they would be—that kind of place of community to bring things and talk about them, but also organize. I think that's the part that's now being built— more capacity to organize and expand the base.

CS: *What has been particularly striking to you in your time in Jackson?*

MT: This place surprises me in all kinds of beautiful ways. I think one is the way in which people hold each other in community. Folks will go, "Southern hospitality!" and act like it's some kind of two-dimensional stereotype. But it's a real thing. It's really beautiful the way people show up for each other, even if they don't personally get along—the level of political maturity that folks have . . . unlike in places that are *supposed* to be so sophisticated, [but then] somebody writes an email [critiquing] them, and they never speak for thirty years; that doesn't happen here.

People struggle together in the ways that you would expect comrades to do, even though they may not use that language.

INTERVIEW WITH MAKANI THEMBA   81

They are clear that life is not to be wasted. That level of maturity, both political and emotional, is something that I love. I see how powerful it is, how it creates the conditions for people to work together for decades. We talk about principled struggle, but folks here literally do it.

The other thing is that it's just a much more progressive place than one would think. I don't mean just Jackson. There are just lots of pockets of longtime radical communities here, and not just [among] Black people. And that gets obscured because of the Confederacy and MAGA [a nativist movement coalescing under the slogan "Make America Great Again"]. Which in many ways is what makes Jackson kind of famous in a way—how it lives in contrast to the dominant narrative about Mississippi. But there is more to it. It's a much more complicated place than people would [think]. It's not just a Black versus White [thing]; it's not as dichotomized or polarized.

CS: *What's foremost on your mind in terms of what needs to be done?*

MT: I wrote an article about that.[13] But even that is now outdated in my mind. I'm going to say two things that are connected. One is we have to build . . . I don't like the term *political home* because you only want certain people in your house . . . So maybe we should use the term *political park*—where people can play together and work together and be together en masse, where folks feel like they belong to something important, and for us to claim the traditions and legacy of left[ist] mass movement building. People act like only the Right does it, and I think that that confuses people, in terms of what there is to do.

Then related to that, the only way to build movement is to also really do the work of contesting narratives that are demeaning, divisive, and disappear who we are, our history. And that's not by countering it or having a demonstration. We have to do the work of uprooting these ideas out of schools and the places where the Right is continuing to rout them, [where] they've been routed for centuries. There is this relationship between building a mass movement and what people learn, what people are told in their churches, what people believe is true.

We have to work on both building this movement and a different kind of set of narratives that help us build trust in each other, help us see a future of love and care, and give us a sense of possibility that things can be different than they are.

cs: *Amid all of this, what keeps you going?*

mt: What keeps me going? Oh my, these people! I work with the most amazing comrades. And—I say this all the time—I always believe [that] we're just a nanosecond away from freedom. I don't necessarily think it has to be a thousand years of struggle. So that gives me hope, that there's more and more people who think in integrated ways, who are trying to do it differently, who are willing to admit they're lost when they're lost, and to ask questions and try to find our way back.

It could happen at any moment. Everybody could look up and be like, *Fuck it. I'm tired. We're free.* That's all that needs to happen. If a billion people say that, then we're free.

PART II

Democracy Is a
Daily Practice

6

No Taxation without Participation

IF BUDGET INJUSTICE runs on governmental opacity and austerity, one antidote might be to vote current elected officials out of office, and to instead elect *into* office politicians who better represent communities' needs. Given dismal voting rates in the United States, that is not easy to accomplish. And then, even when communities do elect officials who purportedly reflect their values, enacting just budgets is not so simple. The austerity urbanism endemic in US cities is reinforced by and actually expands a system of governance where money rules.

Those with resources participate more. Less than half of those with household incomes under $30,000 voted in the 2020 election, whereas more than 70 percent of US households with incomes over $100,000 did.[1] Unsurprisingly, elected officials enact policies that ultimately benefit moneyed interests, often using the ostensibly neutral language of economic development and the "tide that lifts all boats." This occurs even during administrations called progressive. Former New York mayor de Blasio, for instance, ran on a campaign of tackling inequalities, but his affordable housing policies nevertheless benefited real estate developers more than working-class residents. In other cases, even the semblance of democratic governance is ripped away from (frequently majority minoritized) cities. In what Wang calls the financial state of exception, cities under fiscal duress are put on receivership and ruled by euphemistically named emergency managers' consent decrees, not mayors and

86   BUDGET JUSTICE

city councils.[2] In response, budget justice requires radical democratic processes for meaningful, substantive political participation.

Whatever this might look like, it is not by voting. I remember when, days before the 2012 presidential election, I turned to a *Guardian* website interactive feature, calculating the likelihood that my vote might make a difference.[3] I told it my state of residence, age, educational attainment, and so on, and it calculated that according to the feature's data, the percentage likelihood that my vote might affect the election results was a grand total of . . . zero. Apparently, 98,439,860 others were in the same boat. I still voted, partly to feel counted in the popular vote. But it isn't hard to see why so many people in the United States might feel disenchanted with existing channels of political participation. And while these sorts of calculations seem especially pained during presidential elections, they are but symptoms of fundamental issues in our liberal, representative democracy overall.

Voting in the United States is designed not only to be relatively difficult and largely inconsequential but also, "I voted" stickers aside, a lonely and decidedly *un*deliberative process. Popular media coverage focuses more on polling and horse-race-like commentary than explainers of substantive policy positions. The proliferation of super political action committees is but one way in which everyday participation has been professionalized over the past few decades, concentrated in the hands (and voice boxes) of a few. When the larger landscape of engagement is reduced to checkbook participation, the notion that everyday citizens could enact change through civic engagement feels like a farce.

Research backs up the intuitive hunches many citizens feel in their guts. Political scientists Martin Gilens and Benjamin I. Page analyzed 1,799 policy issues considered in Congress, comparing decisions to the preferences of the public and different interest groups; they concluded that the average person's influence on US public policy is "near-zero."[4] The US government's decisions overwhelmingly reflect the preferences of wealthy individuals and business groups, not the wider public.

Locally, too, it hardly feels like voting can make city budgets accountable to city residents. In trying to protest the New York mayor's budget cuts, for example, parents and community groups must work in a roundabout way—pressuring individual city council members, each with their own political affiliations and agendas, to hopefully pressure the mayor in turn.

Viewed in this light, no amount of electoral college or campaign finance reform, or bans on gerrymandering, will cure our electoral democratic woes. According to the Pew Research Center, a historically low 17 percent of people in the United States said that they trust the government in Washington to do what is right "just about always" or "most of the time" in 2019, down from a historical high of 77 percent in 1964. (Though the exact percentage has fluctuated a bit since 2019, it remains near historical lows.)[5] People are deeply disillusioned with US electoral politics and its ability to elect officials who truly represent the communities they serve.

I am by no means claiming that voting is an empty exercise. I sometimes see online posts with the quotation, "If voting changed anything, they'd make it illegal," a statement made by anarchist activist Emma Goldman. (Snopes.com says that it is misattributed, but still.) It is thus telling that many legislators *are* indeed trying to make voting impossible. Indeed, the Brennan Center for Justice has documented record-high numbers of new voting restriction bills and laws since the 2020 elections.[6]

Further, it is substantially easier to vote—with, say, early voting options, voting rights for those who have been convicted of felonies, and short wait times at poll sites—in Vermont, the country's Whitest state, than in Mississippi, with the country's highest percentage of Black citizens.[7] Alongside the disenfranchisement of more than six million citizens (including many no longer on probation or parole), voter suppression disproportionately affects people of color, people with disabilities, and lower-income voters.[8]

———

Might local channels for political participation, like school boards, serve as more meaningful avenues for political participation? Educational

88 BUDGET JUSTICE

governance is helpful to examine in the US context because it is so decentralized; there are over thirteen thousand school districts in the United States, each with their own governance structure. They are emblematic of US federalism, with layers of local, state, and federal regulations along with funding streams to parse through. They are set up in ways that make it difficult for school board members to coordinate across districts and cooperate in terms of budget justice.

Historically, school boards are also a traditional stepping stone for aspiring politicians. They are where many elected officials first run for office and make their reputations. In some districts, board members have substantive powers, shoring up support among nonparents for new municipal bonds or helping to secure alternate sources of funding, negotiating teacher hiring, or taking a stand regarding curricula. School board meetings are common sites of debate regarding proposed bans against books related to age-appropriate sex education and the country's legacy of slavery, for instance.[9]

In many districts, however, school boards are seen as rubber-stamping institutions. For example, New York City has a system of thirty-two community engagement councils for elementary and middle schools, in addition to citywide councils for high schools, certain educational programs, and the Panel for Educational Policy. Yet these councils are seen as largely advisory, without meaningful decision-making power. Although the citywide Panel for Education Policy includes community members elected from each borough, mayoral appointees constitute a supermajority, and the panel regularly passes decisions that are extremely unpopular with the panel's elected members and larger public. Former New York mayor Bloomberg once even boasted, "They are my representatives, and they are going to vote for things that I believe in."[10]

At best, school boards give city residents electoral accountability. Regardless of whether mayoral control exists in a school district or what exactly the school boards look like, few districts give more than a handful of residents opportunities for meaningful participation in substantive policymaking.

Parents are generally encouraged to join PTOs or parent-teacher associations (PTAs), helping to plan activities for families at the school, facilitating collaborations between teachers and parents, and fundraising.

For instance, the PTO at my child's school clearly has a pulse on the school community's needs and coordinates with school staff to meet them in thoughtful ways. In 2022, its work included finding the right donation platforms to get children extra gifts during the winter holidays without making anyone feel self-conscious, talking to individual families in the Spanish-English dual-language program to give up their spots to accommodate newly arriving asylum seekers from Venezuela, sent to Brooklyn by Texas governor Greg Abbott, and giving teachers the opportunity to take a true lunch break by hiring coaches from a local enrichment program to supervise kids playing during recess and prevent bullying.

It regularly raises funds for and secures contracts with different enrichment programs in the school. The PTO has developed an infrastructure of care in the school, so that no family will go without school supplies they cannot afford, without making any family feel self-conscious about their needs; for example, it pooled funds to buy school supplies for all families, paying wholesale prices and saving everyone time as well as money along the way. I, for one, feel grateful for its thoughtful outreach and needs assessment, administrative prowess, and know-how.

But by largely concentrating on and limiting their activities to fundraising, PTAs can also further entrench inequalities and segregation in the city. In New York City, a law mandates PTAs to report their fundraising numbers each year. Unsurprisingly, schools in low-income neighborhoods often receive lower amounts of donations from the lower-income families they serve. The differences are staggering. In 2019, the PTA at Public School 58, in high-income Carroll Gardens, Brooklyn, raised roughly $2.1 million, or more than $2,000 per student, while Public School 6X, in a lower-income section of the Bronx, reported raising less than $6,000, or less than $11 per student.[11]

Because parents like the ones taking leadership at my child's school do not have official decision-making power, their efforts at best blunt rather than replace the logics of austerity and opacity of budget injustice endemic in the city's education budget overall.

———

US liberal democracy emphasizes the importance of elected representatives, the rights of individuals, and procedural justice. But in its founding, it excluded some people from becoming full citizens: slaves, women, undocumented immigrants, and those unable to pay poll taxes or pass literacy tests. And by erecting obstacles to citizenship such as residency requirements, the US government continues to effectively exclude those who lack means. In fact, the liberal representative part of US democracy has undermined its efforts to be truly inclusive and multiracial. Its current system's focus on individuals assumes a color-blind logic that fails to redress the ways in which racism continues to inform our current practices, conditions, and ostensibly neutral budgets.

In clinging to its Enlightenment-based, liberal, representative canon, the United States, in its efforts to "export democracy," has merely exported elections. The country built itself by inscribing a constitutional formula stating that for the purposes of congressional representation, Black slaves counted as three-fifths of a person. This is not a question of fractions or whole numbers. Human beings who did not count as human were used to enhance the South's congressional numbers and add weight to the entire system that kept them in place. What other decidedly undemocratic elements remain in this system of government?

True democracy redresses historical inequities, lends political power to the everyday constituents most affected by public policies, and shifts decision-making away from campaign donors, wealthy elites, and corporate interests. In *We Are the Ones We Were Waiting For*, Peter Levine asserts that many of today's seemingly intractable policy problems can only solved through what he calls *active citizenship*. (The poignant book title comes from a poem by June Jordan.)[12] But this is especially difficult today because there are so few spaces for meaningful political engagement. Labor unions and service clubs, for example, served as potential sites for collective action but have dramatically lower membership rolls than half a century ago.

Another promising terrain lies in participatory democracy, in which constituents themselves help make certain policy decisions. This route is not a betrayal of US democracy but instead at its very roots. When the framers wrote our Constitution, members of the Haudenosaunee Confederacy (called Iroquois by the French) already had working structures to address diverse views and collaboratively maintain resources for "the seventh generation" of descendants after them. After Benjamin Franklin invited Haudenosaunee leaders to the Continental Congress in 1776, the framers adopted the confederacy's federalist design and "bundle of arrows" metaphor, but not its participatory structures. What might newer schools and laboratories for democracy look like?

One striking illustration comes from Ireland, where since 2016, policymakers built on a parliamentary system of proportional representation to enable more dialogue among constituents. In Tionól Saoránach, also known as We the Citizens assemblies, ninety-nine constituents spend multiday meetings learning about a specific policy issue, hearing from experts and diverse advocacy groups, and deliberating over policy recommendations. A 2016–17 citizens' assembly led to an abortion referendum proposing to repeal a constitutional amendment from 1983 that had explicitly conferred a "right to life" to fetuses. Opinion polls suggested that it would be a close call, and news outlets portrayed Ireland as a bastion of Roman Catholic conservatism and emphasized its history of civil conflict. Yet the referendum passed by a landslide.

The assemblies' deliberative process—in which even advocacy groups deemed loathsome by their opponents had the chance to make their case—was likely pivotal to the referendum's success. Participants departed from well-worn party lines, listening to real-life stories and exploring gray areas while fact-checking people's accounts with obstetricians and lawyers. The process allowed participants to reframe the entire debate rather than simply dig in their heels on their preexisting positions—and this, in turn, helped the entire country to follow suit. Meanwhile in the United States, where a majority of people have consistently supported abortion access, the people got *Dobbs v. Jackson Women's Health Organization*, taking away the constitutional right to abortion.

Even when constituents manage to overcome polarization, corporate and state interests can still block the policies that these constituents thoughtfully develop, and can undermine democratic decision-making. In France, President Emmanuel Macron convened people from across the political spectrum for climate change assemblies that took place in 2019 and 2020; he also promised to forward their recommendations, "unfiltered," to Parliament or a referendum. But when the participants recommended a 4 percent green tax on company dividends, Macron reneged on his promise. Out of 149 measures proposed by the assembly participants, more than half were rejected outright; legislators dropped others, like taxes on heavily polluting vehicles, after receiving complaints from French manufacturers.

The French case, especially, suggests that existing governments are open to deliberative democratic experiments and engaging folks beyond the usual suspects, as long as participants do not rock the boat too much. Attention to political economy and economic democracy remain paramount.

After all, a system that sidelines equity normalizes as well as profits off existing social and racial hierarchies. It is no coincidence that so many of the exploitative practices that should be addressed democratically—foreclosures and predatory debts, for instance—developed first as ways of targeting specific, marginalized groups in the United States, such as Black and Indigenous people. This history of excluding racialized groups is a feature, not a bug, in our current system. Taylor calls it "predatory inclusion"—the process by which members of a marginalized group are provided access to a good or service under conditions that threaten their ability to ever benefit from it.[13]

———

I wish that the notion of economic democracy—that people besides the überrich can make a difference in public policy and budgets—did not seem so radical. Reflecting on our communities' various collective needs, thinking alongside rather than competing with others, and questioning city officials should be commonplace democratic practices, not exceptions to the rule. Whereas voting typically closes off conversations about public budgets and delimits collective power, participatory experiments can serve as mobilizing entry points to deeper politics.

For budget justice, cities must develop new, participatory institutions to help the public hold government accountable from the bottom up. How can everyday citizens exercise their right-to-the-city budget I discuss in chapter 5—to not only to access good jobs and work toward homeownership, say, but to help make the policies that make this happen—or more radically, work toward different budgets and different sorts of public policies?

The slogan "no taxation without representation" has been popular in the United States since before the country was formally founded. But "no taxation without participation" might be even more apt. Everyday citizens are capable of connecting with one another and deliberating over local priorities.

In order to get public budgets that help people to thrive, participation in local policymaking must be binding, substantive, and meaningful too, centering equity and avoiding co-optation. In seeking new channels of political participation, communities must also ask, *What is this participation for? What does it ultimately achieve?* The next question, then, is what this participation looks like, and what impacts and outcomes it brings about.

INTERLUDE

An Interview with Tarson Núñez

Porto Alegre's Power Came from Its Social Movement Roots

FOR MANY SCHOLARS working on democratic innovations, Porto Alegre is synonymous with participatory budgeting, giving residents direct say in the city's budget. It's where PB was born in 1989, when members of the Workers' Party won local elections. This took place amid massive changes at the national level as well; Brazil's military dictatorship only ended in 1985, and the country enacted a new constitution in 1988.

Porto Alegre's PB process yielded impressive results. Whereas the city spent most of its investment resources on middle-class neighborhoods in the 1970s and 1980s, PB gave low-income and densely populated neighborhoods the bulk of city funds. This led to a 20 percent decline in local poverty, not to mention significant increases in public goods like the number of paved streets, health clinics, and public housing. In the first decade of PB, the number of residencies with water connections in Porto Alegre increased from 75 to 98 percent, and the amount of schools quadrupled. The process also provided seed money for initiatives like worker cooperatives. And beyond concrete projects, it established new dynamics of political will and democratic accountability, allowing residents to turn down development proposals—such as five-star hotels—that they felt ultimately reflected business interests more than public needs.[1]

From 1990 to 2008, almost half of Brazil's largest 250 cities followed Porto Alegre's lead and adopted PB. Cities that implemented PB produced what political scientists Brian Wampler and Mike Touchton deem "better forms of governance," incorporating citizen input at multiple moments of the policy process, "retraining policy experts and civil servants to better work with poor communities," and rendering city governments more transparent.[2]

Because of its success with PB, Porto Alegre hosted the first World Social Forum in 2001 as well as additional forums in 2003, 2005, 2010, and 2012. It was partly through these forums that practitioners from around the world learned about PB.[3]

Yet even as it was gaining momentum globally, PB lost political support domestically. After the Workers' Party assumed power nationally, it devoted less attention to local PB processes. But then, because PB remained associated with the Workers' Party, the process weakened further after the Workers' Party lost electoral seats in most cities in the 2016 elections, and right-wing Jair Bolsonaro was elected president in 2018. After becoming Brazil's president again in 2023, Lula (Luiz Inácio Lula da Silva) of the Workers' Party said that he would open around one-fifth of the national government's discretionary budget to citizen engagement.[4]

Over Zoom, I spoke with Tarson Núñez about his analyses of Porto Alegre's experiences. Núñez is a social researcher in the Department of Economy and Statistics at the Secretary of Planning, as part of the state government of Rio Grande do Sul. In the early 1990s, he worked as the head of the Porto Alegre Planning Office, overseeing PB in the city, and a decade later, helped launch PB at the state level. He holds a PhD in political science, with work focusing on social movements and social policy.

I first met Núñez in 2019 in Edinburgh, Scotland, at a working meeting for People Powered, a global hub for participatory democracy. I was struck by his ability to reflect critically on his commitments as both a practitioner and researcher. I was especially curious to hear what he learned from PB's spectacular rise, fall, and possible renaissance in Brazil—what he remains particularly proud of, and wishes he and his colleagues had done differently in hindsight.

This interview has been edited and condensed for clarity and concision.

96   BUDGET JUSTICE

CELINA SU: *What has your role been, in terms of work toward budget justice in Porto Alegre? Can you tell us a bit about where you're coming from or how you got started working on this?*

TARSON NÚÑEZ: I was working for CUT [Central Única dos Trabalhadores, the main federation of trade unions in Brazil] as an adviser on popular worker education. In 1986, four state deputies from the Workers' Party were elected. They invited me to work with them as a parliamentary adviser for the state assembly, from 1987 to 1989 or 1990. I was then invited to go to the municipal government, as one of the coordinators of the participatory budget in the mayor's planning office in 1992.

One important aspect of this trajectory was the fact that many of the student activists at the end of the seventies all graduated and started to work with the workers movement in different dimensions. Some of us went to the union movement, like me. Others started to work with the Workers' Party that was starting at the same time; others went to the university as professors. We are friends until this day, and through them, I have worked in different positions.

A radically democratic political culture emerged from the student movements, and at the end of the dictatorship, it spread into different institutions. I would argue that you can work to maintain the same perspective of social change and social emancipation, no matter which space you are occupying in formal terms. This idea of the movement goes beyond its institutional expressions. We always had this unusual approach of being simultaneously very radical and very pragmatic—being outside institutions and inside institutions at the same time.

The more conservative Left always prioritized this pragmatic approach of being inside institutions, and the most radical groups were against it, and we are always trying to be in between. We didn't see this as a contradiction. It was an intuitive approach. I personally was part of a tiny radical semi-Trotskyist group, and

I soon broke with it, because it had this almost authoritarian, top-down approach, like, "We are the leaders of the movement." [By contrast,] the Workers' Party intends to be a very democratic party; there's space for anyone. This reflected the important influence of liberation theology, of Paulo Freire . . . a movement concerned with mobilizing grass roots. [Freire was a Brazilian educator and philosopher who led massive—and successful—literacy campaigns for previously illiterate, poor adults whom others had dismissed as uneducable. His most influential book, *Pedagogy of the Oppressed*, emphasizes that students should not be treated as empty vessels to be filled with facts by teachers, but instead as cocreators of knowledge.][5]

CS: *The story of how PB started in Porto Alegre has been told many times. Why do you think it started there and not somewhere else?*

TN: We managed to have power at the local level. We were elected, partly because at that time you didn't have runoffs. But beyond elections, we had a model that was more connected to territory [and a sense of place]. We wanted to build councils in every neighborhood to discuss and build some alternative power bases to the traditional institutional power structure of city hall. We were elected with this commitment to broaden and amplify democratization.

But the good thing is that we didn't have a recipe for that; [we] only had the political will to do it. We were all concerned about this bottom-up, grassroots approach. And at the same time, there was this huge fiscal crisis. We had to make up some way to deal with the challenge: *OK, we don't have money. So one thing that we can do is to discuss the budget with the people.*

This built the opportunity to come up with a new approach to what we do as a party [the then-ruling Workers' Party]. The good thing is that PB was rapidly successful. After one or two years, because of some changes in the national legislation and good management of public finances, the situation changed from that of a scarcity of resources. We managed to deliver.

98   BUDGET JUSTICE

Then we had money, and we discussed how to spend it with the people, and the people could see things being built with what was decided. It was a real political success. This gave us steam to keep going, and we were reelected four times.

This was again the result of this nonexclusivist divide between pragmatism and radicalism. We were radical in terms of trying to change the way the budget was discussed. But at the same time, PB was a pragmatic solution.

CS: *Were there other factors that made PB so politically successful? While international development experts often discuss PB as a stand-alone process, it was but one of many different democratic experiments happening in Porto Alegre. How did the different democratic experiments and collective struggles come together—or not—for you?*

TN: PB only happened because we already had this strong democ- ratization movement that was pushing from outside the state and from the bottom up. That was related to the idea of pushing democracy beyond the electoral framework in different ways. This was happening all over Brazil.

There were other experiments already in place, especially the sectoral public policy councils. We have this kind of council in every sector: culture, health, urban planning, [and] education, in which civil society organizations can discuss public policies with the government. [At first these councils had voice, but not power.] They started a long time ago; the military government started them, and only gave civil society one or two council seats among many. At that time, the state used to open these spaces where civil society groups could be heard, but without deliberative [decision-making] power; they were just consultative.[6] But still, that was an opening. In my doctoral thesis, I examine the evolution of these participatory spaces. Over time, the composition of these councils changed; civil society groups had one-third of representation of civil society, then half. After some years, they had a majority, with more deliberative power. So there was an evolution.

For example, the health system built by the 1988 Constitution established that this council must have civil society representation to deliberate sectoral policies—at the federal, state level, [and] municipal level. We had this strong health council because no city receives money from the federal government if it doesn't have these councils, these spaces of representation. Through these councils, social movements had a voice and significant control of relevant public policies.

And after Lula first won the presidency in 2002, we started to have these additional national public policy conferences that were open spaces for civil society, starting on the municipal level, with elected delegates to the state-level and national conferences.[7]

CS: *Why was PB so important in bringing about budget justice, in your view?*

TN: PB was part of this bigger, wider process. But it was especially important because it showed fast results; people could see their streets getting paved or receiving water services. PB was less mediated [than other participatory councils like health or education]. And while the other councils had representatives from civil society groups, like the nurses' union, doctors' association, and some client organizations, they did not have direct participation of [everyday] citizens [themselves]. PB had that, in ways that you could see because of its annual cycle. So you could participate, deliberate, [and] evaluate; you see things happening. That's why PB was so important. [It was a different model of government and politics.]

By doing PB, we managed to show results; that, in turn, legitimized the Workers' Party as a successful public manager. We did a survey in 1996, and people liked the Workers' Party not because they were so sympathetic to the Left. But they said, "We like the Workers' Party because it did a good job." PB was very concrete. It was not ideological in conventional terms. It was something objective, where people presented their demands and saw their demands being implemented.

And this also had the side effect of legitimizing a different approach to public policies—a more democratic and participatory one—as part of a wider movement that was pushing for more participation in the public sphere. This all happened because there was this pressure from the bottom for participation. We had organized social movements, demanding voice and power. And this moment, from 1982 or 1983 to the 1990s, was one of huge participation—in the sense that people were really doing direct actions. I think that in the 1980s, more than thirty thousand housing units were occupied in Porto Alegre. So people who didn't have a house, occupied a house.

It was a moment of huge social mobilization that pushed the political actors to innovate, or to new forms of political participation, or to incorporating all of these demands. And this was the main virtue of the Workers' Party being a party built by social movements. It was open to these kinds of bottom-up initiatives.

CS: *Nationally, Brazil witnessed the rise of Lula, complicated political dynamics regarding the Workers' Party, retrograde politics via Bolsonaro, and most recently, Lula's return. In your opinion, what are the most significant recent shifts in politics in Porto Alegre?*

TN: It's something that my friends and I are discussing a lot these days, this whole process of democratization and dedemo-cratization. The most important question is what explains this transformation—from the Porto Alegre of the World Social Forum to the Porto Alegre of the neoliberal hegemony. Because today, the city has been totally taken by the real estate industry. And we are now seeing the dismantling of all the democratic infrastructure that we had.

We were pushing transformations at the institutional level, toward democratization. But at the same time, at the societal level, outside formal governmental institutions, we saw the dismantling of the unions, [and] the fragmentation of workers because of social, political, and technological changes, like automation. The workers were submitted to longer commutes [and] lower salaries. You have less time to be an active citizen. And you have a cultural shift toward individualism. People having to work much more. You have less time to go to your neighbors' association because you work much more. You have less time; you don't participate in your union. You have a more fragmented civil society.

So the very social movements that pushed for institutional and political changes like PB were fading through the 1990s and 2000s. So now, all of this democratic infrastructure that we built no longer has its feet on solid ground.

This is partly because of the bureaucratization of the Workers' Party, which lost its movement base. I see this in a personal way. The guy who was a social militant in the eighties now wears a tie and suit, and is part of mainstream politics. I see the transformation of a guy who was in the circle, organizing grassroots workers to win campaigns for steel metal workers. And now he is a deputy with a personal driver, ten advisers working for him, and his main concern is how to be elected yet again.

I think that this has to do with party dynamics. [Political scientist Angelo] Panebianco discusses parties not with the traditional approaches like ideology and representation; he discusses parties as organizations—how they tend to reproduce themselves.[8] Most of the energy of the Workers' Party militants is now directed to internal, institutional politics. We have fewer organic connections with social movements. We lost momentum.

Meanwhile, as time passes, neoliberal policies are dismantling the state. So we earn more power on a structure that has less power, and we lost what gave us real power—our social base and social movements. This was clear in 2013, when people went to the streets complaining about the system. And this movement was then captured by the Right.

cs: *What do you think has not received enough attention?*

tn: Alongside direct actions and social movements, solidarity economy efforts [emphasizing social benefits alongside financial profits] have not received enough attention. We tended to work for social change within the limits of the current social and economic institutions.

Because of that, the solidarity economy is not part of the government's main strategy. When Lula won the presidency, we already had this strong solidarity economy movement. The government created a secretary of solidarity economy in the government, inside the Ministry of Labor. But the place it occupied inside the power structures was tiny, with a little budget, little power. It was not at the center of the economic strategy of the government. The government incorporated a truly different, "another world is possible" paradigm, but in a marginal way. It did not give the solidarity economy the same status as mainstream economic initiatives, doing business as usual.

The political party's political focus is a traditional one, and this is an untold reason for the dedemocratization in Brazil. In the real world, most of the activists are now trapped in party politics and treat these social movements as accessories. We don't look toward the movements as sources of transformation. The party tends to look at them only as partners that are helpful in electoral terms, which is naive in my opinion. We have to go back to and strengthen movements. Elections are important, but much more important is organizing people at the grassroots level.

So that's my main punch line in every discussion at the international level about PB. The institutional framework and rules of the game may be well designed, but if you don't have pressure from the bottom, you can have a good participatory structure, but you won't have real democratizing effects. You just have shallow spaces. And these spaces are much more frequently controlled by the state, captured by interest groups, the business sector.

I think that the biggest and better example of that is the landless peasants movement [Movimento dos Trabalhadores Rurais Sem Terra, MST, calls for workers to "Occupy, Resist, and Produce!"]. It is a movement that demands land reform. But it doesn't limit its action to that; it has already occupied the land. And it demands other sorts of concrete support from the state. And now the landless peasants movement is one of the biggest producers of food in Brazil. The biggest export of organic rice is the movement. I think there are more than eight hundred schools active at the settlements. It has schools, it has educational projects, and it installs cooperatives.

[Landless peasants] are already changing their reality independently of their relationship with the state. But at the same time, they have this relationship. This hybrid strategy for me is the most interesting thing, that you are [simultaneously] outside and inside. You are in invited [into state-initiated] spaces, but you don't limit your actions to this sphere. You also invent your own spaces, and you have ongoing dynamics between these two strategies.

CS: *What is to be done now, amid all of this?*

TN: In my opinion, there was a shift from social movement dynamics to a representative democracy approach in the Left because it seemed to be an easier and more effective path to power. But the original, movement-based, truly democratic approach, ideologically and politically, is still part of the discourse and identity of the Workers' Party. Fortunately, there wasn't a total divorce between the party and its roots.

The most important problem is that we don't have a transformational paradigm, and we don't elaborate on how we can build power to the people outside traditional political and economic institutions. We need to rethink politics as a whole. We won't be successful if we only manage to get rid of Bolsonaro, go back to electoral politics, and give just a little more space to social movements.

We need to be creative. And I think that the best example of us being creative was PB. We invented something. We are now

104   BUDGET JUSTICE

in a situation where we need, again, to reinvent democracy. That demands a theoretical effort to build a new paradigm of democratization.

I think that the biggest contribution of initiatives like urban occupations is that they manage to establish a different relationship with politics. There's an empty public building. We occupy it first, instead of demanding that the state build more housing. We *do* things first—direct actions. This doesn't mean that we will abandon the state and its political institutions. But nor do we need to patiently only make demands, wait to win elections, and wait for the state to institute new policies. We do both things. We start to *do* things, and also engage the state. Not on the basis that "we have nothing, and you have to do something for us." No. [Rather we assert,] "We know what our demands are, and you have to deal with us."

CS: *I have been thinking about these different spaces—so-called invited, state-initiated processes like PB, alongside so-called invented, extrainstitutional initiatives like worker cooperatives—as part of a larger ecosystem of participation, rather than mutually exclusive or oppositional channels or modes of participation. Does this framing resonate with your observations?*

TN: All of these movements and spaces are connected in a way or another. But some of the movements have a more autonomous approach, and that's important. The biggest and best example of that is the landless peasants movement [mentioned above]. The same is the case with the housing movements; they occupy empty buildings, but they also contest and help shape government housing policies. They struggle for housing, but also create work and housing cooperatives. They make demands from government, but also build kitchens that provide food for people with food insecurity.

They are already changing their reality, independently of their relationship with the state. But at the same time, they maintain this hybrid strategy—outside *and* inside. You are in invited spaces, but you also invent your own spaces, and you have this permanent dynamic between these two dimensions of politics. And the most interesting thing is that they don't treat these dimensions as separate.

CS: *What keeps you going at this moment? What fuels your commitments? You have remained committed for a long time.*

TN: In a more pragmatic and objective way of thinking, I'm a pessimistic guy. I can really see that the threats against democracy are bigger than ever. We have a judicial system that is totally undemocratic. We have a media structure that's undemocratic. We have a political culture that is totally top-down. The army still has lots of power. Social inequalities are bigger than ever. I don't believe, as the Left used to say, that "history's on our side," or "Venceremos!" On the contrary, I think history is not on our side. I think we're approaching a collapse of civilization.

So I'm doing this because we have to. For me existentially, I wouldn't be comfortable if I wasn't committed to social change. I'm not in this for the results; I'm in this for the process. And in subjective terms, I'm still enthusiastic about the resistance, capacity, and resilience of Brazilian people. When I go to a popular kitchen that the housing movement has, it's a structure to give food to the poor. I'm on the side of those who struggle every day to make a different society. I don't think that we will achieve that sometime soon, but I do think that we rebuild it on a daily basis. Social change is already happening. I think that's what [philosopher Antonio] Gramsci used to say in terms of "pessimism of the intellect, optimism of the will."[9] The future is a construction. The past is only lessons. How can I change things here and now? And what can I do at a personal level? I'm doing something for today.

7

An Invitation to Participatory Budgeting

HOW MIGHT CITIZENS BEGIN to demand transparent, equitable city budgets? Since the 1990s, more than eleven thousand cities and communities around the world have turned to participatory budgeting (PB). The process can help citizens to assert a right to the city and its budget by facilitating participation in decision-making regarding public works and public space, rather than pursuing siloed campaigns on issues like economic development or gentrification.[1] I noticed it more after the 2007 financial crisis, when it arguably became the most widely implemented participatory democratic experiment in the world. In 2014, Paris launched the world's largest PB by allocating a hundred million euros, or 5 percent of its public budget, to it each year. This amounts to forty-five euros per capita.[2]

Globally, city governments have used PB under different conditions, resulting in different impacts. At its best, PB disrupts current vicious cycles of budget opacity and austerity, which lead to distrust in government, perpetuating low tax revenues, and thus undermining state capacity to get things done and help cities thrive.

The most common outcomes—seen in cities ranging from Maribor, Slovenia, to Reykjavík, Iceland, to Rosario, Argentina—benefit those who participate in the process. Residents gain considerable knowledge on city government and public funds through their experience, partly because PB feels like an ultimate school of democracy; participants learn analytic, social, leadership, and collaboration skills. Through this, participants then report higher levels of trust in government and each other. That is, PB is not just about surfacing individuals' needs and sorting their budget preferences but also about fomenting collective action. When sustained, PB can help reinvigorate and strengthen civil society too; in Brazil, municipalities that implemented PB developed more civil society organizations than those that did not.[3]

Moreover, PB leads participants to engage in new political practices, like monitoring public budgets, proposing policies as opposed to just choosing between available options, and advocating for community needs through other channels. Cities with robust PB therefore tend to spend money differently. When PB compels residents to think about equity criteria in their decisions, it tends to specifically redirect funds to lower-income communities as well.[4] As people feel more pleased with how public budgets are spent and more confident that they are holding government accountable, they become more willing to pay taxes or vote for tax increases, knowing that they will be getting plenty in return. In Brazil, there was an impressive 30 percent increase in local taxes in municipalities using PB.[5]

In other words, PB can catalyze new dynamics in democratic accountability. Consider, for example, the impressive statement that PB led to lower infant mortality in Brazil. This was not because of any single intervention, like vaccinations or prenatal care. Rather, research shows that when residents demand more health spending and public budgets shift in response, community members build new relationships with each other and new health officials. It is because of a crucial and multidimensional "shift in governance," versus PB alone, that these cities improved local health and well-being.[6]

In this virtuous cycle, PB introduces transparency and democratic capacity building to local governance, which helps citizens and bureaucrats tackle mismanagement, in turn leading to collaboration and trust, bringing in more tax revenues, and nurturing the state's capacity to help a city thrive.

I focus on PB not to advocate for it as a magic potion for budget justice, especially when there is no definitive recipe for it. A lot of what

108   BUDGET JUSTICE

a PB process should look like depends on local political conditions, so some PB processes are organized citywide, and others by district; some are organized around themes like climate change, and others by geography. And so on.

Still, PB can be a crucial intervention—an invitation to a different way of doing local, everyday democracy. In the remainder of the book, I draw on my observations of New York's PBNYC process to examine the fundamental democratic practices essential to budget justice.

The "invitation" in the chapter title references political anthropologist Andrea Cornwall's framing of invited state-initiated and invented citizen-initiated spaces.[7] This framing recognizes and gives credence to collective actions outside protests and elections—like the sorts of housing occupations mentioned in the Nuñez interview—that often get sidelined in analyses of democratic action. To me, Cornwall's framing immediately draws an observer's attention to important questions regarding the rules and norms of participation in the space. How inviting is PBNYC? Who receives and accepts the invitation?

I critically assess PBNYC to pinpoint the practices of deliberation and mobilization needed to make the city's budgeting process more democratic—through official PB processes, if those exist, but also through town hall meetings, people's assemblies, PTOs and other groups, or less formal community organizing. I highlight the main challenges of meaningful PB to argue that PB is one (central) node in an ecosystem of participation (that additionally includes social movements, mutual aid networks, and other collective efforts) that citizens need to activate for budget justice.

———

PBNYC began in 2011, when four council members decided to run PB processes in their respective districts. By 2016, thirty-one of fifty-one council members participated in PB; since then, the percentage of districts involved in PB has remained pretty stable, despite dips in participation during the pandemic and substantial turnover in elected officials.

What does PBNYC look like in practice? Each year, each participating council member devotes at least $1 million of their discretionary funds to PB. For the most part, PBNYC funds so-called capital projects (physical infrastructure, rather than staffing or programming, that costs at least $50,000 and has a lifespan of at least five years).

But the essence of PB does not and should not lie in these technical rules of eligibility and process; PB comes to life in small group deliberations taking place in school cafeterias and gyms, community halls, or even outside, whether at portable tables set up on a Sunday after church services, at local farmers' markets, or by supermarket doors.

In the fall of each year, council members host neighborhood assemblies throughout their districts, where thousands of New Yorkers pitch proposals for community projects. Frequently, a simple question gets them started: "How would *you* spend $1 million of the city's budget?" Since New York's long-running PB process is managed by district, each district has a list of hundreds of project ideas to vet by November. Over each winter, some residents volunteer to become budget delegates, conducting feasibility and needs assessments to curate the proposals that will end up on the ballot, and working with city agencies to develop ideas into full-fledged proposals. Each spring, residents vote for the proposals that then win funding via PB.

At meetings I observed, many residents have immediate complaints. The arts program at their kid's school was cut in the mayor's latest budget. An intersection two blocks away feels unsafe and needs a curb extension. The blacktop at the playground basketball court is in disrepair. Library hours were cut short on Sundays, and people need somewhere easy to go on winter weekends, especially with little kids bouncing off the walls of their small New York apartments. Some residents pitch other ideas—such as a tool library (where residents could borrow expensive, rarely used tools like floor sanders), mental health services, and birth doulas for all pregnant people. The participants forwarding these ideas usually justify them with bits of concrete experience or information as well. They visited their cousins in Oakland, California, and were impressed by a tool library there, their sibling needed affordable therapy because they graduated and could no longer access the college clinic, or they read an article that poor people have higher maternal mortality rates and learned that birth doulas reduce incidence rates of C-sections by more than 50 percent.

Trained facilitators provide information on the concept and process of PB as well as the local district (with maps and statistics on who lives there). They invite participants to brainstorm ideas in small groups. Sometimes the groups are organized by some sort of affinity—such as age (for youths or the elderly), neighborhood, or fluent language spoken. Most of the time, attendees are grouped randomly. They then bounce ideas off each other, comparing notes on their experiences and emerging themes.

PB engages folks by helping them practice deliberation, articulating ideas and discussing or debating them in ways that feel unimaginable in the typical politics of elections and voting booths.

———

By facilitating events like this hundreds of times each fall, PBNYC broadens notions of citizenship, engaging traditionally disenfranchised constituents. As but one example, the first rulebook dictated that youths could not vote in the process. I was present during the "writing the rules" workshop that determined this rule, and almost all the attendees had wanted youths to help make decisions. But one of the participating city council members had stated that they would not allow their discretionary funds to be determined via PB if youths were allowed to vote. Their veto was successful that year. Yet even then, the rulebook did allow youths to attend and deliberate in neighborhood assemblies.

At one assembly in East Harlem, approximately two hundred middle and high schoolers gathered at a school gym on a gray afternoon. Some of the adults doubted that youths could participate meaningfully. They stated that youths do not possess the cognitive functioning or maturity for this level of debate.

Still, a PB coordinator spoke for five to ten minutes about the process, and the students then scooted their metal folding chairs into circles of twelve or so people each. I stood just outside one such circle. I saw an adult roll their eyes when the facilitator in their group first asked for ideas. "They just want skate parks," they mumbled under their breath. Indeed, two of the children in the group suggested skate parks.

I could have imagined an untrained facilitator dismissing the idea as too self-serving; a self-possessed and quick-thinking teenager could then rebut that they did not have enough fun spaces to hang out after school, and their lower-income neighborhood did not have the same amount of green space that richer neighborhoods did. They could not afford to buy expensive lattes so as to hang out in cafés and were often accused of "loitering" in commercial spaces.

But that isn't how the scene played out. The facilitator nodded and transcribed each and every idea on a giant pad of paper taped onto a wall, adding asterisks next to ideas that were echoed by others. They also pointed to a map of the district and asked where each proposal would be implemented. The children started to shout out ideas in rapid succession; the facilitator could hardly keep up. They wanted spaces for parkour. Murals in the parks. New elevators in public housing at Jefferson, Lexington, Johnson, Carver, and Wagner. Free college prep classes. Boarding schools. Handicap accessibility at bus stops. For all school buses to become handicap accessible. They talked about the experiences of their friends, siblings, and cousins. They specified specific blocks, like how a particular block between Lexington and Third Avenues sometimes felt unsafe in after-school hours.

After just fifteen minutes of brainstorming, every group had dozens of ideas to deliberate. They spent half an hour discussing which neighborhoods in their district seemed better off, which playgrounds seemed to be in greatest need of attention, and how different folks in their community might react to each proposal. They then informally voted on three to share with everyone gathered at the assembly. The event ended with some of the attendees volunteering to become budget delegates. Delegates work together to vet thousands of project ideas gathered at assemblies, developing just a few to become ballot items.

That school gym near the northern end of Manhattan, with a neighborhood median household income of $34,060, felt a world away from the financial district at the southernmost tip of the island, with a neighborhood median household income of $170,330.[8] But at least some of the students immediately recognized the connections between their conversations that afternoon and the larger ones happening downtown at the Occupy Wall Street encampment. One high schooler wore a white T-shirt that they had handwritten on with permanent marker: "WE ARE THE 99%." When I asked them about their shirt, they talked about banks being "too big to fail," and how in the meantime, without opportunities to press elected officials on community needs, it felt like their families and neighbors were being set up to fail.

And although some of the ideas seemed far-fetched for PB (see "boarding schools"), it was clear that the children took the brainstorming exercise seriously, heeding both the formal spending rules (college prep classes are considered "expense" spending, not infrastructure, and thus disallowed) and local knowledge (their personal observations of which places felt unsafe and when). And in retrospect, I also wonder about the housing and school conditions that led that one youth to beg for boarding schools.

Enthusiastic youth participation in neighborhood assemblies was instrumental in convincing adults to lower the PB voting age to sixteen and participation age to fourteen in 2012, as mentioned above. When adults observed more substantive youth participation, they lowered the age of eligibility again. Currently, participants must be at least eleven years old or in the sixth grade.

In many ways, PBNYC succeeded in engaging traditionally marginalized constituents other than youths, too. According to research by the Community Development Project, constituents from traditionally marginalized subpopulations participated in PB at much higher rates than in traditional elections in every cycle thus far. For example, in District 8, which at the time included high-income Upper West Side neighborhoods alongside lower-income East Harlem and South Bronx neighborhoods, the very poor—those with incomes of $10,000 or less—constituted

4 percent of voters in city council elections but 22 percent of PB voters. Along lines of race, PB also engaged traditionally underrepresented constituents. For instance, 11 percent of PB voters identified as Asian, compared with 4 percent of local election voters, and 24 percent of PB voters identified as Latine, compared with 14 percent of local election voters.[9]

In addition, survey data suggest that strong outreach efforts pay off; lower-income and foreign-born constituents were more likely to learn about PB through word-of-mouth or targeted campaigns, rather than online or through traditional, governmental channels like city council announcements. Notably, half of PB voters surveyed state that they had never worked with others on a community issue before. One-third were foreign born. In one district, over two-thirds of distributed ballots were in languages other than English.[10] Strikingly, almost one-quarter of PB voters in 2015 had a barrier to voting in regular elections, largely because of age or lack of US citizenship.[11]

PBNYC has successfully engaged New Yorkers beyond the usual suspects because city council staff, participating community organizations, and others made concerted efforts to conduct targeted outreach. The operation's limited resources were largely devoted to contracts with experienced community organizers. These organizers worked with specific demographic groups, such as LGBTQ+ communities or Spanish speakers in East Harlem. In some districts where a substantial percentage of residents speak languages other than English, neighborhood assemblies were held in those languages, such as Haitian Creole and Yiddish in Flatbush, Brooklyn. Important notices, ballots, and surveys have consistently been distributed in nine languages. Such efforts created what some scholars call *safe spaces* for deliberation, especially by those without the public speaking skills, confidence, and educational background to speak up at more typical public forums.[12]

Indeed, budget delegates repeatedly emphasized that the PB process allowed them to participate in discussions with neighbors they may not have met otherwise, and to work with the proverbial "other" in deliberations. They stressed how PB was deliberative in that it encouraged the exchange of ideas and compromise. PB's tenor contrasted with that of electoral politics, even for those already politically active. For one delegate, the combination of working with others unlike themselves toward binding budgetary decisions gave the PB process a sense of impact lacking in their usual civic engagement: "Every four years, I . . . vote . . . [but] feeling like this process is . . . responsive to community input . . . you don't often feel."

As one youth delegate remarked, "At the meetings you meet people from all over the community. You may walk by them on a daily basis and not know what they're into. It was a good gathering for people to interact, those for women's rights, LGBT, you have all of these organizations and representatives, and say, 'Cool, you're trying to do that, maybe I'll participate in that.' So it really helped me understand how I can help my community." Delegates noted the substance and tenor of their conversations through PB, and the fact that they now worked with neighbors from different backgrounds "repeatedly, on a serious but still social level," felt different from, say, organizing block parties. They were not just collaborating on a single event or project but instead on public policies—ones that might tell elected officials more about their prerogatives on the city's budget. Several participants noted that they learned a lot about local community priorities because of both needs assessments and informal conversations. One delegate from East Harlem comments, "I was able to see the needs [of] the community in a way I've never seen before. . . . I didn't know how bad of an asthma cluster there was in public housing. I don't have kids, so I don't know about needs at school. I don't have any relatives who live in senior housing, so I didn't know about the issues they faced."

Remarkably, among roughly one hundred delegate interviewees my colleagues and I spoke with, none cited friction with other delegates as a barrier to further participation. In fact, many took pains to assert that despite feeling disappointed when their project proposals did not win enough votes to be funded, they felt that their relationships with fellow budget delegates were more collaborative than competitive. One delegate stated that because the committees' topics and target populations tended to vary, "it's not a competition; it's about understanding other populations' needs." Another young delegate, who stopped participating after the first cycle because of time constraints, reminisced, "Doing the budget, it was cool. You can actually come together; voice your opinion, and get something done good. It was hell of an experience, and I hope I can participate in upcoming cycles. I do miss it. I miss the people getting heated, *I want this project! No, I want this project!* . . . I miss that; [that] whole friendly competition is cool."

———

In New York, PB has resulted in hundreds of millions of dollars invested in over a thousand community projects. Some sorts of ballot items became more common; these include technology upgrades and air conditioners for school classrooms, curb extensions and pedestrian islands at specific intersections, renovations to make facilities wheelchair accessible or sensory friendly, infrastructure for contained science labs like hydroponic farms, countdown clocks at street bus stops, green roof installations, upgrades for libraries, and equipment renovations at playgrounds and parks.

PB is an invitation, extended by local governments to everyday citizens, to engage public budgets in new ways. But exactly what sort of space, process, or political project is the local administration inviting citizens into, and to what effect? At the heart of my analysis is a long-running conundrum of participatory democracy: Can top-down (government-led) democratic initiatives really facilitate bottom-up participation? Or is that an oxymoron? Is it possible to create a formal space for political participation and institutionalize it, without then containing it?[13]

The story of PBNYC suggests that governments can make their decision-making more democratic and participatory, but within limits and not without contradictions. One part of this story can be told through observations of participation on the ground level, as in the assemblies above. Another interesting part can be traced through the evolution of PBNYC's leadership and coordination.

PBNYC's different administrative eras reflect shifting prerogatives, orientations, and levels of funding dictated by city council. While the

116 BUDGET JUSTICE

city council speaker's office has always provided support, PBNYC's early years were also marked by substantive cogovernance with citizens. When council members introduced the process to New York in 2011, they housed PBNYC coordination in the Policy and Innovation Office of the New York City Council. Community Voices Heard, a community-led organization focused on social justice in New York, and the Participatory Budgeting Project, an organization building on existing research and expertise as well as provide technical support, helped anchor the process. From 2011 to 2014, the steering committee meetings I attended as a member focused on ensuring that the process encouraged meaningful deliberation among residents, different districts got to learn from one another, and the citywide committee could reflect and act on the strengths and challenges of the PB process so far. City council staff asked for meeting agenda items well in advance, and committee members spent precious meeting times making binding decisions. The first portion of each meeting revolved around central staff presenting data and background information that committee members would need to make decisions during the remainder of the meeting.

In 2015, the city council transferred PB coordination to the Office of Community Affairs. This allowed the city to move PB beyond a "pilot project" phase. It also allowed central staff to take on some of the jobs previously performed by the district staff of individual city council members; this would ideally then help them to keep individual districts more accountable. But to the steering committee, the move felt like a demotion to a shallower process. Even the term "steering" in the committee's name became controversial; the committee was now called a "citywide" one instead. It moved from being a governance board, making decisions like the age for voting eligibility, minimum standards for neighborhood assemblies in the annual rulebook, and which vendor to use for online voting and why, to supporting the implementation of decisions already made by central staff. Sociologist Isaac Jabola-Carolus, who spent a year attending and examining PBNYC's administration, observes that "dissatisfaction was expressed by every [civil society organization], council district staff member, and community representative that regularly attended meetings." He quotes one committee member as asking, "Is this the Council Members' process, or is this the people's process?"[14]

Then in 2019, coordination of PBNYC moved once again, this time to the participatory budgeting advisory committee hosted by the newly formed Civic Engagement Commission. Coordinating meetings for the PB advisory committee became less frequent. By the time the pandemic arrived, PBNYC no longer received the resources needed to implement the process well or conduct proper evaluations. Without such resources, meeting facilitators could not receive proper training, organizers would not receive contracts to conduct outreach for the process, and surveys could not get printed, collected, and analyzed. The citywide committee members therefore spent meetings writing letters to the mayor, asking for PB funding. Over time, even anchor organizations like the Participatory Budgeting Project participated less. At the same time, the Civic Engagement Commission was tasked with implementing a new mayoral PB process alongside the decade-old city council PBNYC one I focus on. By 2024, the commission was no longer as actively involved with PBNYC.

Democratic participation was now supposedly high on the city agenda, but the proliferation of participatory spaces—especially without a clear mandate or sufficient additional resources—ended up confusing or frustrating previously enthusiastic PB supporters.

Through these various stages, PBNYC successfully got a wide range of New Yorkers to participate, but crucial questions remain. Which PB projects tend to win? Beyond PB project results, are there larger or ancillary effects? Does PB help residents to identify and assert different priorities, so that the larger city budget might better help their communities to thrive? In the following chapters, I tackle these questions to examine whether, when, and how PB might enable citizens to move closer to budget justice.

8

Terms of Deliberation

REACHING AND INCLUDING New Yorkers beyond the typically higher-income usual suspects in PB is impressive. But it does not necessarily ensure their *meaningful* participation. Initiatives must attend to sustained opportunities for deliberation; even explicitly antiracist and justice-oriented initiatives are shortchanged without adequate attention to questions of political economy—such as the austerity policies and budget obfuscation I discuss in part I. Here I pay attention to how social constructions of the "good project" shape the discourses around winning projects, especially in the areas of education and community safety.

Some groups of participants ended up dominating their local PB processes by drawing on social connections and cultural capital, the know-how regarding what language to use along with what cultural touchstones and references to share, in their campaigns. Schools appeared to be especially vulnerable to this dynamic because their constituents are often already formally organized into parent groups, and because schools and libraries consistently represented the largest category of ballot items in PB.

One former facilitator complained of how wealthier, predominantly White parent groups in their neighborhood worked to mobilize such social and cultural capital to tailor (or even create) projects to fit city agencies' PB project criteria, and then launch campaigns in comparatively well-resourced schools: "I ended up dropping out of PB. . . . I was so disgusted with [education projects at high-income schools] being contorted to look like—to be defined as—'need' for technology. That made me crazy." Technical criteria are thus most easily manipulated by those with legal and bureaucratic connections and experience with writing grant proposals to "massage" their desires into PB-eligible "needs."

They described how the process intimidated even them, a former government lawyer: "I was sitting in this lawyer's office at a big white-shoe [prestigious] law firm having a sushi lunch talking about our issues. I thought, *this is really unfair* because I'm a pretty resourceful lawyer who knows to go to [a specific nonprofit] and get a law firm" to contribute pro bono services.

In interviews, both budget delegates and city agency representatives discussed the underlying logics of successful "good projects," helping to articulate which projects tended to move forward and why. Through the complex process of project proposal and selection, constituents negotiate whose ideas should take priority. Along the way, the predominant criteria they use to set priorities also appear to shift.

When community members first articulate their proposal ideas, they concentrate foremost on whatever they believe their families, neighbors, and neighborhoods need most. Quickly in the process, however, the lens of budget delegates, city agencies, council staff, and voters shifts to what is eligible, "feasible," and "reasonable." By the end, the remaining "reasonable" policies have become whittled down, doing little to challenge austerity in the city budget.

Budget delegates complained that their original project ideas, which spoke to dire community needs, were frequently sidelined and replaced by questionably needed projects that appeared easy to implement. Predictably, these projects were also those prioritized by city agencies or championed by already powerful groups. For example, one former delegate (identifying as Black and working class) complained that they had been trained to "think small," and when they tried to put forward employment ideas, people "say, 'Oh no you can't, it's going to be too big!' . . . We don't think, we behave small." They continued, "People need . . . shelter. . . . [The process ultimately] didn't progress anywhere. Where was it going? It was just people debating and speaking about minor things like traffic lights, like garbage pails. . . . And when you suggest a reasonable thing you get verbally shut down." To this delegate, the process ultimately "didn't progress anywhere." Their comments question whether budget delegates can be empowered to develop projects that explicitly address substantive community needs and equity. Can they and their neighbors fund what they believe to be right for the city and treat the city budget as a moral document?

———

Besides education, the other category of PB projects consistently mentioned by participants was community safety. If PB is supposed to bring meaningful change to the city budget, why did it keep funding police-run surveillance cameras? These win funding every year. At first glance, the popularity of surveillance cameras administered by the NYPD may be surprising, given widespread street protests against police violence, coupled with long-standing complaints about police surveillance, stop-and-frisk policies, and aggressive tactics.[1] At the same time, the prominence of body, dashboard, and cell phone camera feeds in documenting police brutality highlights potential roles for cameras in bottom-up accountability too.[2] How and why have surveillance cameras emerged as perennial, winning "good projects" in PB?

When I interviewed PB participants who had advocated for surveillance cameras, they reported that they did not do so in naive, unquestioning ways. Their visions of community safety included greater police accountability and economic support as well as surveillance, and they crucially included bottom-up accountability and access to the data (the video footage) captured by cameras. To them, PB should allow constituents to shape not just *what* programs are administered, but also *how*.

Community members who advocated for surveillance cameras conveyed nuanced takes on "safety" in their neighborhoods as well. They stated that they needed interventions for their neighbors, who let their dogs defecate in the elevators and did not clean up after them, engaged in petty crimes, or damaged building amenities. They hoped that security cameras would help them to ascertain who was doing what so as to hold these folks accountable.

In addition, they emphasized that their ideas for public safety should not be reduced to surveillance. One delegate, a middle-aged Black immigrant in the Bronx, asserted that "right now my main focus is to bring more programs into the neighborhood. Education, education. Jobs, jobs. . . . I think that cameras are a necessity in the community because we're a high-level poverty [community] and people tend to do stupid stuff . . . when their back [is] against a wall. . . . Security is bigger than this, cameras."

Their statements tie individual-level behaviors to macrolevel inequalities, pointing to structural forces such as poverty as potential root causes of criminal acts. Indeed, some interviewees first discussed these surveillance camera projects as just one element of a much broader vision of community safety. As one White, former facilitator in their twenties put it, "The whole dialogue with safety [goes] beyond policing, so this leads to a much broader conversation . . . tied into the Black Lives Matter campaign, against the one thousand new cops, and all the hundred millions [of] dollars for the however many new police officers and the whole safety beyond police campaign. But there's this assumption that, 'Oh yea, PB was going to fund the new cameras that's going to make the whole community safer.' . . . Rather than fully funding robust social programs and services, and wraparound services and community schools that our young people need to actually prevent crime and violence."

Over time, the jobs programs and other components of more holistic visions for community safety gained less attention in PB, partly because they fell outside eligibility criteria. These contestations over community safety reflect the extent to which later stages of the PB process did not fully reflect these residents' lived experiences, give them the ability to articulate the root problems they wished to address, or analyze the criteria by which their project proposals were judged.

Further, Bronx public housing residents who did receive PB-funded cameras expressed frustrations over not being able to access, own, and interpret the camera footage, the data, themselves. They wanted to access footage of police brutality as well as crimes, and protested the fact that police did not make footage public. One delegate, the Black immigrant quoted above, lamented that "they're putting [in] all of these cameras, we don't have access, there's nobody to monitor them.... It's only when they [have] a big shoot-out of that nature, the camera is being looked into.... The murders and stuff, we'll leave that to the professionals, which is the cop, but [for other incidents,] when the police is against our people and [our community] has a lot of police brutality. We can get community leaders [to] get an opportunity to view that and form a community to even do a protest if they wanted—[a] peaceful demonstration ... a not-breaking-the-rules protest. We are not given that opportunity."

Another PB participant, a Latine in Brooklyn, expressed similar disappointment with the lack of access to camera footage. "I mean, everybody wants to feel safe.... A lot of the people who I spoke to, who voted for these cameras, they themselves told me that if they had known beforehand that there's no way that we'll ever get access to this footage—they would never have voted for that." They went further to argue that without bottom-up accountability, the cameras not only expanded the city's carceral policies, but also made them feel *less* safe: "$680,000 was chosen to go into putting up more cameras in the neighborhood.... How does the community feel safe when incidents like this happen and the authorities are the ones committing these crimes against citizens, and there's no accountability, there's no transparency, there's no access to this footage? So ... public funds are being used to surveil the public."

———

For PB to serve as a meaningful exercise for budget justice, participants must be able to not just articulate their needs and propose specific projects, but also help shape the criteria by which projects are judged, the underlying logics of the city budget as a whole, and the rules by which they are governed. Put together, the experiences of budget delegates and their resulting projects pinpoint ways in which engaging constituents from historically marginalized communities is necessary but insufficient for racial equity. How can residents build racial solidarities and remake politics from below?

On the one hand, budget delegates spoke about how PB helped them build some unexpected, crosscutting alliances of groups of residents or organizations, which might usually lobby for funds independently. Specifically, PB deliberations allowed them to emphasize more than one aspect of their lives and identities along with issues of intersectionality, rather than a single identity—by race, gender, or other social axes. More than one interviewee stated that they ended up backing projects they would not have otherwise thought of or supported.

On the other hand, PB deliberations do not always address power inequalities embedded in communities. Some delegates warned that stressing how PB helped people get along distracted participants from the larger structures that perpetuate inequalities. In fact, some activists and scholars have dubbed an emphasis on mutual support as "intersectionality lite," arguing that a deeper intersectional approach would force deliberating groups—like budget delegate teams—to adopt new analytic lenses on community issues, starting from the lived conditions and bodily experiences of those most vulnerable.[3] They would not only form unexpected coalitions but also forward substantively different solutions.

Indeed, the PBNYC case highlights profoundly intersectional dimensions of participation, especially by race and class. The intersections here go beyond the fact that native-born, White residents report higher incomes than other residents, and that higher-income, higher-educated residents may have the social networks and legal skills to more easily navigate bureaucratic procedures.[4] They pointedly underline how, as Hall writes, race continues to serve as a fundamental "modality in which class is 'lived,' the medium through which class relations are experienced, the form in which it is . . . fought through."[5]

After all, in both education and community safety (the two PB project categories where budget delegates repeatedly raised issues of race), policymakers draw on racialized lines of public discourse to justify neoliberal welfare retrenchment policies and status quo class inequalities. In popular

124 BUDGET JUSTICE

debates on the "racial achievement gap" in education, a "culture of poverty" discourse helps to shift public scrutiny away from egregious inequalities in school funding, to how students from "the hood" purportedly refuse to study, work hard, or "act White."[6] In conversations on community safety, popular tropes around "criminality" and "broken windows" similarly shift the unit of analysis from structural forces to individuals.[7]

Community deliberations for budget justice were especially fruitful when participants engaged in *intersectionality as method*—not just noticing overlaps between participants' respective sets of identities and interests, but centering the distinct experiences of participants from multiply marginalized communities as jumping-off points for further analysis. The limits of failing to do so become obvious in court cases on workplace discrimination, as but one example. Cases forwarded by Black women have failed when plaintiffs are forced to cite either sex discrimination statutes or racial discrimination ones, and neither White female nor Black male colleagues face the same sorts of harassment.[8] In discussing intersectionality as what she calls a power analytic, social theorist Patricia Hill Collins writes, "Social actors who are subordinated within multiple systems of power are in a better position to see how the power hierarchies, social inequalities and social problems that characterize one system of oppression not only resemble those of other systems, but also that multiple systems work together to shape their experiences."[9]

Thus centering intersectional analyses was about more than garnering support for, say, a playground and soccer field by joining sports enthusiasts and local parents in an aggregative way. It was about reshaping what the project might look like, noting not only the lack of green space in the neighborhood but also the ways in which most playgrounds and sports fields remain inaccessible to children with special needs. Intersectionality as method forces participants to look at aspects of local built environments that otherwise tend to remain hidden in plain sight, and articulate different solutions that by serving the most vulnerable, should eventually benefit everyone. The new policy solutions do not have to explicitly benefit each and every community member to strengthen communities as a whole in equitable ways. As articulated by legal scholar john a. powell (the lowercase name is purposive), *targeted universalism* uses targeted processes to set universal goals.[10]

These frames for discussion are pivotal because identity politics can be flattened or contorted to promote essentialist assumptions or entrench neoliberal principles of individualism rather than nurture collective power. As activist Maurice Mitchell writes, a common trend in so-called identity politics involves "using one's identity . . . as a justification for a political position. You may hear someone argue, 'As a working-class, first-generation American, Southern woman . . . I say we have to vote no,' . . . [as if] that identity is evidence of some intrinsic ideological or strategic legitimacy." But, Mitchell continues, "We infantilize members of historically . . . oppressed groups by seeking to placate or pander. . . . Genuflecting to individuals solely based on their socialized identities . . . deprives them of the conditions that sharpen arguments, develop skills, and win debates."[11] The *method* part of intersectionality as method is essential to creating such conditions and centering equity in budget decisions.

Such deliberations also differ from more common exercises in empathy. Some magazine features incorporate "behind-the-scenes" looks or photography to invite readers to relate to undocumented immigrants, for instance. In response, readers often offer personal help, especially if those profiled seem "deserving." By contrast, intersectionality as method and targeted universalism invites participants to reflect on lived experiences not to judge one another, but instead to pinpoint what *structural* changes could make a difference for them and others.

Here, the miner's canary serves as an apt metaphor. The people in communities most vulnerable to violence, illness, opioid or substance abuse, debilitating work hazards like toxic chemical exposure, or other causes of premature death—young Black men, elderly Asian women, folks with disabilities, unemployed or underemployed adults lacking formal educational attainment, and so on—are canaries in the mine. In campaigns for budget justice, citizens work to not only improve their respective situations as individuals and shepherd others to flee danger, but to change the mine in ways that help canaries thrive too, along with less vulnerable birds and beings.

Intersectionality as method helps communities ensure that they pinpoint not only policy needs that might otherwise get overlooked, but policy innovations as well. In practice, centering intersectionality to articulate policies of targeted universalism can be accomplished at different scales, with profound effects. A common example of target universalism is that of the curb cut—a dip in the sidewalk originally designed to help cars enter driveways. Centering people who use wheelchairs, curb cuts at street corners benefit not only those who have physical disabilities but everyone too—including though not limited to parents pushing strollers, people being pulled by enthusiastic squirrel-chasing dogs, people dragging home luggage or heavy grocery carts, postal workers transporting packages on dollies, or people distracted by their phones.

Likewise, using intersectionality as method, the fact that only one-fourth of New York's subway stations are wheelchair accessible becomes not just frustrating, but revolting. Escalators and elevators help people with limited mobility, such as the elderly, parents with young children, someone who broke their ankle playing pickup basketball, or those suffering from vertigo, postural orthostatic tachycardia syndrome, or long COVID. The fact that escalators are seen as extras rather than the bare minimum of our public transit system erases the needs of a large swatch of the city's residents.

In the context of PB, intersectionality as method helped budget delegates examine proposals for playground repairs and think more imaginatively about what accessible playgrounds and communal spaces might look like. As a result, several newly funded playground projects included new equipment engaging senior citizens and children as well as adults with disabilities, especially those who might not be able to afford specialized physical therapy or gyms.

Budget justice calls for residents to use intersectionality as method on a neighborhood or city scale. As one example, a group of queer youths of color called FIERCE has repeatedly protested new luxury developments in the West Village neighborhood of Manhattan for two decades. These youths also consistently identify homelessness and too much policing as persistent issues. (While surveys of the unhoused are extraordinarily difficult to conduct well, ones that do exist report that while roughly 4 percent of the city's population identify as LGBTQ, 42 percent of youths accessing homeless youth services in New York identify as LGBTQ. A notable 95 percent identify as youths of color.)[12]

As the retail spaces in the West Village neighborhood have become increasingly higher end (designed to cater to tourists and a coveted, higher-income clientele imagined as older, White, gay, and male), queer youths of color have reported simultaneous increases in stop-and-frisk tactics and aggressive policing, greater harassment by shop staff and clienteles, greater use of "hostile" or "defensive architectures" in parks and public spaces (like spikes on ledges outside stores, so that people cannot sit while waiting for friends), and the closure of historically important shelters and social services providers, so that there are fewer safe spaces available to these youths. Centering FIERCE's intersectional analyses articulates different structures of inequality—and different proposals for budget justice—than analyses based on class, race, gender identity, sexual orientation, or age would on their own.[13]

Communities are unlikely to construct adequately nuanced policy proposals or strong racial solidarities without accounting for the ways in which, say, recent anti-Asian violence has specifically, disproportionately targeted elderly women, and deportation proceedings disproportionately targeted Black immigrants. (According to the Black Alliance for Just Immigration, Black immigrants constitute just 5.4 percent of the undocumented population in the United States, but one-fifth of those facing deportation after a criminal offense.)[14]

And as feminist urbanist scholar Leslie Kern writes, such intersectional analyses belong in all aspects of city planning, not just infrastructural decisions typically associated with specific groups—ramps for those using wheelchairs, say, or playgrounds for mothers. After snowstorms, for instance, "most cities will [center able-bodied male drivers commuting to work in their analyses and] plow major freeways first to clear space for car traffic and . . . leave residential areas, school zones, bike lanes, and sidewalks until the very end. And this has very obvious gender

128 BUDGET JUSTICE

implications. So some cities have started to ask: what if we did the opposite?"[15]

———

Studies on deliberative democracy often focus on the "force of the better argument," and indeed, the priorities articulated by many of the groups in PB suggest that such deliberation is fruitful and essential.[16] Such deliberations can help constituents to think collectively, collaborate rather than compete, and even become politicized in ways that electoral politics typically do not.

But as the PBNYC case study shows, the best assertions or projects do not automatically "rise to the top," as some advocates for deliberative democracy hope. First, there are questions regarding "the better argument." Participants can draw on their own and experts' observations, opinions, and analyses to eliminate poor choices, but best choices are not always apparent. Some problems are "wicked" ones—complex and lacking a right answer. Is there a clear answer to whether women should have their own women-only sections on public transit in attempts to reduce sexual harassment, as is the case in many countries? Especially in the context of austerity budgets and increasingly regressive federal funding policies, are there obviously better arguments for which anti-poverty program to fund and which *not* to fund? Or which climate change remediation project to undertake next? Or which mural design to select?

Besides, because there are many decisions to be made in a city budget, perhaps the sort of consensus underscored in theoretical deliberative democracy models is neither realistic nor necessary. Yet a lack of consensus lays bare the fact that disagreements sometimes reflect power dynamics, not substantive contentions.

Second, relatedly, there are questions regarding the better argument's "force." When does it triumph over centuries of patterned disenfranchisement, frequently encoded into law? When I quip, "May the Force be with you," I sound snarkier than I mean to. Still, I fear that this force, like the one in the *Star Wars* universe, can be similarly romanticized. It has undeniable allure as an ideal. It sounds almost mystically righteous, particularly in contrast to undemocratic assertions against average citizens as unfit for decision-making. But unlike the Jedi Force, the force of the better argument is not guaranteed.

In fact, I have observed it being invoked by gatekeepers and self-selected representatives, sidelining and ignoring power inequalities, especially those of race, gender, class, and other social forces. My concerns go beyond who gets to wield the lightsaber-like skills of eloquent oratory, sure to galvanize others as well as win approving applause and finger snaps in neighborhood assemblies or town hall meetings. It concerns whose arguments, what sorts of contentions, and what sorts of problems are carefully considered in the first place.

In these cases, it becomes imperative to center equity, attend to power dynamics, and resist the glamor of deliberation; otherwise, "consensus" becomes another mask for domination. Critical race theory scholars have repeatedly investigated how facially neutral "objective" criteria might have racially and intersectionally disparate effects, particularly when there are state policies involved. Amid dynamics of interest convergence, policies or reforms aimed to promote equity are usually implemented only when they also serve the interests of White elites, as well as help maintain status quo racial hierarchies.[17]

When questions of community safety are framed first as those of safety, then more narrowly as those of policing, and then simply as those of surveillance, some participants feel that their needs never made it onto the deliberative agenda in the first place. Often after some deliberation, neighbors acquiesce to a group decision to move a particular PB project forward, not because they agree with a specific argument, but because getting something is better than nothing. Or they are simply being polite.

Such civil, constructive dialogues could be counted as an achievement, especially with rising right-wing authoritarianism, violent populist movements, and political polarization around the world. But helping citizens to get along will not get to the root causes of their discontent or help achieve budget justice.

130　BUDGET JUSTICE

This sort of specious inclusion—one that ultimately reifies status quo inequalities—occurs even when participatory decisions are binding rather than advisory, and even when the process is deliberative as opposed to electoral. Intersectionality as method and targeted universalism, in turn, serve as principles to reorient budget deliberations away from feasibility and ease as the ultimate criteria for good projects. They are guideposts in thinking about budget justice and a right to the city. They draw on participants' lived experiences and attempt to build on new neighborly connections in specific ways—but with universalist aspirations other than lowest-common-denominator appeals to humanity or heartstring-pulling details about an unusually deserving, exceptional case.

Substantively different visions for education policy, community safety, neighborhood planning, and other policies are born through sustained community deliberations. And PB provides a promising venue, as long as communities get the resources they need to work across differences and collectively examine contested visions for a right-to-a-city budget. The New York case, however, also forces citizens to ask crucial questions regarding participatory and deliberative democracy, including, *Participation for what? Whose projects get taken seriously, move forward, and get funded?*

9

Actionable Knowledges

TO AVOID SHALLOW gestures toward democratic governance, budget justice requires that citizens and bureaucrats work together in a new way—moving away from a dynamic in which facially neutral technical knowledge and what Lefebvre calls the "science of the city" reign supreme.[1]

"Although necessary, policy is not enough."[2] Social anthropologist Manuel Delgado Ruiz stresses Lefebvre's critique of an ostensibly value-neutral science and knowledge.[3] To Delgado, planning that emphasizes such scientific knowledge results in spaces by and "of planners, administrators and administrations, and also of the doctrinaires of citizenship and civility . . . [with] clear, labeled, homogeneous, safe, obedient territories . . . disguised behind complex languages that make them unquestionable," replete with technical jargon and what might colloquially be called legalese.[4] Because this type of planning tries to render citizens and their actions legible to government, it creates "spaces of power" from which certain forms of knowledge are expelled.

Budget justice requires epistemic justice—whereby different ways of knowing are actively valued, and all constituents hold credence as producers of knowledge.[5] If, as the 1980s' *GI Joe* cartoons intoned, "knowing is half the battle" (granted, this is a big *if*), then epistemic justice focuses on the other half of the battle. When is knowledge taken seriously and acted on? Epistemic justice creates and is enabled by new citizen spaces for claims making, meeting needs, and thriving.[6]

Epistemic justice is important not only for its normative functions in the name of democracy, but for instrumental ones as well. Local, experiential, and "traditional" ways of knowing—based on careful observation, and often born out of necessity and survival—help communities to account for context and make do with what they have.

Urban dwellers draw on local knowledge to navigate the city every day. Many residents take certain routes to work not only to save time but also to avoid dangerous intersections, or get more sunshine in winter and shade in summer. Over time, food delivery workers decide when and where it is safe enough and worthwhile to "salmon"—bicycle against the flow of traffic—to cut travel times and earn sufficient tips to survive.

Citizens can inform public policies with local knowledge too. Neighborhood groups frequently have their own sense of where farmers' markets, community gardens, food distribution sites, or mobile health clinics should go. Furthermore, they might, with coordination and resources, have different models for effectively de-escalating about-to-turn-violent crises without police.

Epistemic injustice has implications for scholarly understandings of government as well. In fact, political scientists Joe Soss and Vesla Weaver argue that some communities, especially working-class Black and Latine ones, have long been rendered "marginal to the subfield's account of American democracy and citizenship." Scholars working on US politics mostly failed to adequately predict and analyze Black Lives Matter protests. They were so focused on liberal-democratic dimensions of the state (like elections) that they largely overlooked an equally crucial dimension disproportionately experienced by lower-income communities of color (namely, the police). As Soss and Weaver point out, Du Bois quipped over a century ago that "police were our [African Americans'] government, and philanthropy dropped in with periodic advice."[7] Without epistemic justice, dominant theories of urban government, democratic governance, and US citizenship remain woefully distorted and incomplete.

The value of epistemic justice is clear in the biological sciences too. One striking example comes from Chinese scientist Tu Youyou's search for a cure for chloroquine-resistant malaria. Tu found a breakthrough not in cutting-edge laboratory experiments but instead a sixteen-hundred-year-old text called "Emergency Prescriptions Kept up One's Sleeve," which referenced sweet wormwood in treating fevers. After replicating the treatment from AD 317, Tu extracted the compound artemisinin; in 2015, without a doctorate or medical degree, she received a Nobel Prize in medicine.[8]

Another example, from Indigenous Potawatomi thinker and botanist Robin Wall Kimmerer, highlights implications for how different constituencies might relate to one another. Buffalo herders and traditional Passamaquoddy sweetgrass basket weavers have long asserted that harvesting might facilitate rather than impede grass growth. When some of Kimmerer's university-based colleagues first heard this hypothesis, they scoffed. But once scientists conducted experiments that took the traditional practitioners' knowledge seriously, they learned that indeed, moderate harvesting triggers what is called compensatory growth; further, buffalo spit actually contains an enzyme that stimulates grass growth.[9] The local knowledge originally seemed counterintuitive partly because the laboratory scientists tended to consider variables only in their respective subfields—that is, botany, animal husbandry, and enzyme chemistry—in siloed, nonecological ways.

I find these anecdotes particularly instructive because they have immediate implications for how holders of local knowledge might relate to holders of technical knowledge, for everyone's benefit.

———

In PBNYC, the city agencies' racialized practices—especially regarding local versus technical knowledge—help forward a model of *managed participation* as opposed to community organizing and mobilization. Combined with the context of austerity addressed in part I, these practices suppress substantive citizenship.

134 BUDGET JUSTICE

Official policy is only as good as how it is implemented—and the latter is determined by the administrative personnel and contractors who interpret and enforce policy. Nonprofit and public administrators—city managers, social workers, and agency representatives—are also concerned with improving participation, and how policy designs construct citizenship and affect the wider public.[10]

In public administration, the model of new public management introduced by Reagan in the 1980s remains dominant.[11] In the 1990s, US president Bill Clinton further institutionalized this model through the large-scale implementation of performance metrics and incentives for a "customer-driven government."[12] In this model, "entrepreneurial" public managers develop a combination of insurance, subsidy, and other products to deliver government services to recipients deemed "customers" versus citizens.

This has consequences. Ill-implemented attempts at democratizing public administration may further discredit community input, or "ultimately reinforce and extend neoliberalism by embedding market logics more deeply in progressive uses of state power."[13]

Widening inequalities and deepening distrust of government prompted calls for another model of public administration in which public managers "*govern*, not just manage, in increasingly diverse and complex societies."[14] In what Partners for Dignity & Rights coexecutive director Kesi Foster emphasizes as cogovernance, citizens are not just customers or voters but instead partners in policymaking; public managers act as collaborators and capacity builders.[15] Ideally, government responds to active community participation to deliver collectively defined public goods—though unsurprisingly, it remains challenging to achieve the conditions necessary to make participation possible, politically acceptable, and administratively sustainable in an era of austerity.[16]

Indeed, a key, undervalued element of the Porto Alegre PB experiment lies in changing how city bureaucrats and government workers viewed their jobs as well as themselves, shifting from what sociologist Boaventura de Sousa Santos calls a model of "technobureaucracy" to one of "technodemocracy," and renewing, however infinitesimally, the public administrative state from inside.[17]

PBNYC gives citizens a forum to speak, but that does not necessarily mean that these citizens are truly listened to. It becomes a situation of, as journalist and poet Alissa Quart puts it, "Too many words, not enough ears."[18] For a technodemocracy, city bureaucrats must put their technical expertise in service of democratically determined priorities. But can bureaucrats take seriously everyday citizens' views? Research shows that citizens remain consistently perceived as "emotional, illogical, and lacking in credibility."[19]

In the PBNYC process, budget delegates stated that city agencies were sometimes difficult to work with because, first, many representatives were slow to respond to inquiries. Second, many organically developed project proposals were deemed ineligible. One constituent complained that "agencies . . . don't allow the team to change their proposal to be realistic." Third, other delegates felt frustrated by the lack of coordination between agencies or because the same project idea—for example, a green roof—might involve different agencies, depending on who owned the parcel of land. Several delegates spoke about struggles to build new community gardens on identified vacant lots: "[PB] wasn't really impactful. . . . We searched . . . a number of areas; some . . . we chose were under [two agencies]. . . . It became very difficult . . . because of all the agencies involved."

Granted, the city agencies participating in PBNYC did not interact with constituents in monolithic ways. Some agencies prepared helpful flyers for budget delegates, including typical projects eligible for PB funds. Several agencies' presentations graphically dimmed more ambitious projects, so as to manage PB participant expectations. Later in the cycle, after project proposals were developed and before residents voted on them, some of the agencies also conducted outreach on behalf of the PB process.

Still, many delegates suggested that agencies rejected their proposals because of technicalities, in contrast to collaborating with them to make the project feasible. As one delegate recounted, "It's a jurisdictional nightmare. All the agencies . . . say, 'It's not our problem, talk to [this

136   BUDGET JUSTICE

one, that one].' So a lot of them know more than they're willing to let on, I think."

Delegates wanted more specific guidelines for city agency decisions to help them develop better proposals, but they also asked for more dialogue overall. They requested an "appeals process. . . . [W]e felt the agency misunderstood or misrepresented the projects." Budget delegates did not view agency representatives as neutral parties but rather as simultaneous facilitators and gatekeepers with distinct interests.

These tensions speak to how citizens' lived experiences, local knowledge, and priorities were sidelined by technical rules and dismissed as pejoratively "political."[20] Cumulatively, city agencies did not just reject specific proposals; they denied citizens the ability to assert their own hard-earned lessons about their needs or remedies as valid.

In managed participation, city agency representatives do not formally exclude residents from invited democratic spaces like PB; instead, they limit residents' ability to instantiate substantive citizenship within these spaces through epistemic injustice, in the guise of "rising above the fray."

Indeed, as they become adept at navigating the PB process, some participants give up on changing budget allocations or demanding more from government. Instead, they simply forward whatever proposals they now know to be most palatable to city agencies, even when these proposals sideline the concerns that compelled them to participate in the first place. They risk becoming easily placated, educated "model citizens" as the state would define them.

In any case, should it really be the job of busy New Yorkers to "choose" which curbs should receive extensions to be safe, or which schools "ought" to get basic repairs, and by extension, which do not?

In such a scenario, discussions regarding taxation along with the shape and size of the figurative public budget pie are sidelined by competitive exercises determining the slices. PB reduces constituents to citizen-consumers. In PBNYC, several city agencies quickly tailored their information sessions to lobby participants for funds with prepared "menus" of projects that suffered from budget cuts and needed a relatively small PB top-up for implementation. They in effect told constituents exactly what projects needed funding in their neighborhoods.

———

A number of city agency representatives spent considerable time asserting that PB promises to be a great democratic experiment, but that they work in an exceptional policy arena in which local knowledge plays little role. Technical expertise trumps all.

At first glance, such statements corroborated budget delegates' frustrations and impressions that agency representatives stonewalled them. But interviews suggested that epistemic injustice typically played out in more subtle ways. Representatives pointed to a range of conditions that shaped their ability to meet alongside PB imperatives. For instance, agencies varied greatly by organizational structure and funding streams (especially regarding the level of government funding them).

City agency representatives acknowledged that PB allowed community members to identify local priorities and draw on local knowledge. One representative, for instance, stated that "the community is good about identifying the need and saying, 'Yes, this is a really dangerous [spot].'" Different constituents drew on different bodies of local knowledge in their deliberations; for example, youth budget delegates were particularly adept at pinpointing locations that felt unsafe right after school in ways that planners working at City Hall downtown were unlikely to know.

Nevertheless, almost all city agency representatives I interviewed bemoaned what they felt were outsized expectations by PB delegates. As one quipped, "I think the[ir] weakness is [a] champagne taste with a beer pocketbook." These bureaucrats felt that they were easily villainized, and that the PB process punished the messengers of high-cost figures. Representatives thus repeatedly asked for more participant education before meetings with them. As one agency representative stated, "These are the relative costs of certain things. . . . To build a new sewer costs this . . . much per foot."

138 BUDGET JUSTICE

This view narrows the definition of potentially useful knowledge to solely that of laws, codes, and existing agency directives. It negates residents' articulations of their needs, their theorizing about causality, and their potential solutions—say, why a curbside rain garden might be better than a traditional storm basin at this location. Maybe children already have trouble traversing the intersection safely and would have difficulty navigating the basin, but are likely to play and even help care for the tiny garden plot. Or maybe someone used to garden there and knows that the plants couldn't thrive unless some old tree roots were properly removed.

When one bureaucrat remarked that citizens "should be put in a room and *educated*" it also sounded like they wanted citizens to be *schooled*—that the meetings have socializing and disciplinary functions alongside informational ones.

In any case, budget delegate training improved within the first few years of the PBNYC process, and representatives, too, have prepared helpful presentations on eligibility criteria. Hence delegates avoided the most common technical mistakes in their project proposals—thinking that electronic tablets are eligible, for example, when the city rules that they are not. Furthermore, even agency representatives who complained that the PB process felt like "a waste of time" enjoyed this educative role, conversing with well-versed policy "geeks."

Over time, reports of deliberation with delegates became more common. One reported, "In this case, it was obvious the green roof would come through us and not [the Department of Environmental Protection] because it was on our property. The delegates already knew that much." Another noted that by the third year of the process, groups "came to us with projects . . . with . . . specifications. . . . [T]he more homework they do, the better. And we . . . were able to show up to the meeting with cost stuff and have a much better discussion."

Other common frustrations involved technical details that were difficult for lay constituents to grasp. Several representatives stated that they could not work on certain improvements because, for instance, "it's a combination of state land, parkland, [and an agency] facility." There thus remain questions regarding how much "typical" citizens should be expected to know in order to be taken seriously by city bureaucrats. To what extent should participants—many of them volunteering amid holding one or more full-time jobs, and many of them from traditionally marginalized constituencies—limit their proposals to ones that perfectly fit individual agencies' respective criteria?

After all, many meaningful projects—like tackling chronic homelessness—require interagency coordination in ways that are challenging for city agencies, since they can be set up to work independently. Epistemic justice demands that constituents and bureaucrats look beyond the sort of siloed technical expertise cultivated in laboratory settings, universities, or city agency performance indicators, to better recognize condition-specific, synergistic effects in everyday life.

———

This overreliance on technical expertise results in antidemocratic epistemic injustice, even when city bureaucrats bear no ill will or unjust intentions. In keeping with technocratic discourse around policymaking, many of the agency interviewees asserted that they are apolitical, neutral actors: "We have no vested interest in any of the projects that are being voted on or . . . discussed. . . . I don't want to give any information that would . . . alter plans." Another representative implored, "Just tell me what you need done, and we'll go fix them if it's an issue." Such statements, while friendly, also worked to limit delegate expectations. They dovetail well with scholars' findings that regulators "feared commitment to ideas or decisions reached by non-expert . . . stakeholders" as inevitably distorting definitions of the "public good."[21]

Bureaucrats spoke about how PB might encourage rent seeking or situations where citizens took public wealth to redistribute it to themselves. One hypothesized that a small group of active constituents might end up with "millions of dollars" to build its "own clubhouse" rather than a facility to serve a broader range of residents. "That's a waste of money. . . . [T]he groups that bang on the table the loudest, won." The agency representatives' aversion to contested politics could be seen as an attempt to protect "quiet wheels" from proverbial "squeaky" ones that "get the grease." This view of contested politics denigrates disagreements as inevitably destructive. It implies that there are clear, objective ways to define the "public interest," and that there can be a science of the city.

Yet when pressed, bureaucrats cited no real-life examples of such rent seeking in PB. In actual PB meetings, conscientious constituents frequently disagreed on top priorities in respectful ways and still, they managed to successfully have constructive discussions. Participants implied that sometimes, there is no one right answer; deliberations can facilitate *generative conflicts*, exercises in incorporating different worldviews as well as competing and potentially overlapping interests, in decision-making. In such cases, a consensus on a "best" project might even seem suspect.

Furthermore, some issues framed as "technical" by public agency representatives sure looked political to participants. For instance, participants regularly asked for closed stairwells in certain highly trafficked, public buildings to be reopened. In response, agency representatives stated that reopening the stairwells was impossible because they would then technically have to build elevators to be compliant with the Americans with Disabilities Act. The latter would be too expensive. To agency representatives, this was an unfortunate situation to which they resigned themselves.

One budget delegate, however, claimed agencies "seemed to make up data compared to research that we had done. For example, [they made] disingenuous claims that a project wasn't possible due to the Americans with Disabilities Act, when that wasn't really true." To this delegate, the agencies might have deemed the project feasible if they looked harder for alternative solutions, or if constituents with disabilities had more political power.

As this anecdote suggests, some groups' views tend to get sidelined more often than other ones. These questions are inextricably tied to equity; after all, well-resourced constituents may be the ones to master technical criteria more quickly. Besides, their preferences are probably already well-documented; they may have even helped shape existing city standards.

At the same time, the agency representatives repeatedly stated that they themselves were struggling to combat budget cuts. This serves as a reminder not only of the conditions in which they work, but also the fact that the state is not any more monolithic than the citizenry is. I was reminded of this at a lunchtime Zoom meeting with city agency representatives; I had invited them to anonymously report on how budget cuts were impacting their daily work. Around a dozen workers called in. Most of them had their cameras turned off, some got quiet whenever colleagues walked into the break room they were calling from, and one person called from a bathroom stall.

Their informal testimonies were heartrending. Someone spoke about how they had been working on an evidence-based social services initiative for five years. They finally finished developing it, getting it approved, hiring for it, and prepping for implementation in key high-need neighborhoods—a feat. Now this initiative was suddenly defunded. The person hesitated to tell me the name of the initiative, but they did note that it was the sort of "violence interruption" that experts assert would have prevented several high-profile deaths in New York's subway system.

A social worker in the Bronx spoke about working in a zone that should have sixty-five social workers, but at that time, had just thirty-four. Accordingly, they rushed through their home visits, trying to see as many families as possible, knowing that the public already mistrusts the city's foster care system, and feeling terrified that they made a mistake and left a child in an unsafe situation.

Such testimonies stress the city workers' thoughtful application of hard-earned experiential knowledge alongside technical knowledge. Multiple callers talked about how they were losing people with decades of experience (and knowledge on how to properly diffuse tense situations) because of budget cuts. In the meantime, they had less discretion and more paperwork each day, making it virtually impossible to do their job well. To them, administrative burdens had shifted from merely annoying to intolerable. This corroborated what I heard from others working in city agencies.

When I asked what they wanted New Yorkers and the general public to know about New York City government workers, they replied, "We are not the foot soldiers of the mayor."

———

The agency workers' testimonies show how austerity policies sideline local knowledge within government too; this dynamic, combined with the prevailing technobureaucratic practices in the agencies' public-facing work, reifies respectability politics. An overemphasis on technical knowledge risks sidelining not just "dirty politics" but also democratic deliberation, on-the-ground ingenuity, and neighborly collaboration.

Underrecognized reservoirs of local knowledge are not equally or randomly distributed throughout the population; they are gendered, racialized, and neurodivergent. (In using the term *neurodivergent*, I think of how my friends with learning challenges like dyslexia constantly adapt to user-*un*friendly presentations with ingenious, homemade assistive devices or tactics—creating auditory accompaniments, for instance, to all visual cues. Wide swaths of the public, including "neurotypical" people like me, benefit from assistive devices and tactics like open captioning during public forums or in movies.) Epistemic justice goes hand in hand with the sort of intersectionality as method and targeted universalism I discussed in chapter 8 on terms of deliberation.

After all, it is no coincidence that historians are still setting the record straight on how Rosa Parks, Ella Baker, and Fannie Lou Hamer contributed to the radical politics of the civil rights movement, building solid grassroots bases on which more familiar names, like Martin Luther King Jr., stand. Their efforts sometimes get denigrated as less intellectual or simply secondary. This is true even when their practices and discourses—through mutual aid during the pandemic or the community organizing "with heart" in the people's assemblies in Jackson—are integral to success.[22]

If budgets are both moral documents and wicked problems, then they need government workers along with everyday residents to draw on different bodies of knowledge to develop programs and policies that work. And critical citizens need both innovative solutions and thoughtful ways to adjudicate as well as implement them. They must assert their own ways of knowing and technodemocracy in policymaking.

10

No Algorithms, No Shortcuts

THE LIMITATIONS OF NEW YORK'S PB process have implications not only for the city's budget process, but other democratic experiments as well.

First, PB must be expanded and deepened beyond its current design. As sociologist Caroline Lee writes, "Political equality—the chance to be decision-makers for a day—is not worth much when making decisions means budget cuts as far as the eye can see."[1] Currently, PB often remains the exception to typical municipal budgeting: a way for constituents to voice concerns, let off steam, and see some of their ideas come to fruition while most of the budget remains opaque and predetermined.

If New York were to match the 45 euros per capita PB funding in Paris, for instance, it would invest around $50 for each of almost 8.1 million residents into PB, yielding $400 million to be decided by New Yorkers each year. This robust version of a New York PB process would be roughly ten times bigger than it currently is. It would thus not be a side exercise, but instead a core budgeting process for the city.

Second, by focusing exclusively on the invest side of the equation, PB remains incomplete. It therefore risks propagating the myth that the problem is solely a scarcity of funds, rather than austerity as policy. PB in the United States is not consistently tied to explicit questions of funds' origins; eligible funds are frequently those deemed easy, limited, regressive, or discretionary. In Vallejo, California, the citywide PB process allocates proceeds from a sales tax. Other PB funds have come from Community Development Block Grants. In other places, community groups have campaigned for PB processes to allocate the proceeds of court cases where firms had to pay hefty damages. PB's attention on investments must be accompanied by attention on revenues and divestments.

PBNYC funds come from city council members' discretionary budgets; when the pandemic hit, all but a few paused their PB processes. In 2018, a referendum to change the City Charter and establish a mayor-coordinated PB process was approved by a landslide, but Mayor de Blasio failed to adequately fund it. In 2022, Mayor Adams launched a new citywide process called "the People's Money," but the small pot of eligible funds remains too small to prompt meaningful conversations about the city budget as a whole.[2]

A deeper lesson is that there is no foolproof algorithm for PB. Communities must resist discourses of best practices or perfect institutional designs. PB must be practiced, maintained, and regularly tweaked to stay strong as well as relevant to changing political conditions. Searching for perfect procedural rules deems PB a technical project for "good governance," not a political project for racial and economic justice.

In fact, Brazil's decades-long experiences with PB suggest that even institutional designs and rules that are nearly perfect in one context can flounder in another. The scope along with the role of PB in local governance must be adjusted to fit local and current needs.

In the case of Porto Alegre, the original scope of the process focused on capital infrastructural projects because that is what the city needed at the time. PB-funded projects involving street safety, water, and utilities helped the city to make remarkable progress in lowering infant mortality over a relatively short span of time. Further, the PB process was designed in a way that fit the political moment. The city boasted of a strong civil society—including social movement groups that helped topple the military dictatorship in Brazil in the late 1980s—that could be relied on for high rates of participation. The city also closed some other traditional channels of feedback, so that local organizations had to appeal to the local government for funds, in front of everybody else, through the local PB process. That is, there were no

146 BUDGET JUSTICE

backroom city budget negotiations because the local government closed the back rooms.[3]

In contrast, most of the community needs articulated in New York concern services and programming, not infrastructure. Quite a few constituents have complained that project eligibility rules have not fit their needs.

And within a city, local agencies develop in different ways, often shaped by racist histories of segregation, land-grabbers, and displacement. Two adjacent neighborhoods might hence be in the same city council district, different police precincts, two school zones that nevertheless send residents to schools in the other neighborhood, the same community board (which makes decisions regarding business liquor and restaurant licenses, zoning, and other land use policies), and different congressional districts. Practically speaking, these sorts of borders make formal politics even more intimidating to the average citizen. Local policymaking in these contexts can become more difficult to coordinate, vulnerable to what political scientists call *forum shopping*. If a citizen group does not get a friendly response to a local initiative via, say, the community board, perhaps it could try the local council member instead.

PB cannot bring about budget justice as a democratic experiment in a larger administrative state and political context that otherwise remains unchanged.

Another lesson from Porto Alegre is that when political conditions change, the process needs to as well. To be successful, PB must be continually supported with both meaningful implementation and political will. The process worked well for decades in Porto Alegre, with mayors from competing political parties supporting it. But the city failed to adjust the PB process to help poor residents to participate in decision-making regarding larger-scale projects, like building federally funded stadiums for the World Cup. One of these projects involved the relocation of 1,550 families.[4] Nationally, residents began to feel frustrated that PB was no longer aiding them to realize helpful and meaningful projects, and they expressed this discontent at the polls. That, in turn, diminished enthusiasm for PB as politicians returned to top-down policies.[5] In other words, even when a seemingly insurgent democratic experiment develops within a state, it does not necessarily remain so for long.

———

As experiments like PB become widespread or even trendy, communities must also remain vigilant against their elite capture and co-optation.[6] City governments can no longer make major decisions or approve large developments without at least the semblance of community input, but that does not mean that the processes are truly participatory, even if they call them so. This increases the chances that they become "technocratically canned," robbing them of the reason and power of why they were invented in the first place.[7] As Lefebvre notes, perfunctory public participation "allows those in power to obtain, at a small price, the acquiescence of concerned citizens. After a show trial more or less devoid of information and social activity, citizens sink back into their tranquil passivity."[8]

Or perversely, they risk further alienating rather than engaging citizens. In particular, sociologist Francesca Polletta notes that a view of participatory democracy as middle class and White has in the past discouraged some activists of color.[9] For instance, community input sessions mandated before public works projects like affordable housing developments frequently yield antidemocratic outcomes, often with predominantly White homeowners' associations exacting not-in-my-backyard politics.

Quite a few paradoxes of participation arise—that in most cases, those who might benefit most from political participation tend to participate least, and relatedly, that in contrast to holding politicians accountable, participatory channels sometimes give them the cover (or less generously, the gall) to wash their hands of the provision of essential services. In such instances, some policymakers attempt to claim that all negative outcomes should now be attributed to citizens since they helped inform decisions.[10] While some pundits proceed to claim that "community input is bad, actually," democracy scholars show that it is by no means inherently so.[11] At the very least, participatory venues must not be set

148   BUDGET JUSTICE

up to fail—with insufficient funding, crunched timelines, little outreach, little training or helpful information provided, incompetent facilitation or attention to power inequalities and preorganized groups, and tokenistic representation.

Since many of these experiments originally developed in the Global South, it is useful to look at their experiences with this "participatory turn." Many of the calls for participation in foreign aid were inspired by the need for constituents throughout the Global South to have a say in the mass-scale dam projects, economic policies, and other governmental decisions being made by elites as well as the Washington Consensus institutions like the World Bank, IMF, and US Department of the Treasury.[12]

Yet by the early 2000s, practitioners and scholars had already begun to call "participatory frameworks" the *new tyranny*, a way for funders and institutions to pay lip service to participation, and to quiet protests. This new tyranny perpetuates status quo inequalities, benefiting Global North professionals in what some have dubbed a nonprofit industrial complex and burdening individuals to assume responsibilities that had traditionally been those of the welfare state.[13]

In the United States, the nonprofit industrial complex includes museums, soup kitchens, and a dizzying array of organizations with tax-exempt, 501(c)3 status. They are often contracted to administer programs that have traditionally been the purview of government. Austerity measures have taken funds away from comprehensive social safety net programs; in doing so, they have instead created a market for social service providers working in small, piecemeal ways.

Less cynically, many professionals and organizations in the nonprofit sector provide essential services and do as best as they can under difficult circumstances. Well-meaning consultants need funding to survive, and so it is understandable that they try to get contracts to facilitate strategic planning retreats, administer citizens' assemblies, design outreach campaigns, and write a lot of reports. These consultants frequently provide helpful technical support; without such support, for instance, many local governments might neglect to plan a realistic timeline for ideas collection for neighborhood assemblies or put aside money for proper outreach.

But because democratic participation can be good business, participation consultants vary greatly in quality. The particular slice of the nonprofit industrial complex most directly relevant to budget justice constitutes what I call the *participation industrial complex*. Some work to make sure that new citizens' assemblies or PB processes are implemented well; others have little experience with democratic facilitation, but have jumped on the deliberative democracy bandwagon and branded themselves experts. Some win contracts by promising fodder for flattering local news headlines, explicitly *not* asking questions about data ownership, racial inequalities, building substantive solidarities, or initiating systemic change.

I have witnessed firsthand all sorts of consultants facilitating meetings and pitching their services to local governments. Because they rely on government contracts, foundation grants, and philanthropic gifts to stay afloat, many end up developing boilerplate templates for "success."

Lee calls this participation industrial complex a *do-it-yourself democracy*; after examining a number of deliberative forums and programs, she issues a stern warning that "deliberation contains more potential for social control than liberation, even in cases where collective action is an explicit goal and processes are generally found to be satisfactory."[14]

Spaces for democratic participation must themselves be democratically governed. As Hall wrote while analyzing English Labour and Social Democratic Party strategies, "'Participation' without democracy, without democratic mobilization, is a fake solution. 'Decentralization' which creates no authentic, alternative sources of real popular power. . . . function[s] . . . to dismantle the beginnings of popular democratic struggle, to neutralize a popular rupture."[15]

One meme that emerged online in 2021, a year after the uprisings in Floyd's name, declared, "We demanded racial justice; we got an Office of DEI [diversity, equity, and inclusion] instead." One can imagine many corollaries, at different scales: "We wanted to budget justice; we got PB instead." "We demanded PB; we got laptops and water fountains instead." When do such compromises set the stage for their own undoing?

Indeed, because the PBNYC process remains so limited, many of the more interesting and profound outcomes thus far take the form of spillover effects—that is, proliferating demands and practices that formally fall outside the PB process, but would not have happened without it.

Based on my research, constituents routinely became informed citizens *through* PB, but they also became so indignant or even enraged by the budget injustice they witnessed during the process, that they became politicized in new ways *because of* it. For instance, from 2011 to 2013, PB participants—perhaps especially those who had no personal connections to local schools—were shocked by the conditions of school bathrooms, with issues like stalls without doors. They were upset about putting PB discretionary funds toward such basic needs. The PB process mobilized them around this concern; in 2014, the Department of Education doubled its allocation for school bathrooms. This was explicitly because of PB.[16]

In another example, Lander's own experiences as a council member inspired him to develop an online tracker for the timelines and spending of PB-funded capital projects in his district. He then advocated for a citywide version and sponsored a law mandating its creation. The online Capital Projects Dashboard, which came out during Lander's term as city comptroller, merges budget information from the city's Financial Management System with cost, current phase, and details from agency project management databases.[17] It is exactly the sort of interactive, accessible information portal I yearned for when I first tried to make sense of the city budget.

While such spillover effects cannot be designed or predicted, their presence is crucial. They serve as reminders of PB as both a school (and boot camp even) and laboratory of democracy.

While no perfect model PB process exists, it remains imperative to examine whether a specific PB process has mobilizing or delimiting effects. The national Black Lives Matter protests led to a new wave of PB around the country—one that centers power analyses and racial justice in newly explicit ways. In several cities—such as Nashville, Seattle, and Raleigh—local governments have established PB processes, but community groups continue to advocate for more robust versions. In these cases, PB has helped communities to articulate alternative budgets contrary to the status quo—as part of an emerging and significant movement of people's budgets around the country.

These people's budgets feel like a movement because active campaigns using this terminology have emerged, without central coordination, in over a dozen cities—and not just in large, coastal ones like Seattle, Los Angeles, New York, and Philadelphia. I read about people's budgets in Norman, Ypsilanti, Sacramento, Nashville, Raleigh, and Cleveland. The exact names of their campaigns vary a bit; some call themselves *solidarity budgets*, for instance. But I was struck by how so many of them took off in a short span of time, during or after the pandemic, and how they articulate the sorts of #carenotcuts, divest-invest, or defund-refund framings at the heart of budget justice.

It feels like no coincidence that most of these campaigns are led by grassroots coalitions that include both organizing and services groups, and that they aim to, as legal scholar Jocelyn Simonson writes, "bring together local community knowledge with large-scale thinking about government spending."[18] In other words, in addition to forwarding alternative policy or budget platforms, they pay attention to participatory democracy, helping everyday residents to forward *their* perspectives and have a say in policymaking. Most, if not all, of these cities also pursued PB or people's assemblies (like the ones Themba discusses in her interview in this book) as part of their campaigns.

Two of the campaigns I have found especially inspiring so far hail from Nashville and Seattle, partly because they insist on the radical spirit of PB to engage structural changes in city budgets. For years, starting in 2016, a group called Metro Nashville tried to bring PB to the city. In its campaign, it emphasized residents' identities as taxpayers and how the process might work.[19] Then in 2020, the historic uprisings after the police murder of Floyd brought a record number of Nashvillians to

152 BUDGET JUSTICE

hearings about the city budget, including a marathon one that lasted through the night until dawn.[20] A new coalition called the Nashville People's Budget Coalition launched that summer to analyze the mayor's proposed budget and demand PB for the city. Unlike previous efforts to initiate PB in Nashville, the new campaign explicitly cited PB as part of a larger strategy to divest from policing and invest in social services.[21]

In 2021, the mayor put aside $2 million for PB processes to be spent on infrastructure in the historically underserved and Black neighborhoods, Bordeaux and North Nashville. The mayor renewed the same process in 2022. In 2023, the mayor expanded the process to involve $10 million to be spent around the city. But the Nashville People's Budget Coalition continues to push for a more substantive PB process—one that explicitly divests from policing while investing in education and housing. It hosted a "radical proposal writing party," for instance, to help residents develop ambitious proposals despite "inadequate funding, inaccessibility, & burdensome control by the mayor's office," and "build momentum toward a PB process true to its radical roots."[22] And the Black Nashville Assembly, another project founded in 2020, has been combining calls for participatory democracy with people's assemblies, issue-based campaigns, and political education. As the assembly puts it, "The participatory democracy *we* are talking about is unlike anything we've seen in Nashville because it fundamentally changes the power dynamics between our communities and elected officials."[23]

In Seattle, the city government started a small, citywide, youth-focused PB process with $700,000 in 2015.[24] In 2020, a statement signed by seventy-five local organizations demanded a solidarity budget—one that not only allowed residents to articulate potential projects for the city but also affirmed that any money divested from the police be allocated by a robust PB process led by Black Seattlites, and that the city reject an austerity approach overall.[25] In 2022, the Solidarity Budget Coalition continued to advocate for a 50 percent reduction in the police department's budget, especially by eliminating 240 "ghost cop" positions, which the Seattle Police Department stated would remain unfilled for years. The coalition helped the city to secure the elimination of 80 such ghost cop positions, as well as over $1 million for eviction prevention and defense, and over $3 million for climate resilience hubs. These wins relied on revenues from a new JumpStart Seattle corporate tax.[26]

The Seattle Solidarity Budget's demands articulated both policy goals and constituent programs, with price tags attached. For example, it demanded a "budget to end deaths of houseless people," with a moratorium on sweeps, improved harm reduction practices, a $20 million investment into community-based responses to public safety, five mobile pit stops, and nine recreational vehicle safe lots. Beyond a "budget to live," the coalition articulated a dream "budget to thrive," asking that the city double its commitment to PB from $30 to $60 million, and that this commitment increase each year until it reaches $200 million.

I especially admire these two cities' campaigns because of how they meld community budget priorities with participatory democratic practices. Grassroots groups in these cities articulate PB as a way for citizens to become engaged in larger struggles for budget justice.

These campaigns constitute a movement by citizens nationwide—as individuals or members of organizations—to forward alternative visions for city budgets and understand how budgets get made in the first place. They also pointedly suggest how, when combined with ideas and logics from invented spaces along with larger struggles for people's budgets, PB cannot be easily defanged by local governments or the participation industrial complex.

———

When the means determine the ends, there can be no shortcuts. In order to enact public budgets that facilitate collective care and well-being, cities need what Lefebvre calls "real and active participation."[27] They must mobilize citizens to think together about collective needs, learn about city budgets, articulate what they wish to divest from and invest in instead, and work beyond small, "cute" projects. Meaningful PB only takes place when policymakers invest resources, thoughtful designs for engaging interactions with citizens, and real decision-making power into the process.[28]

With those nonnegotiables in place, communities that put in the effort reap rewards in spades—in fruitful projects that improve material conditions in the city in sensitive ways, new social and political connections, greater trust in one another and government, and even greater public willingness to pay taxes.[29]

Deliberation here is not so much about airing a best argument that somehow rises to the top, but instead collective thinking about root causes and emergent strategies. This book examines PB experiments as one overt way in which this can happen, and cities around the country—and world—have been demanding PB to help constituents make binding decisions on public budgets. PB is not—and should not be—the only path to budget justice.

If the process is not messy, if it is easily accepted by power holders as safe and doable, then it is not truly working. Budget justice requires grassroots politics that takes up invitations like PB, but that also refuses to be managed from above. (Some political scientists aptly dub the latter *astroturf* politics.)[30] The driving question of means and ends for budget justice thus shifts from, *Is participatory democracy possible?* to, *Are these participatory democratic institutions, like PB, mobilizing?* Do they help communities to organize themselves to combat austerity and opacity, articulate divest-invest formulations for city budgets as moral documents, and propose different logics for a right-to-the-city budget?

Paying attention to context does more than help PB practitioners to implement more appropriate, sensitive, substantive, and therefore successful processes. It also helps citizens to attend to struggles over budgets outside PB or elections, across a whole range of democratic spaces, and to practice instances of budget justice that PB simply cannot contain.

PART III

Citizens Make Cities

11

Neighborly Citizenship

IN NEW YORK CITY, each family must submit lists of up to twelve schools on their applications for public kindergarten. Although unlikely, some students do not receive placement in any of the schools they list. So my family researched local schools to decide which ones to put on our application. We read online reviews, toured schools, and mapped walking commutes.

The morning after kindergarten applications were due, another parent commented, "I put down this school as my top choice. It's our local school," with an almost apologetic tone. "I put one other one. But I feel badly that I didn't put down more. I feel like I'm being a bad parent / school shopper."

This parent made explicit what I had previously taken to be the subtext of many public policies these days—namely, that our roles as public citizens have been remade to those of private consumers. My role as a parent is to comparison shop and pick the best school I can afford for my kid, rather than send my kid to a local public school and work with other local parents to make our neighborhood school one that serves the whole community.

School choice as a policy treats public education like a private good when it is really a public one—exhibiting many of the characteristics that economists dub "market failures." First, markets work best when goods are consumed individually; the cookies I eat go only into my body, for instance. And when demand goes down, manufacturers can scale down in response. By contrast, public goods like roads, emergency rooms, and schools are not quite so divisible or scalable. Second, I can easily compare the relative sizes, selections, and levels of scrumptiousness of cookies across local bakeries. But with public goods, I frequently don't have good information to comparison shop among competing providers. Third, when bakery cookies feel too pricey, I buy grocery store treats on sale instead or simply stop buying them altogether. But what economists call price elasticity tends to be lower for needs than for wants. I'm unlikely to forgo transport, health care, or college because it's pricier, until I simply can't afford it.

Besides, highway, medical, or school fees are as likely to reflect political environments as they are the "product" or service at hand. The usual market rules of supply and demand don't apply. Put together, in policy landscapes regarding public goods, market dynamics are often unlikely to reflect public interests.

And yet even though I believe primary education to be a public good, policies like school choice make me treat it like a consumer one. Such notions of the citizen-consumer fuel budget injustice, and communities need new models of bottom-up citizenship.

I am not immune from marketplace-like thinking as a parent; I cannot help but read clamor for a certain local school as a signifier for its quality. And I certainly do not begrudge parents who choose to opt out of their local schools, trying to secure the best education they can for their kids.

Still, I cannot help but wonder whether our individual decisions add up to what is good for the community. I live in an economically mixed neighborhood, and 37 percent of the students at my kid's school are eligible for free or reduced lunch. If parents with the time and experience navigating bureaucracies disproportionately decide to send their kids to magnet, charter, or other schools outside the neighborhood, then nurturing a sense of the commons—public resources and shared fates as a community—becomes much more difficult.

I realized that what bothered me was not that parents were making these difficult decisions about school, but instead that they are made to do so in the first place. With school choice, the default is that each family needs to opt in to, as opposed to opting out of, a local school. The moniker of "school choice" masks and normalizes racial as well as economic disparities.

After all, some parents have more consumer power than others. On an episode of NPR's *This American Life*, Chana Joffe-Walt states, "I don't think I've ever felt my own consumer power more viscerally than I did shopping for a public school as a *White* parent."[1]

I thought back to a vocational high school in Boston I visited in my graduate student days. There, students ostensibly "chose" their areas of study to reflect their interests. But an assistant principal explicitly told me that "the smart [mostly White] kids go into legal studies, we put the Chinese kids into the informational technology program, and we put the Hispanic kids into an events and hospitality program—like the special education kids." I did not object to vocational programs existing alongside more academically oriented schools, but I did object to entire racialized categories of people being funneled into them. Most instances of tracking are not so explicit, yet my larger point remains.

These versions of mandated school choice and vocational program tracking may be extreme, but they are by no means unique. Emphases on choice and the de facto marketization of schools can take many forms. In post–Hurricane Katrina New Orleans, the vast majority of schools under the purview of the city's public system are actually charter ones. (Charter schools receive government funding yet operate independently, exempt from many of the public accountability channels, curriculum and labor requirements, and mandates of typical public schools.) This notion of shopping for public goods is familiar to us as we shop for college or health insurance (whether via employers or on the Obamacare marketplace), though in ways that feel strange to citizens in many other countries around the world, especially industrialized ones.

———

As I briefly discuss in the introduction, I do not use the word *citizen* to denote the passport someone holds. Rather, my framing is similar to the one that writer and comedian Baratunde Thurston utilizes in his

160 BUDGET JUSTICE

podcast series *How to Citizen,* using the word as a verb.[2] Citizenship, in this framing, is defined not by nationality but instead practices that can be engaged by anyone. In part III of this book, my attention shifts to the crucial role of what some scholars call *citizen subjectivities*—how citizens understand their positions and practices as citizens—in budget justice.

Outside education, other public policies shaping our cities' daily lives also encourage notions of citizenship as shopping or "voting with your feet," versus acting as a citizen in shared fates—an active participant who helps to shape and remake the city.[3] It is no accident that while official governmental budgets remain difficult to parse, popular financial reports and city rankings often construct members of the public not as citizens, but instead as consumers. Where should households "choose" to live? (I use scare quotes because many families live wherever they can afford to, or have family nearby; it hardly feels like a meaningful choice.)

This citizen-consumer mentality both sows and feeds on racial and social divisions. Writing about the US context, policy advocate Heather McGhee pinpoints the fomenting of racial resentments as a crucial political move to undermine both public goods and racial solidarities. She writes about how "the American landscape was once graced with resplendent public swimming pools, some big enough to hold thousands of swimmers at a time." But when these public pools could not remain whites only, many communities chose to drain their pools rather than racially integrate them. McGhee quips, "Public goods are seen as worthy of investment only so long as the public is seen as good."[4] Using the public pool as an analogy for public goods writ large, McGhee documents how racism hurts everyone, and how solidarities are crucial to well-being.

Yet citizenship continues to be invoked in decidedly antipublic ways. One might naively guess, as I did, that a popular phone app called Citizen might enable civic engagement—with information on how to register to vote, dates of upcoming school board meetings, or street closures for local 5K races. Instead, the app sends users real-time safety alerts and encourages them to send in reports of break-ins. It is telling, then, that Citizen was originally called Vigilante. It boasts of a paid, subscription feature called Protect, which allows users to contact virtual agents for help.

Citizen the app has been criticized for encouraging racial profiling and encouraging users to treat their communities like gated ones. And like many online forums writ large, these platforms have been critiqued for producing echo chambers rather than spaces for generative deliberation. These phone apps illustrate the impoverishment and perversions of citizenship that political theorist Wendy Brown has dubbed "undoing the Demos"—emphasizing *homo economicus* above all other citizen identities or roles, away from collaborative thinking about common goods, toward private consumption and action.[5]

I do not mean to trivialize individuals' pained choices—far from it. Nor do I minimize political actions that harness and leverage citizens' identities as consumers, especially when constituents hold little power via more typical political channels. The Montgomery bus boycott of 1955–56, partly sparked by Rosa Parks's famed act of defiance, and the Delano grape strike and boycott of 1965–70, which helped make labor organizer Cesar Chavez famous, are but two reminders of the importance of consumer actions. Further, as historian Lizabeth Cohen notes, formations of women and African Americans as bread-and-butter consumers helped lay the groundwork for the civil rights and women's liberation movements.[6]

Here I do not focus on questions of consumers as citizens so much as the reduction of citizens as consumers, sidelining other forms of political action. Public policy has not only become more neoliberal in terms of substance by emphasizing "choice," competition, and the sorts of austerity discussed earlier in this book. It has, in turn, helped limit the roles, social dynamics, emotional valences, and political possibilities of what it means to be a citizen in a democratic society.[7]

———

What might it look like to use *citizen* as a verb—to relate to one another as neighbors as opposed to consumers? More than voting for public budget priorities with one's feet, citizens routinely come together to care for one another in the face of disasters.

For example, when Hurricane Sandy hit New York in 2012, dozens of people died, and thousands of people were left without homes. While the Federal Emergency Management Agency, other state entities, and established nonprofits like the Red Cross could not overcome logistical hurdles in their work, local groups joined Occupy Sandy, pulled together by activists who had been part of Occupy Wall Street, to distribute food and medical care much more quickly.[8] They organized themselves in participatory democratic ways, drawing on local knowledge and networks, and jointly making decisions instead of leaving it to a few appointed representatives.

During the COVID-19 pandemic, too, everyday citizens stepped up to supply essential services when the state did not. Governmental authorities failed to provide sufficient personal protective equipment like masks, leaving people unable to attend to basic needs. (Between 2020 and 2022, the United States reported around 1 million deaths from COVID-19, hundreds of thousands more than any other country, including far more populous ones.)[9] Thousands of people lost jobs or could not physically go to them. Public agencies and nonprofit organizations paused operations like soup kitchens. Masks, COVID-19 test appointments, hospital ventilators, and even acetaminophen (especially in liquid form for children) were in short supply. Nor did the supposed invisible hand of the market do a good job in weeding out inefficient or unscrupulous providers; price gouging and shortages were commonplace.

Suddenly, food cooperatives, community gardens, and other experiments in solidarity were no longer seen as cute social experiments. They took on urgent registers and high stakes. Neighbors distributed diapers and set up community fridges on the street. Because green space was in high demand, neighbors self-organized maintenance crews when parks and sanitation departments could not keep up. They also shut down streets to cars, opening them to kid-friendly activities when schools closed and families had no backyards or outdoor spaces of their own.

They collected funds and redistributed them to people who asked for them, no questions asked.

Neighbors quickly organized groups to offer grocery delivery services, especially for senior citizens lacking mobility, immunocompromised persons, or anyone who could not afford groceries or buy them in person.[10] When neighbors became sick with COVID, these local groups were the only way they could ask for and receive help without endangering others.

In my neighborhood, I quickly saw posts on social media and cardboard signs on the street announcing both websites and local phone numbers to which one could text or call to request groceries, or volunteer or donate. In neighboring Crown Heights, a newly formed mutual aid group raised and redistributed $400,000 in its first year and a half, mostly in the form of grocery deliveries.[11] One Brooklyn mutual aid organizer reported serving food to about one-quarter of their neighbors during the pandemic's first year.[12]

Such efforts have implications for citizen subjectivities and budget justice when they are not exceptional—when they are the result of not a heroic few but rather the many. Indeed, between 2020 and 2022, at least a hundred mutual aid groups formed in New York State alone.[13]

Further, these mutual aid efforts have been sustained. They are more than single acts of altruism or solidarity. Four years later, the local community fridges are still in effect. One Brooklyn group continues to distribute around six hundred meals every month "because," as it maintains, "food security is always needed," not just during the onset of a pandemic.[14]

The fact that these emergency responses have translated into longer-term habits and democratic formations also hints at how participating in mutual aid can be transformative. Writer Rebecca Solnit notes that in her research, after people who participated in postdisaster mutual aid "went back to their jobs in a market economy . . . that changed perspective stayed with them."[15]

These citizen-neighbor practices push back against the logic highlighted by McGhee, of public goods being available only to publics deemed good. Instead, they work toward the construction of new public narratives of "us," demanding public budgets and the provision of public goods—from basic groceries to affordable housing—not just for themselves and the neighbors they have gotten to know, but *everyone*.[16]

———

In earlier chapters, I argued that democracy is better defined as a set of situated practices and solidarities than institutions. After all, there is no perfect institutional design for government—even one with checks and balances across multiple branches of government. In fact, democratic institutions and citizens are mutually coconstitutive. Democratic practices for budget justice—whether elections, PB, mutual aid, or something else—have meaning and shape only when citizens demand and enact them.

Here, I come back to Cornwall's framing of invited and invented spaces, which I reference in chapter 7. Namely, if part II focuses on state-initiated, democratic experiments in invited spaces like PB, then this final part of the book follows citizens as they move back and forth between PB and invented spaces outside the state, such as the mutual aid collectives I discussed above.

Whatever its terms of deliberation, PB cannot democratize democracy on its own. I thus consider its role in a broader and richer landscape of grassroots action—a whole ecosystem of participation.

My ecosystem framing is partly inspired by work on deliberative democracy, especially by social scientists who look across institutions like Congress or a parliamentary body in their analyses. Advocating for what they call a "systemic approach to deliberative democracy," political theorists John Parkinson, Jane Mansbridge, and others point out that the media, advocacy groups, and nonprofit organizations all perform important political work, and that a deliberative institution, "such as a well-designed mini-public [a randomly selected, demographically representative people's assembly], can look less beneficial in a systemic perspective when it displaces other useful deliberative institutions, such as partisan or social movement bodies."[17]

Political scientist Josh Lerner, codirector of People Powered: Global Hub for Participatory Democracy, emphasizes that viewing electoral, direct, deliberative, and participatory democracy as competing and not complementary hurts democracy overall. Further, Lerner notes that societies need a "just transition" to healthier ecosystems—one that does not sideline citizens' current needs in the meantime.[18] An ecosystem perspective helps communities to think about the constituent practices and processes that make democratic institutions meaningful.

Part III therefore follows part II both temporally and substantively; it builds on my analysis of PB in part II to reconsider its role as a crucial entry point in a larger ecosystem of participation. In this last part, I examine how ecosystems of participation for budget justice must be enlivened by a new ecology of citizenship. How might citizens engage each other and different spaces of political action in more productive ways?

If *ecosystems* in the natural world are the biomes and landscapes—like deserts, rainforests, coral reefs, and wetlands—that host living beings, then *ecologies* refer to the symbiotic, collaborative, competitive, and other relationships between living beings in the context of a particular ecosystem, and between beings and the larger environment in which they live.

While my knowledge of ecologies is quite limited, the importance of ecosystemic diversity and ecological interdependence consistently stands out to me.

Political anthropologist Anna Lowenhaupt Tsing examines how the matsutake mushroom, a delicacy coveted in Japanese cuisine, thrives not in undisturbed forests or on domesticated farms but only in human-disturbed forests. It is called "pine mushroom" because it is typically hosted by pines, but not in a straightforward symbiotic or parasitic way. Along the way, the matsutake reshapes the uneven landscapes in which it grows.[19]

In my mind, mushrooms become an analogy for a particularly unpredictable and nourishing sort of grassroots politics; after all, mushrooms literally sit on the forest floor, hosted by (and seemingly at the mercy of) powerful, towering, stately trees.[20] At times they seem to crop out of nowhere, but their spores actually spread through wind—discourse/conversation—or mycelium—underground networks. Like democratic practices that cannot be contained by either invited or invented spaces, they almost appear to be spread through word of mouth, scaling sideways rather than up.

Citizens constantly adapt their strategies and attempt to reshape their interactions with more powerful, institutional gatekeeper-facilitators, like city agency representatives, in deciding or making policy on the ground. Sometimes they take the logics more likely to be developed in invented spaces, developed without state constraints, and sneak them into PB, using public moneys for new public goods. Perhaps, like bees in a dance, they take tiny specks of ideas from wildflowers and pollinate them in the official botanic garden nearby.

Although scholars have long examined attempts at cross-class and multiracial alliances in electoral politics and social movements, I am curious about attempts at provisional and principled alliances in everyday democracy—like those between colonies of matsutake mushrooms, between colonies of mushrooms and the grasses and flowers of more intentionally cultivated invited spaces, or between mushrooms and stately pines, amid precarious and quickly shifting conditions.

———

Policymakers know how to render social goods private—to *privatize*—but not how to render them public again; *publicize* is certainly not the right word. With so much overt and de facto privatization of public space and private provision of what should be public goods, it is no wonder that when it comes to what citizenship practices should look and feel like, many citizens are out of practice.

The public goods and public policies at the heart of budget justice—schools, green spaces and the environment, prevention of infectious diseases like COVID-19, and community safety—cannot be parceled and consumed individually like cookies from the shop. They thrive off our interdependence and coordination with our neighbors.

Public policies focused on choice rob communities of meaningful change and enfeeble the popular imagination on what could be. I argue that budget justice requires a model of citizenship that situates everyday residents as citizen-neighbors, so that communities can articulate different public policies, cities, and ways of relating to one another.

The work of strengthening popular imaginations begins with quotidian practices. As poet and scholar Mónica de la Torre questions, "People read the paper in the morning; / at night they turn to fictions. / What kinds of dreams / would reversing this simple habit / precipitate."[21]

What might substantive citizenship for budget justice look like? Because my knowledge of the nonhuman ecologies is so limited, I will stick with familiar realms of human activity here. As with playing soccer or the guitar, the muscles and skills needed for substantive citizenship grow and strengthen with use; unfortunately, they can also atrophy from disuse. Technical prowess is important; there is no defying gravity in throwing a ball or compensating for imprecise finger play across guitar frets. The analogies of team sports and music highlight other important aspects of substantive citizenship and city making too: the endeavors are magnified when collective. Participants build solidarity and feel appreciation for one another—strangers, even—in quick, half-hour pickup basketball games and campfire jam sessions. But even in well-planned, seemingly regimented games or multimovement symphonies, there remains room for specificity and the unexpected—the elements of pacing, simultaneous collaboration and friction, harmony and dissonance, beats and syncopated rhythms and groove and swing, and building momentum or saving energy for the grand finale.

This work is play. It builds on technical knowledge and prowess, yes, but also muscle memory, practice, yearning, and bodily as well as local knowledges. Elite athletes and musicians consider the context at hand— the current weather, whether the tennis court is made of clay or grass, or what the acoustics in a concert hall are like. We most admire the feats of those who have studied and practiced with multiple epistemologies (ways of knowing)—who are "book smart" in music or sports history, theory, and strategy, *and* "street-smart" in real-life tactics and plays.

168 BUDGET JUSTICE

Substantive citizenship for budget justice similarly enacts this sort of collective play, meaning making, and world-building in action.

To transform budgets, citizens must change as well. As historian Robin D. G. Kelley writes, "Without new visions we don't know what to build, only what to knock down. We not only end up confused, rudderless, and cynical, but we forget that making a revolution is not a series of clever maneuvers and tactics but a process that can and must transform us."[22]

12

Inventive Solidarities

THE LITMUS TEST for a new democratic process for budget justice is not, *Shall we be civil and get along?* but rather, *How do we mobilize, share resources and power, and better address residents' needs?* In lieu of either elections or a participation industrial complex, budget justice requires a diverse ecosystem of participation that keeps popular contestations and struggles alive.

The New York case study suggests that because of the limitations and power struggles embedded in invited spaces like PBNYC, budget justice requires that everyday citizens pay attention to both invited, state-initiated and invented, citizen-initiated spaces.[1] As political scientists Rod Dacombe and Phil Parvin write, "For some people democracy does not reside in its formal institutions but instead is focused on other forms of participation."[2] Compared to invited spaces, invented ones give citizens more wiggle room to be imaginative.

Invented spaces are fertile soils for new solidarities and the social basis of policy change. Through these experiments, everyday constituents can work on what J. K. Gibson-Graham (a pen name shared by two economic geographers) calls the politics of language and politics of subject, with an "intermixing of alternative discourses, shared language, embodied practices, self-cultivation, emplaced actions, and global transformation" to create new social as well as political dynamics within the shell of the old.[3] This focus is inspired by what Grace Lee Boggs called "living for change," and what activist adrienne maree brown (the lowercase is intentional) calls "emergent strategy"—"how we intentionally

170　BUDGET JUSTICE

change in ways that grow our capacity to embody the just and liberated worlds we long for."[4]

———

Communities need spaces of genuine connection, deliberation of community needs, and binding decision-making. They need public spheres for claims making vis-à-vis the state, and PB fits the bill as such an invited space. But even when they are implemented well, invited spaces cannot shift power dynamics on their own.

For example, as I discussed in chapters 8 and 9, many PBNYC participants were disappointed by the continued popularity of police surveillance cameras in the process. They felt that their original visions of community safety were much more robust and multi-issue, including job training programs, safe spaces for youths and young adults, intergenerational dialogues, and many other ideas that never got onto PB ballots.

It was striking, then, to see exactly such projects realized all around me during the pandemic. This time, neighbors mobilized such initiatives on their own. They had limited financial means because they did not have access to state resources, but they *were* able to work on their own terms.

These mobilizations show how, in addition to invited spaces like PB, citizens need spaces to meet immediate materials needs, forward different criteria for what "good projects" look like, and rehearse alternative ways of relating to one another. As urban scholar Faranak Miraftab puts it, "Within . . . invented spaces . . . grassroots actions are characterized by defiance that directly challenges the status quo: in one [invited] space strategies of survival are sought within the existing structural system, and in the other resistance is mounted to bring it down."[5]

———

Invented spaces are integral to budget justice. First, invented spaces help constituents weave stories about their struggles and nurture what political theorist Nancy Fraser calls *counterpublics*.[6] Counterpublics are discursive arenas that operate in parallel with the official public sphere, "where members of subordinated social groups invent and circulate counter discourses to formulate oppositional interpretations of their identities, interests, and needs."[7] For instance, Fraser argues that late twentieth-century feminist counterpublics were essential to women developing new, counterhegemonic terms to describe their social reality and make claims vis-à-vis the state. These new terms included "sexism" and "sexual harassment."

In budget justice, one current counterpublic arena might be the mutual aid initiatives I discussed above.[8] I increasingly heard an emerging theme of "we keep each other safe." This refrain counters the dominant discourse that police remain the only viable and realistic response to community safety concerns, and anything else is laughable or even dangerous.

The "we keep each other safe" theme is notable because these groups work with diverse participants with a range of political opinions. Both sociologist Allison Goldberg and geographer Laura Landau note that mutual aid participants often disagreed about whether they wanted to "defund" police or work toward police abolition, for example. Still, as they deliberated over how they might spend their resources and focus their energies, participants did agree on giving care and working on housing stability. In their view, these priorities were clearly relevant to community safety, thus broadening their vision of the term *safety* beyond policing.

As one organizer put it, "So yeah, de-funding the police was not our thing, but food security is universal."[9] To me, these points of agreement are also significant because they resemble many of the sorts of project proposals that were repeatedly deemed ineligible or unfeasible in PBNYC.

Second, invented spaces allow citizens to try new forms of organization and alternative policies—especially those that might meet resistance from state entities. By giving room for experimentation, mutual aid can play a pivotal role in what writer and organizer Mariame Kaba calls "prefiguring the world in which you want to live."[10]

172   BUDGET JUSTICE

For instance, when several women reported being attacked near subway stations in Brooklyn in 2021, an activist and DJ named Peter Kerre founded SafeWalks, through which volunteers escort people walking to or from the subway, particularly at night. When incident rates of anti-Asian violence also rose, SafeWalks quickly expanded to Manhattan's Chinatown. Again, participants likely have different political positions regarding the police, but they foremost rely on one another in their vision of community safety. In doing so, their initiatives are in stark contrast to elected officials' continued emphasis on law enforcement and hate crimes legislation.

Further, SafeWalks poignantly resists narrative tropes that valorize its efforts yet fail to hold elected officials accountable for the social programs, such as mental health services, needed to help keep communities safe. As members of SafeWalks declared after one TV news story, "As long as those [mental health and other needs] are NOT addressed, nothing will change. We spoke about this during the [TV] interview but it was cut out of the above story."[11] They complained that fearmongering media coverage—centered on violent incidents in ways that rile up audiences thirsting for punishment in place of prevention—undermines the very solidarities they aim to embody.

———

The details matter. In invented spaces, citizens focus not only on *what* to prioritize; they emphasize *how* they operate and implement their programs. The groups insist on helping people unconditionally, say, regardless of their legal status or whether they appear "deserving."[12]

And as compared to the official ballot item project proposals in PBNYC, many of the local projects from invented spaces are more likely to explicitly tackle larger questions of political economy, reach out to community members overlooked by most public and nonprofit programs, and work to build relationships of care along the way.

For instance, La Morada operates as a restaurant specializing in Oaxacan food in the South Bronx; in spring 2020, it transformed itself into a mutual aid kitchen that served five thousand meals a week. It also partnered with local farms as well as with local tenants' associations to deliver meals, especially to vulnerable neighbors in buildings without gas and asylum seekers quarantined in shelters on the peripheries of the city.[13] La Morada is run by the Saavedra family, which has a history of community activism. While still undocumented, Marco Saavedra intentionally got arrested by authorities in Florida in order to help other detainees who qualified for asylum (but did not have the resources to pursue it) in the for-profit Broward Transitional Center. Saavedra has since won political asylum.[14]

The initiative Heart of Dinner began during the pandemic to address isolation, loneliness, and food insecurity among Asian American elders in Manhattan's Chinatown, one-third of whom live below the poverty line. It procures produce from local farms; one of the Asian heritage crop farms that Heart of Dinner partners with is even called Choy Division, in nods to bok choy the vegetable and Joy Division the English band. It also buys meals from local restaurants that struggled to survive during the pandemic, and includes handwritten notes in one of six Asian languages in each and every meal delivered. Four years later, the group has delivered over two hundred thousand "meals and love notes," and continues to feed 650 elders a week.[15]

Through examples like these, it suddenly became easy for me to recognize public budgets as moral documents. I admit that previously, I might have dismissed initiatives like Heart of Dinner as "cute"—but during the pandemic, they helped me to finally recognize ecologies of care in concrete terms.

Further, their careful consideration of supply chains reminded me of comments made by one of the PBNYC participants I worked with. This interviewee, who identified as a Black woman, originally *did* advocate for surveillance cameras in her public housing project but was nevertheless disappointed by the outcomes. She clarified that she had wanted surveillance cameras only with community control of how they were used; she had also hoped that public housing residents, many of whom worked in the skilled manual trades, could have helped install and operate them. In other words, she, too, had hoped for deeper and broader notions of community safety and community wealth through

174   BUDGET JUSTICE

PB. (I later read that even though Black New Yorkers constitute almost a quarter of the city population, just 1.57 percent of the city government's contracts go to Black-owned business enterprises.)[16]

———

Although other sorts of invented spaces, such as community organizing groups and trade unions, are relevant to budget justice, I focus here on how solidarity economy initiatives help neighbors to practice cooperation and different models of citizenship, imagine different ways to organize collective budgets, and maybe inform PB projects. The term *solidarity economy* encompasses a wide range of economic activities centering some notion of social benefit, like affordability or ethical environmental and labor practices, alongside profit or basic solvency.[17] It is part of the *diverse economies* framework forwarded by Gibson-Graham; they argue that while market capitalist activities dominate popular debates on "the economy," these activities actually form just the tip of the economy iceberg.[18]

Indeed, economic cooperation is more common than many realize and underrecognized as a source of grassroots power.[19] Organizing in "informal" spaces outside workplaces, especially, has received less attention.[20] In the United States, it is practiced by worker cooperatives (like Equal Exchange foods), employee-owned businesses (like King Arthur Baking), producer cooperatives (like Ocean Spray), consumer cooperatives (like REI), mutual insurance companies (like State Farm and Liberty Mutual), credit unions, community land trusts (nonprofit entities that hold land via community control and for permanent affordability), housing cooperatives, and community gardens. The world's largest worker cooperative, in Spain's northern Basque region, employs around eighty thousand workers.[21]

Like mutual aid, other formations in the solidarity economy have also grown considerably since 2020. The number of worker cooperatives in the United States grew by almost a third from 2019 to 2021, and the number of community land trusts increased by 40 percent from 2005 to 2024.[22]

As social scientists Maliha Safri, Marianna Pavlovskaya, Stephen Healy, and Craig Borowiak note, solidarity economy initiatives can play critical roles in gentrifying areas, creating what they call solidarity cities. Housing cooperatives and community gardens, for example, serve as bulwarks against displacement. Those land parcels, at least, will not be replaced with luxury condos anytime soon.[23]

———

The solidarity economy has played a long-standing role in movements for cooperation and self-determination in the United States, especially in Black, Indigenous, and immigrant communities. For example, popular informal rotating savings clubs—such as *sou-sous* in some African and Caribbean communities, and *huis* in Chinese ones—have operated in the United States for centuries. Political economist Jessica Gordon-Nembhard examines how, before the Civil War, servants and enslaved people pooled money to buy one another's freedom, even as "their cooperative networks were mostly invisible to masters."[24] After the war, they likewise worked to jointly purchase farm equipment, medical and funeral services, and pensions.

Other antecedents to contemporary efforts include the Free African Society of Philadelphia, founded in the 1780s; Chinese mutual aid associations organized by last name so that newly arriving workers could find a social network to join during the Gold Rush; and collectives and settlement houses by and for eastern and southern European communities in the early twentieth century.

While solidarity economy initiatives have played long and significant roles in helping marginalized communities practice collective care, their records of influencing public policy and contributing to budget justice—combating the sorts of opacity, austerity, and carcerality I discussed in part I—are not without tension.

First, not all such initiatives are outward looking, working toward the larger-scale distribution of public resources. In fact, some support networks that start off as efforts for survival may, as they strengthen, turn

176 BUDGET JUSTICE

inward and remain closed off to those outside their network—in effect, resource hoarding rather than resource sharing.

Writers and activists Leah Hunt-Hendrix and Astra Taylor argue for *transformative solidarity* across difference versus unity or exclusionary solidarity.[25] Indeed, much of the renewed attention on solidarity economy initiatives since 2020 has emphasized work tackling racial and income inequalities along with geographically defined communities, as opposed to those defined by race or identity. This can be quite difficult, particularly when groups operate in gentrifying neighborhoods.[26]

Further, negotiating the relationship between mutual aid services delivery and other forms of political action—like community organizing, legal action, and advocacy campaigns directed at the state—remains a challenge. In the twentieth century, some solidarity economy efforts became divorced from policy demands. Mutual aid came to be largely dismissed as apolitical service work in the United States, implying a distraction from "real" direct action work and protest (partly because it was less confrontational). Indeed, as community organizer and journalist Rinku Sen writes, "Combining mutual aid and direct action might seem like common sense, but in today's corporatized and professionalized nonprofit world, this model had disappeared almost completely. The roots of this split lie in the increasing professionalization of the sector over half a century, driven by no small amount of sexism, classism and racism."[27]

Indeed, like PB, solidarity economy initiatives in New York are disproportionately the purview of women, trans femme / feminized people, and lower-income residents.[28] In the US context, they have historically been practiced by feminized, racialized nonwhite, and queer communities—those left out of state resources, those who could not risk protesting in the streets for fear of arrest or detention (often because they were especially vulnerable to police repression or mob violence, or because they had to care for others at home), and those trained to keep the proverbial ball rolling (providing childcare, cooking meals when neighbors get sick, organizing spreadsheets on who should do what when, paying bills or dodging collection agencies for debts owed, or filling out forms for various programs) in what scholars call social reproduction. Correspondingly, such efforts have historically been denigrated as too service oriented (at least in the United States) to be counted as political action.

Because of such tensions, it should not be surprising that such efforts can also be weaponized to let government off the hook, abetting neoliberal policy. Historian Benjamin Holtzman documents how this happened after the New York fiscal crisis in the 1970s, when landlords literally abandoned thousands of buildings when they ceased being profitable. "In response, Latinx, African American, and some white residents directly occup[ied] and [sought] ownership of abandoned buildings through a process they called urban homesteading."[29] As Holtzman notes, homesteading won support from both the political Left and Right. It could be framed as a stinging indictment of governmental failure, or as can-do, pull-yourself-up-by-the-bootstraps initiatives, showing others what could be done even without "handouts" and governmental largesse.

Important exceptions, like the Black Panthers' provision of free breakfasts, pointedly demonstrate how pooling resources and serving free hot meals can constitute political action, mobilizing people and pressuring government to respond. Although the Black Panther Party first formed to address police brutality in cities, it quickly mobilized to address local needs as part of its work. Soon, women made up the majority of Black Panther membership, and many of them led initiatives like their Free Breakfast Program for children.

In the Federal Bureau of Investigation's Counterintelligence Program, Director J. Edgar Hoover warned that the program "represents the best and most influential activity going for the [Black Panther Party]" and chose to target it in particular.[30] In Chicago, police urinated on the food to prevent its distribution.[31] At its peak in 1971, the Black Panthers fed more children than the state of California did, operating in thirty-six cities across the country.[32] This put pressure on the US government to address widespread food insecurity; simultaneously, more mainstream women's groups participated in invited spaces (testifying in Congress, for example) to advocate for free breakfasts, and the United States established a permanent school program in 1975.[33]

178 BUDGET JUSTICE

The Black Panthers also worked with other marginalized and vulnerable groups to meet community needs. For instance, to protest abysmal hospital conditions and the inability to access their own medical records, they teamed up with the Puerto Rican group the Young Lords to draft the original Patient's Bill of Rights, a "watered-down" version of which now hangs in every US hospital.[34]

And one of the most poignant moments of the documentary *Crip Camp: A Disability Revolution* shows footage from a 1977 sit-in, when almost 150 people with disabilities occupied a federal Health, Education, and Welfare building in San Francisco. Some of the protesters were blind; some were quadriplegic and needed to be turned over to avoid bedsores. The government officials cut off their original supplies of electricity, food, and water. Despite this, and even after they were threatened with arrest, over 120 remained. They refused to leave until Health, Education, and Welfare secretary Joseph Califano signed regulations for disabilities rights into law. Members of the Black Panther Party played a decisive role in sustaining the protest by providing hot meals every day, until Califano signed the regulations on April 28, after twenty-five days of occupation.[35]

———

Contemporary solidarity economy initiatives contribute most to budget justice when they center democratic practices and the *solidarity* part of their name. Many of these self-organized collectives further cooperate with other groups to assert a culture of collective care, counter the logics of existing austerity policies, and tackle community needs in holistic ways. Stoop watches by groups such as Brooklyn Eviction Defense, for example, encourage neighbors to gather and sit on the stoops of families facing eviction—sometimes knitting or just hanging out, and sometimes educating one another on housing experiences, rights, and policies—in order to "watch for landlord activity" while keeping each other safe from violent sweeps and evictions.[36] These efforts append support for families facing eviction in housing courts; they also involve practices like tenant organizing, assemblies to discuss priorities and strategies such as rent strikes, and campaigns for community-owned housing for the unhoused.

Such invented spaces not only help constituents attend to material needs, as noble as those achievements are. Many build new democratic citizenship practices, forge solidarities across difference, and mobilize for new state policies and resources too.

When viewed alongside voting and protests in an ecosystem of participation, these mutual aid efforts and solidarity economy initiatives constitute not acts of charity or "mere" survival but instead politics in another form.[37]

———

Communities can only achieve budget justice by practicing such politics from below wherever and whenever they can. Indeed, some of the New Yorkers active in mutual aid efforts since the pandemic became adept at nonhierarchical organizing and decision-making through PB, and several of the more recent PB projects funded during the pandemic build on mutual aid and other solidarity economy initiatives.

Invented spaces can also be crucial incubators for the ideas and practices that citizens can then introduce into invited ones. These bottom-up practices set precedents for established institutions as well. During the pandemic, foundations began to administer at least some grants by lottery rather than ranked merit—saving applicants and judges many hours of time as well as possible headaches and heartaches. City agencies cut down on the paperwork needed to receive unemployment benefits. Then President Trump's administration sent checks to every person in the United States in what amounted to the sort of basic income that Andrew Yang helped popularize in his 2020 presidential campaign. Moreover, pandemic relief included childcare credits that almost made it into the Build Back Better legislation. New York City helped move unhoused individuals into otherwise empty hotels for temporary housing.

Budget justice relies on such effects—not as errant or serendipitous spillovers, but as central synergies. It demands not only freer elections or invited spaces like PB but invented spaces as well, and the democratization of an entire ecosystem of participation.

———

Each sort of node in an ecosystem of participation plays an essential role. Self-determined, democratic spaces are essential when invited ones all blare "the same tunes" and "leave little room" for some citizens' experiences. Writer John Keene, for one, declares that in such situations, "I've learned to thrive on . . . exile, cunning, / past surviving, fashioning my *own* spaces . . . where . . . chords / from *every* singer conjure our common futures."[38] Such invented spaces allow citizens to shape the rules by which they are governed and practice new ways of relating to one another.

Still, while crowdfunding can avoid co-optation by the state or philanthropic foundations, it can also risk relying on the poor to help the poor. Invited spaces give citizens structured opportunities to hone as well as rehearse practices and ways of being they invented elsewhere, and demand more from the state along the way.

A particular challenge, then, lies in nurturing the practice of what Astra Taylor calls "living in the tension," critically assessing liberal representative democratic structures, but continuing to engage with the idea—and work—of democracy.[39] In the following chapters, I examine the sort of citizenship needed for citizens to connect invited and invented spaces, and traverse them for budget justice.

13

Budget Lines of Desire

AUSTERITY PERVADES the New York PB process. As one agency representative emphasized, "For every dollar that we spend, we probably could spend another ten . . . to actually meet our needs. So . . . the [PB] discretionary projects are . . . very helpful . . . [for] 'quality-of-life' [projects] that, you know, we normally would have trouble funding." In this context, PB is not so much a way to engage citizens; it is a means to address budget shortfalls.

Managed participation embodies contradictory dynamics; several agency representatives' remarks reflect what political scientist Deborah Stone calls the "rationality project," a framework in which policymaking is scientific, leaving little room for citizen participation and alternative ways of knowing.[1] Yet the agencies' actions also revealed political savvy. Rather than letting citizens present their needs, agencies sometimes presented hyperlocal projects in need of additional funding; citizens could then "shop" for and "choose" the exact projects the state already forwarded anyway so as to get "extra bang for [their] buck." Agencies were thus "weaponizing" reforms for unintended purposes.[2]

As one budget delegate described a hypothetical but archetypal set of responses, "'I want new streetlights. My streetlights aren't broken, but I want prettier streetlights' . . . [since] funds are available for that purpose." Some of these participants appear to have given up on budget justice, but have instead either dissented via exit or succumbed to governmentality, forwarding proposals they know to be most palatable to city agencies—even when these proposals sideline the concerns that

182   BUDGET JUSTICE

compelled them to participate in the first place.[3] Discussions regarding taxation along with the shape and size of the figurative public budget pie are sidelined by competitions determining the slices of the pie.[4]

Through their interactions with residents, though, city bureaucrats help create not just informed citizens but indignant ones too. Namely, PBNYC prompted at least some citizens to pay greater attention to the sort of epistemic justice that I discussed in chapter 9, and then develop policy proposals centering their own everyday desires and strategies for survival, not what was officially legal or permissible.

———

In a healthy ecology of citizenship, citizens refuse to stick to either invited spaces like PB or invented spaces like mutual aid collectives. Rather, they move between them, taking values and citizen-neighbor habits from invented spaces, and making them public—that is, accessible to strangers unlike themselves, using government funds.

Projects that won funding in PBNYC largely fall into three roughly hewn categories. The first consists of projects that make up for budget shortfalls, reflect managed participation, and reify existing priorities. The second category consists of projects that articulate new ideas, but do not clearly challenge existing budget priorities and power dynamics. The third offers new ideas that counter austerity logics through *insurgent budgeting*.

The vast majority of PBNYC ballot items fall in the first category. They consist of the same project ideas, again and again: audiovisual equipment and technological upgrades for schools and libraries, surveillance cameras, and curb extensions and park benches. These are ideas that city agencies would themselves have likely funded, if they had access to greater funds.

I do not wish to malign these project ideas; citizens have specific reasons for advocating for them. Some of these projects—like repairs to playgrounds and schools—were put on the ballot to address funding inequities in the city budget. Indeed, many of the PB ballot items explicitly state that proposed projects will be implemented at federally designated high-poverty Title I schools.

Other projects in the first category reflect needs deemed lower priority by city agencies, or what one agency representative deemed "nice-haves" rather than "must-haves." One example might be the restoration of Endale Arch, an archway in Brooklyn's Prospect Park called "a thing of beauty" by the *New York Times* when it debuted in the 1860s.[5] The restoration replaced rotted wood panels and eroded stone retaining walls that had suffered more than a century of water damage, and peeled away layers of paint that revealed a color motif not seen since the early twentieth century. In a context of austerity, agencies might have been surprised that local citizens prioritized such a restoration versus more "basic" needs. Nevertheless, by and large, these projects do not challenge prevailing budgeting norms. In fact, some would argue that by finding alternative funding for Endale Arch, the PB funds alleviated pressure on the parks department to maintain the monument on its own.

The second and third categories of projects consist of a small yet significant minority of funded PB projects that despite such norms, attempt to bring innovative project ideas to the city. The second category of project ideas are the budget policy equivalents of so-called lines of desire. In the fields of landscape architecture and urban planning, *lines of desire* are unplanned trails made by foot traffic rather than marked by pavement. One way to figure out where people's desire paths might lie is to wait for a snowfall, when paved paths through a park are covered and obscured, and then observe how passersby wish to travel from point A to point B. Spanish poet Antonio Machado wrote, "Se hace camino al andar," or "You make the way by walking." In grass, it takes as few as fifteen passages over time to create a new trail.

Lines of desire are acts of civil disobedience. They only appear when people refuse to stick to the anointed path or "within the box." And they are reflective of epistemic justice in that they demonstrate local knowledge gained through experience, rather than official, paved paths and technical, textbook knowledge. Residents walk according to their needs, observations (maybe the official path has a tree branch or pothole obstructing the way), and contextually developed solutions.

Good urban planning attempts to heed and accommodate such lines of desire. This is not always possible; some lines of desire might, for

184 BUDGET JUSTICE

example, exacerbate erosion, threaten a site's structural integrity, or endanger wildlife. Still, in a technodemocracy, planners might look for patterns in lines of desire to better attend to epistemic justice in their decision-making. Both local and technical expertise are valued; neither is romanticized.

In PB, cultural projects can also act as desire lines. With such projects, citizens demand respect on their own terms, in their own languages, forms, and aesthetics. Again and again, elected officials were taken aback by residents' fervor for cultural projects, not just bread-and-butter ones. This manifests in how PB projects included not only vans for mobile showers for unhoused people, but also vans that served as studio spaces for visiting artists over the summer. Other cultural projects varied from an outdoor storytelling garden featuring a beloved children's book character, Mo Willems's 'Knuffle Bunny, in the neighborhood where the *Knuffle Bunny* books take place, to a Shaheed Minar or martyr's Mother Language Monument to honor Bangladeshis' struggle for Bangla language recognition and self-determination. Although the Shaheed Minar monument did not win PB funds, it did help residents mobilize enough resources and interest to commemorate International Mother Language Day and "linguistic freedom."

Indeed, these projects represent a potent retort to questions of citizenship and epistemic justice. When tackling issues of "otherness," they represent historically marginalized communities' struggle to belong on their own terms too. They refuse to flatten all knowledges into technical discourse.

Urban planning should take heed of figurative lines of desire in public budgeting alongside literal ones in spatial planning. In PB, budget lines of desire might be those project ideas reflecting infrastructure and services that do not yet exist, but should. Some examples of PBNYC projects in this category include freeze-resistant water fountains in the parks to operate through the winter (when most are disabled to avoid frozen or burst pipes), a study of endangered bats in Prospect Park, and fitness equipment for senior citizens and other people with physical disabilities.

Spatial lines of desire often meet urgent needs, but they are not necessarily political. A middle schooler might, for instance, take a locals-only shortcut through a public garden simply to play video games as soon as possible. Cultural projects, too, might be consistently underfunded in austerity budgets, but this does not mean that they are inherently justice oriented. They are controversial because people create them in part to reflect, shape, and revise how cultural histories are told as well as how social identities are felt and internalized. They can do work toward imperialist, White supremacist aims, toward decolonizing aims, or neither. And they could do little or a lot to challenge existing racial inequalities, hierarchies of power, and the stories used to justify them.

The third, final category of PB projects I look at here consists of a subset of budget lines of desire, with an overt justice orientation. These projects also have a counterpart in architecture and planning—tactical urbanisms. Like spatial lines of desire, they offer bottom-up solutions to local challenges and urgent needs. In addition, they reflect a short-term tactic as a deliberate, strategic step toward longer-term policy changes. Tactical urbanisms reflect coordinated, collective efforts for a different city, building dynamics of amiable proximity and collaborative connections—some might call it solidarity—between residents.

Examples of tactical land use urbanisms include guerrilla crosswalk paintings at intersections marked dangerous by residents, open streets (sometimes called *ciclovias* in South America to emphasize new pathways for bicycling) that use chairs and barriers to block car traffic and provide safe spaces for walking, cycling, and play, and pop-up parks on annual "park(ing) days," when residents take over street car parking spaces and transform them with planters, decor, and lounge chairs into mini gardens and parks. In Oakland, California, students from the Technical High School used chalk to draw a rainbow-colored crosswalk in front of their main campus so as to encourage the city's Department of Transportation to install a permanent one.[6] Like lines of desire, tactical urbanisms heed epistemic justice and put it into practice; they come to being not through grand, bird's-eye view blueprints, but rather on-the-ground design and iterative action.

———

It is impossible to neatly distinguish projects in the third category from those in the second; the lines between "apolitical" lines of desire and tactical urbanisms are sometimes blurry at best.

Mobile showers for unhoused individuals and nature walks for neighbors with dementia, for example, could be amenities for these community members to feel a bit more dignified as well as address personal hygiene and health needs. They could also serve as oblique critiques of the dearth of services offered by the city; this dearth effectively criminalizes being an unhoused person in New York City during the day, when shelters mandate that residents vacate the premises until nightfall. With nowhere to go, unhoused individuals often struggle to find spots where they can sit for more than a few minutes before being shooed away.

A justice orientation combines means (including a focus on deliberation) and ends (meeting urgent needs). Because intention is quite important here, interviews with PB budget delegates helped me to discern certain instances of tactical budgeting. But even if I were to interview every participant in PB, I would not always be able to confidently judge whether any certain project idea has a justice orientation.

Besides, taking the principle of epistemic justice seriously, it is not up to me—no matter how many interviews I conduct—to judge alone.

Still, a distinct, third category is important to underscore that not every line of desire is political. Acts of trespassing, transgression, or disobedience—like so many lines of desire—should not be summarily dismissed or suppressed because they do not abide by the rules of respectability politics. Anthropologist James C. Scott calls these acts infrapolitics because like infrared light, they attempt to remain invisible.[7]

But nor should they be romanticized. Rather, political scientist Cathy Cohen emphasizes that "counter normative behavior" should be examined and "recogniz[ed]" for "its *possible* subversive potential"; these acts are not inherently subversive or insurgent but instead must be "mobilized in a conscious fashion to be labeled resistance."[8]

Besides, insurgent budgeting relies in part on acts of subterfuge, fugitivity, and stealth—creating pockets of neighborliness and city making in an otherwise inhospitable policymaking environment. If these campaigns get too loud, they get rejected or repressed. This is why some interviewees state that they did *not* make their project descriptions too explicit or critical, so that they would not attract scrutiny from city agency representatives. They wanted to make the projects look more innocuous than they actually are, in order to sneak radical projects into the public budget.

Indeed, interviews with delegates suggest that they adapted their citizenship practices to use loopholes, technicalities, and existing rules to forward project ideas with explicit equity goals. In one committee, the delegates generally refused to advance project proposals that addressed what seemed like endemic needs like bathroom repairs.[9] They told residents to lobby the city rather than go through PB for such repairs, stating that the city must be held accountable.

But they made an exception for a proposal to reappropriate an existing school bathroom into an all-gender one, and did so as states around the country pushed legislation to ban transgender people's use of gender-affirming bathrooms.[10] At the school, members of the gay-straight alliance planned to make it so not just with new signage, but also by all using the bathroom—a sort of tactical urbanism. They especially wished to do so exactly so that youths who were not yet out to classmates, teachers, or family could do so without feeling self-conscious. The committee submitted the project to the School Construction Authority simply as a "bathroom upgrade."

I argue that in the context of public budgets, these policy-oriented tactical urbanisms are insurgent. They not only deviate from the norm; they are direct critiques. They resist common citizen-consumer practices and

188   BUDGET JUSTICE

austerity logics, demanding change from within government. They walk tightropes to avoid both being dismissed as illegitimate (with ideas too radical to be immediately recognized as respectable) and getting co-opted by the state (with projects like surveillance cameras, which ultimately work to reify status quo policies). And they demand shifts in resources that government officials might balk at or condescendingly dismiss otherwise.

At least some ballot items explicitly started as community-led initiatives in invented spaces. A diaper distribution network, for example, first developed during the pandemic as a collaboration between several mutual aid groups. The organizers noted that "diaper need affects 1 in 3 families and diapers are not covered by [federal food assistance] benefits." In the version funded by PB, the diapers are housed in brightly colored "hubs" that look like newspaper kiosks (or community fridges) on the sidewalk. Built by formerly incarcerated neighbors and hosted by local partner organizations, the hubs declare in bright pink letters, "Give what you can, take what you need." In other words, they implemented a small solidarity economy project using public funds. Other ballot items taking inspiration from the solidarity economy include "Worker Cooperatives 101," a housing policy lab for youths, and a project to connect a local soup kitchen to local farms.

The PBNYC case study reveals other glimmers of insurgent budgeting hiding in plain sight. Every year, there are a handful of project proposals on ballots marked by phrases like "pilot," "down payment," or "exploratory study." These phrases hint that these ballot items do not go down well-worn policy paths but instead attempt to make new ones. They render explicit that these projects serve as short-term tactics aimed at longer-term, strategic change.

Some citizens developed them as proofs of concept after being told by city agencies that the projects were unrealistic, in order to demonstrate that they could be done—and with PB votes, that they had public support. A ballot description for an elevator at a subway station in Park Slope, Brooklyn, for instance, clearly states that winning PB funds alone could not possibly pay for such an elevator; rather, people used PB to "put pressure" on the public transit authority to fund the remainder of what would be needed to create the first accessible station in the council district.[11]

Indeed, quite a few project proposals focus on political organizing for social change. These include a successfully funded youth-led project called Youth Organizing for Menstrual Equity. Period, intended to "create youth-led workshops for middle-schoolers to discuss period stigmatization [and] medical racism," and another described as "organizing together for dignified work: domestic workers and employers."[12] The latter "aims to cultivate care by bringing together domestic workers, employers, and allies . . . to identify and enforce the standards we want to uphold in our community."[13] Like the mutual aid initiatives I explore in chapter 12, this project works to negotiate and change power dynamics through self-governance.

And like the mobile showers mentioned above, quite a few winning proposals take amenities or services usually provided to individuals through the private market and shift them to the public sphere. Compared to the sorts of capital projects typically funded by PB, these tended to be smaller in scale, but more impactful in changing relationships between residents within a neighborhood through a sort of prefigurative, "other-worlding" politics—building another world in which, for example, unhoused people have places to get clean, or just to be.

Such projects run counter to the growing privatization of public spaces. Take privately owned public spaces like plazas in front of office buildings. According to a study by the *New York Times*, special agreements allowed developers to build 20 million square feet more than zoning regulations typically allowed, usually by permitting them to build more floors in skyscrapers. In return, these developers were supposed to make roughly 3.8 million square feet in privately owned public spaces accessible.[14] But a Department of Buildings study showed that around one in five of these properties violated their agreements—for instance, they blocked off what should have been public plazas with fences or employed elements of hostile architecture such as stoops studded with concrete spikes. Such moves mean that members of the public cannot sit down to wait for a friend or eat a bagel on the go.[15] In general, they often come with rules of behavior that serve a few as opposed to the many.

As private property codes of conduct, exclusion, and surveillance become ever more widespread, PB projects insist that even marginalized constituents should be welcomed in public spaces like parks; in doing so, they reappropriate what is, in effect, privatized public property to serve everyone. They aim to engage in practices of *commoning* to make small pockets of the commons more, well, common. One ballot item asked for $12,000 for workstations with attached cribs/play stations for babies and toddlers at a local library. This proposal does not mention the need for universal childcare; it does, however, acknowledge that the childcare affordability crisis is a public issue, and parents often suffer alone and isolated in their respective homes.

Unlike private sector platforms in the "sharing economy" like Airbnb and Uber, these efforts operate with principles of mutuality. They work to change relationships between citizens from those of consumers to those of neighbors—not necessarily friends, but living in the city in solidarity.

———

Together, these projects offer visions of a different sort of city in which to flourish. In place of competition, deservingness, and surveillance, these projects uplift values of unconditional universal access, camaraderie, local pride in cultural diversity, and self-determination.

Finally, these projects demonstrate that practices of epistemic justice—reflected in how projects are developed (and by whom)—help build racial solidarities among citizens. Projects aimed at addressing sensitive issues in Brooklyn's Bangladeshi community, for example, included self-defense workshops developed by and for Muslim women, and sewing circles for victims of domestic violence in the community.

Asians (including East Asians) constitute only 13 percent of the district's residents, so in order to win PB funding, these projects needed to win the votes of most district voters *not* identifying as Bangladeshi or Muslim as well. Based on conversations with district residents, they successfully did so because they were not only culturally sensitive, but also developed in part by people from within the community. Residents I spoke with said that they would not have presumed to know what their

Bangladeshi neighbors needed to address gender-based violence, nor how to broach issues of stigma. This was not a question of language barriers but rather respecting neighbor's careful, yearslong analyses of their own experiences and how different practices of care would make a difference. No "best practice" exists; the women's articulated desires—what they were ready to do to counter violence for themselves, without turning to police that they felt misunderstood by—made all the difference.

In heeding different knowledges, participants in PB can build solidarities between groups of citizens who previously competed with one another for resources. In a winning project for a plaza in front of a large school building, five small schools housed in that building came together to advocate for an outdoor plaza.[16] Getting five principals and school communities to collaborate on a project like this—focused not on repair or addition, but the conversion of a space and amenity—is a feat.

By tying school funding to student enrollment, institutional rules frequently pit small schools against one another; sometimes, too, the existence of several schools in a building creates tensions, especially when it looks like one has more resources than the others. The students watch the other schools' students walking by in the hallways, comparing their experiences. In such a context, it is notable that the participants chose to create a proposal that benefits not only everyone at school, but others in the neighborhood as well. They scaled back previously separate efforts in order to join forces.

This stands in contrast to zero-sum games, winners, and losers. Moreover, these tactics help participants to think in terms of "we" and "our district" rather than just their own respective, divisible interests. The latter is essential for a more equitable distribution of resources.

Indeed, interviewees noted that over the years, they adapted to city agencies' attempts at managed participation and developed new tactics in response. For example, they began to bundle smaller projects into larger ones in specific, strategic ways, precisely to sneak in equity-oriented projects that would have been difficult to get approved otherwise. Participants used these tactics as quietly as possible. They did this to spotlight issues that cut across locales in order to advance the logic that working together increases chances of success, and encourage dynamics of innovation, comparative analysis, and collaboration along the way. When public administration scholar Carolin Hagelskamp, sociologist David Schleifer, and I examined whether PB-funded projects were more likely to benefit high-needs schools, we found that delegates' strategies for equity—especially bundling and equity-focused descriptors for ballot items—were associated with winning PB votes.[17]

These citizens pursued these project ideas even when they knew that city agency representatives might bristle in response and even (or especially) when they were sure that these project ideas would have little chance of approval under typical, non-PB circumstances. They used specific tactics to try new ideas, moving quickly with the logic of "beg forgiveness, not permission"—knowing that once implemented, they might not have to beg forgiveness. It is almost as if they snuck radical projects and policies into the public budget by subterfuge, if not quite sabotage. Residents enact a new ecology of citizenship and assert their right to the city through insurgent practice.

It is no accident that most of the projects I have labeled as budget lines of desire are concentrated in certain districts. I do not believe that those districts have more inventive residents, though I'm guessing that their organizers have more resources to help mobilize them. Rather, my analysis suggests that districts where elected council members and city agency staff continually tweak PB protocols also nurture imaginative project ideas in PB. They sustain higher rates of participation too.

For instance, after a few years of PBNYC, constituents in some districts demanded that PB funds be used for expense (or programming) projects alongside capital (or infrastructural) ones. In districts that expanded the range of PB-eligible project ideas, participants sought to innovate policies, provide proofs of concept, and meet urgent needs.

———

The iterative changes in official PB rules and budget delegate tactics as well as strategies show that citizens and state institutions inform each other; they are mutually constitutive. In some cases, citizens can build fugitive spaces within the state, akin to what critical theorists Stefano Harney and Fred Moten call the *undercommons*, counterpublics *in* but not *of* the larger institutions in which they dwell.[18] These spaces encourage work toward budget justice, even when surrounded by bureaucracies and politicians accustomed to the status quo.

In an ecology of citizenship for budget justice, residents reorient themselves from acting as citizen-consumers to citizen-neighbors. They work across an ecosystem of participation to enact provisional, temporary alliances with elected officials, city bureaucrats, and others in a technodemocracy. With grassroots solidarity economy campaigns or funded PB projects, they remake little parcels of the city, perhaps like replacing individual bricks in a house, one by one, until entire rooms and floors are redone. Or returning to the metaphor of lines of desire, these citizen-neighbors make new walking paths, in stark contrast to the sorts of highways that dominate national policy. They continue to press policymakers to codify and expand these changes. And in the meantime, they do not wait around for explicit permission.

INTERLUDE

An Interview with Marc Serra Solé

Barcelona's Citizens Forge Solidarities through the State

I STARTED PAYING more attention to protests in Barcelona in the months between the Arab Spring and Occupy Wall Street, when millions of citizens calling themselves the Indignados—the indignant ones—poured into streets and plazas across Spain. Also called the 15M movement (named after May 15, 2011, when mass demonstrations spread around Spain), the Indignados impressed me with the scope of their policy demands, spanning domains from housing to public space—while explicitly insisting on participatory democracy throughout.

In 2015, I heard that a crowdsourced citizens' platform elected a new mayor in Barcelona. *How could a platform elect a mayor?* I wondered. Activists had formed a grouping of electors, a temporary group of citizens aiming to forward a candidate in a specific election, even when they had no political party. Drawing on mass movement assemblies like the ones from 15M, they developed a new citizens' platform called Barcelona en Comú (Catalan for "Barcelona in Common," abbreviated as BComú) to expand community rights as well as develop alternative models of economic development and tourism for Barcelona. BComú won enough votes to appoint Ada Colau as mayor. Until then, Colau had been an anti-evictions activist and founding member of Plataforma de Afectados por la Hipoteca (Platform for People Affected by Mortgages), which used both policy campaigns and nonviolent direct actions for housing reforms.

In 2017, Barcelona began a municipalist informal global network of Fearless Cities, with "over 100 municipalist organizations from every continent."[1] In 2023, as part of a European Union initiative, it was declared the inaugural European Capital of Democracy.

I was struck by BComú's refusal to choose between process (insisting on "real democracy") and outcomes (greater resources for social policies). For instance, it worked to "radicalize democracy, feminize politics." According to activist Kate Shea Baird, "The idea is not to be essentialist" or simply aim for female representation.[2] Rather, Colau stresses dialogue and listening, that "politics done collectively are better than those done individualistically," and incorporates a gender analysis into all policy—from park designs to antipoverty programs.[3]

BComú's work highlights a joining of solidarity economy work with political organizing, and an emphasis on community leadership alongside public administration support. In two terms, BComú quadrupled the budget for social housing and recovered €150 million in corporate tax revenues. It formed a municipal childcare program, sustainable public energy company, publicly owned dental clinic, the city's first municipal LGBTQ center, and new systems for city procurement to source *from* cooperatives. Also, it allocated funds to new cooperatives, especially migrant- and refugee-led ones, and halted fines on sex workers.[4]

BComú declared that "we took the social networks, we took the streets, and we took the squares . . . to win back the city," but wanted to change how city hall operates as well.[5] Still, while Colau's administration made significant strides for budget justice in Barcelona, it lost local elections in 2023.

I was eager to glean lessons from BComú's experiences and spoke with Marc Serra Solé over Zoom about what he had learned. Serra Solé holds degrees in law, sociology, and advocacy, and has worked in various organizations defending social and environmental rights. In 2019, he was elected councillor for citizen rights and participation on the Barcelona City Council, a position he held until 2023. He also served as secretary general of the International Observatory on Participatory Democracy. Serra Solé is deputy area chair for climate action and energy transition as well as deputy councillor for citizens' participation on the Barcelona Provincial Council. I was eager to hear Serra Solé's reflections on BComú's attempts to do politics differently, both inside and outside city hall.

196   BUDGET JUSTICE

This interview has been edited and condensed for clarity and concision.

CELINA SU: *What has your role been in terms of work toward budget justice in Barcelona? How did you get started working on this?*

MARC SERRA SOLÉ: I am a lawyer, sociologist, and social activist. I joined the Barcelona City Council when BComú won its first election in 2015 and remained for two terms. I am currently in the Provincial Government [Diputació de Barcelona] in charge of climate action, energy transition, and participation.

Before we won the elections, I had never participated in a political party. My career was always linked to social associations and movements—as founder of a platform for the closure of the CIE [Centro de Internamiento de Extranjeros, or Immigrant Detention Center] or in the Platform for People Affected by Mortgages. Also in my neighborhood, [where] social activism was always present. My connection with immigration detention centers, for instance, was through my neighborhood social center.

CS: *Was this social center run by the municipal government?*

MSS: No, it was run by members of the community—in a rented space, operating like a neighborhood group. I live in a neighborhood where 45 percent of the residents are immigrants. One of the community center activities is Spanish and Catalan languages. At that time, I was studying law, and some of the neighborhood people who came in for the language classes also asked about their regularization [immigration visa] process. Because here in Spain, the laws on foreigners are a bureaucratic and terrible thing.

One day, one of the students didn't come to class. We found out that she was [being held] in the detention center and activated the community to help her. Back then, a lot of people didn't know that these immigration centers [even] existed. Now a lot of people know. We created a campaign and eventually got majority support in the Catalan Parliament. We did a lot of advocacy to close these detention centers. While we didn't achieve that, we were able to mobilize a lot with this issue.

CS: *The case of Barcelona is remarkable for moving beyond established political institutions and electing a mayor out of a platform instead. Why do you think this came about?*

MSS: What happened in 2015 in Barcelona—and in many other cities around Spain—was incredible. Citizen candidates, such as BComú, ran in elections for the first time and won. And we did it without having media or financial support.

There are two [main] reasons. [First,] the erosion of the Spanish two-party system: the People's Party on the Right and the Spanish Socialist Workers' Party on the center Left, the two large parties that have alternated power in Spain for the last forty years, were in crisis. Second, the Indignados movement that occupied the squares, seeing that its proposals were not listened to by the large parties, forwarded citizen candidacies with broad social support.

The victory of BComú is also explained by the leadership of Ada Colau. With Ada, we gathered academics, lawyers, and activists, all active in city movements, and from there emerged BComú. We were generating a new political space in which citizens could participate with the maximum of internal democracy, without electoral quotas or coalition agreements.

CS: *How did this "maximum of internal democracy" develop? Sometimes, progressive movements lose support because they're not engaging the public well, or doing things on behalf of people and not with people. How did you work to avoid this?*

MSS: It was important that all the little political parties, like left-wing and environmental parties, were committed to this new space—without controlling it. Everybody had to deliberate on each issue.

198 BUDGET JUSTICE

In Spain, we have a long history of progressive left[ist] parties [that] tried to make [electoral] coalitions and tried to negotiate visibility in these coalitions. And it was not working well. So we said, *Political parties, we need you [as a legal form to get elected and hold office]—but we need to create something bigger.* Something with a citizen form, not a professional political form.

This means that our terms of transparency and communication were very important. Our organization was more similar [to] a social movement than a political party.

CS: *What did this look like?*

MSS: BComú was created in 2015, and the elections were in 2016, so in just one year, we created a group and won elections. So our issue was, *Let's prepare for the elections with open assemblies in the neighborhoods to create the candidate's political program.* We did that using the same organizing strategies as the Indignados and 15M movements: open assemblies.

This assembly culture was very important for citizen participation and connected everything we did. Everybody says, "I was there in 2011, when citizens occupied the squares." And now we approached the [BComú] platform in this same way—not as [a typical] protest, not to take command of [existing] institutions, but to articulate new terms.

We made sure that leaders of existing movements agreed that it was an important moment to seize the institution [of elected office]. We worked on ensuring mass participation—not just by top [or] medium-level advocates [but also rank-and-file people in grassroots movements along with everyday citizens]. We wanted our platform to earn the trust of the people. Here were people who have been fighting for the last twenty years in social movements, who want a change in the city. We needed to earn their trust, for them to say, *BComú could be a good tool to build power; it feels different from the city council.*

cs: *The city's Decidim and PB initiatives since then have received a lot of attention. Did they help make the city budget more democratic?*

mss: When we won the elections, we promised that we would not [single-handedly] develop the Municipal Action Plan as long as we held office. [This plan is the traditional policy road map for each new term.] We wanted it to be prepared in a participatory manner by as many citizens as possible. So we created Decidim, an online platform for citizen input. In the beginning, the platform helped thousands of people to make proposals and interact with one another, critiquing and improving proposals. It aimed to be a complement to deliberation and in-person participation. Forty thousand citizens participated in this process, making around 10,000 proposals that had 156,000 supporters—figures that were unprecedented in the city's participation system.

We soon saw that the Decidim tool had so much potential that it could have more functionalities and transcend Barcelona. The fact that we had created it with free, open-source software allowed us to share it with other cities that could also make improvements, providing feedback on the tool. [This contrasts with the typical practices of hiring private contractors.] Today, Decidim is in more than twenty countries around the world, in hundreds of cities, with more than three million users around the world.

And we inaugurated participatory budgets here in 2020. But just when those budget deliberations began, the COVID-19 pandemic arrived, eliminating face-to-face deliberations and significantly reducing the budget from €75 to €30 million. Still, around sixty thousand people participated in that process.

The PB process in Barcelona served us most through a lot of teaching on how public investment works in the neighborhoods and generating a democratic culture, especially in sectors that were not [previously] organized. For example, citizens saw this tool as an opportunity to achieve improvements in their schools, small sports facilities, parks, bike lanes, and so on. It also served as a powerful experience of collective intelligence and innovation because among the two thousand projects that citizens proposed, there were some that would never have arrived via traditional spaces of policymaking, such as the construction of a cricket field (remember that cricket is not a common sport in Spain!), and this became *the* most highly voted project—mobilizing young girls from Bengali, Pakistani, and Indian communities, who not only engaged the process but participated massively and helped lead it [too], and the city getting a project that would definitely not have been included in a Municipal Action Plan.

cs: *Beyond specific institutional designs, what cultural connections do you see between radical democratic practices and Barcelona's political trajectory?*

mss: Barcelona has a long history of worker, neighborhood, and feminist movements. The cooperative movement starting in the late nineteenth century managed to build a parallel society of production and consumption athenaeums and cooperatives to respond to the needs of workers. [These athenaeums have been likened to citizenship schools in the US civil rights movement, operating in contexts where access to formal education remained limited.][6] In 1919, a successful general strike established the eight-hour workday here, and this opened the doors of success to many other countries in Europe. One of the most prominent unions then was the CNT [the National Federation of Labor], an anarchist trade union that in the 1930s had more than eight hundred thousand members, the majority in Barcelona. The CNT played a very important role in the resistance against fascism, becoming part of the state government in the middle of the civil war. It did so with the leadership of women like Frederica Montseny, the first woman to hold a ministerial position in the history of Spain—and one of the first in all of Europe—in 1936.

There is definitely some continuity between the cooperative, anarchist history of the early twentieth century and the democratic radical movements from these last twenty years. Both are sets of movements that try to oppose the havoc caused by savage capitalism—whether in the form of Fordism or its digital version, in the form of platforms such as Amazon or Uber. People see how the liberal democratic system is incapable of providing answers to inequalities or channeling the desires of a social majority for emancipation.

Through the city government, we have promoted the democratization of the economy through cooperativism. In the last eight years, the number of cooperatives has increased by 55 percent [with women constituting 60 percent of workers and worker-owners], and today, Barcelona has Can Batlló, the largest cooperative center in Europe.

CS: *You say that the public sees "how the liberal democratic system is incapable of providing the answers to inequalities." How did citizens in Barcelona see the limits of the liberal democratic system and turn to cooperative efforts?*

MSS: Barcelona has a population of almost two million. You have the market, you have state institutions, but then you have the citizens, or as we say, *la comune*, the community. We have a lot of associations, around five thousand in the city, and a lot of public facilities that are important to community. For example, we have seventy-three neighborhoods, with public civic/social centers in each.

More than fifty of these neighborhood centers are *autogestionados* [self-determinations]—civic centers, athenaeums, sports facilities—managed directly by groups of citizens. Most of these facilities are public today thanks to yearslong neighborhood struggles. When neighbors get a new facility, they tell the city council: *We won the facility, and we want to manage the facility*. We call it *gestion civica*, or *gestion comunitaria*, community management. So in government, we try to contribute public resources to support these communities.

These public facilities today reflect the radical democratic story of Barcelona—even when that history is quite unknown to the social majority. We see the same practices of self-management, cooperativism, and mutual support. It's a revindication that citizens want the community [to] have spaces to develop projects with the support of the public administration, but the leadership of the community.

CS: *In your view, what are BComú's greatest accomplishments and challenges?*

MSS: From the city government of BComú, we increased the budget for social rights by 74 percent, placing Barcelona as the administration in Spain with the greatest social investments. This facilitated the development of new rights such as energy advice, psychologists, and public dentists, which are now progressively assumed by the state or regional government.

Likewise, we achieved a 62 percent increase in the budget for education and culture, which enabled the opening of fifty new public schools, so that public education offerings in the city now exceed private ones. Public transport has also been a priority; fares have been frozen for the last six years, and the budget has been increased by 85 percent to improve our network. The housing budget has increased by 68 percent, so that the Barcelona administration is the country's leader in new public housing construction. Likewise, we created an antieviction unit (focused on mediation and social support) that managed to stop 93 percent of evictions.

Regarding the city's physical transformation, one of the most obvious legacies of BComú is the superblock project. Many city streets have been transformed into green space [spaces for walking and play]. It is also a way to realize social justice in public space. Children, the elderly, and those most vulnerable were prioritized; cars were not.

Still, there remain challenges. Rents increased by 50 percent in recent years throughout the country. This means that [even our increased] social investments have often not been enough to help many families to make ends meet. Social movements, with the support of BComú, have been insisting for years on the need to regulate rental prices, prohibit abusive increases, and protect tenants. Finally, and after overcoming the resistance of the real estate lobby in 2023, we passed a new housing law to cap rental prices. This has been, without a doubt, one of the main battles of the last decade, and the challenge will be for new administrations to actually enforce the law and burst the speculative bubble.

CS: *Where did the money come from for these investments? How did you do this?*

MSS: In Spain, local administrations have significant problems with funding because we don't manage most taxes; the main ones are at the regional and federal levels. So we do different things; for example, each tourist who sleeps in Barcelona now pays around three euros per day, much more than before. It doesn't sound like a lot, but it's important. [In 2022, there were around ten million tourists and thirty million overnight stays in Barcelona.] Then we work toward agreements with the state or federal governments for some of these projects, especially when our political party is holding the majority at those levels.

This reflects our priorities. Maybe other governments [prioritize] other activities, like promotion of tourism. That has historically been very prominent in our budget. We spent so much money on selling the city, telling everybody in the world to come to Barcelona. We reduced that part of our budget; our investments focused instead on social provisions. We also increased property taxes in a progressive way, asking those who own big properties to pay just a little more, and increased transaction fees for estate transfers and property sales.

204 BUDGET JUSTICE

CS: *What are some of your key challenges now, especially in the face of rising authoritarianism worldwide?*

MSS: Making sure that progressive forces are those framing the problems to be addressed, in ways that resonate with the social majority. If I have learned anything from politics, it is that ideas are ultimately judged by their ability to concretely improve people's quality of life and generate new rights. Radical ideas are of little use if they do not manage to be shared by a social majority and get translated into public policies that, in turn, transform social reality. And this applies both to the institutional policies of political parties and those forwarded by social movements.

During and after the 2007 financial crisis, we were the ones to define and frame the crisis: *We are the 99 percent. And we have problems with the 1 percent; we are the people with problems with jobs, evictions.* From 2008 to 2015, all around the world, this framing helped garner social support for progressive proposals.

[In some ways, that framing continues to resonate.] Defending the right to the city in Barcelona today means protecting it from international investment funds that see the city as a commodity—purchasing entire residential buildings, renovating them, and renting them at exorbitant prices, especially as tourist rentals. Many families are being displaced from their neighborhoods and even the city because they cannot afford rent.

[But in other ways,] we have a different political moment now. Progressive movements are not the ones [forwarding popular] frameworks; now it's the far right. The same families facing evictions now say that immigrants are their enemy, not market speculation.

[We have to work to not only attain power but maintain it too.] One challenge for BComú is that we were not professional politicians. We felt pressure [as activists] to produce results: *We have the government, we have to transform everything.* For example, one important issue for us is the transformation of public space. We had a clear model of the city we want—whereby most space will be for pedestrians, for families, without pollution. So we started a lot of public works to transform the city. I do think that our model is the model of the future, for the planet, for our lives. But maybe we went too fast, without sufficient communication and deliberation, because some of the citizens didn't understand this transformation. This model also implies reversing privileges and changing consumption patterns, and some sectors saw the projects as interference [and a threat to their social positioning].

In higher-income neighborhoods, car owners wanted to keep their cars, [and have] more security, fewer immigrants, all of that. All the right-leaning parties worked together with that vision, and I think that their electoral win can be explained as a reaction to our attempts to transform the city. We went into election season with a lot of construction and public works in progress to reclaim public space, with [temporary] chaos in the city center. [This made us vulnerable to critiques and reframing by right-wing parties.] I think that political parties would have never made this kind of mistake ... but we are not a political party; we are a group of social activists. In the end, we didn't [win]. The current mayor beat Ada by only two hundred votes. There was no runoff election.

CS: *Amid all of this, what is to be done for budget justice—in Barcelona and elsewhere?*

MSS: Without BComú in government, the new administration immediately questioned the continuity of the participatory budgets. Those selected projects that open up public spaces in the city—such as bike lanes or street pacification—are being canceled by the new government. Likewise, the new administration's vetoes on certain projects are putting the public's trust in PB at risk. If the citizens who vote in a process like PB see that their will is not respected, they will not participate again. This would be a major setback. [Meaningful

206 BUDGET JUSTICE

institutions are never permanently won; they have to be won over and over again.]

I don't think, however, that the city's organized citizens will allow this to happen. Neighborhood associations and social groups have already been organizing to demand that the new government respect the will of the thousands of residents who voted for the winning projects. This is one of the neighborhood struggles that is really galvanizing citizens around the city.

Now, we are in a moment of reflection. What we have done in the past is organizing, mobilizing social movement opposition in neighborhood movements. Now, BComú is an additional tool we can use in the opposition. But our origin [as a grouping of electors] and our spirit is in the government. So we are working on winning the next election by working with social movements, with communities in all neighborhoods, and defending all of our projects so that the current government does not endanger the participatory budget process, for example.

CS: *What keeps you going now?*

MSS: For me, the community. I have lived in the same neighborhood for the last twenty years. That's not easy in Barcelona because of [real estate] speculation. You constantly have to move if you rent. I am a part of the citizenry, so that I ultimately work not for the political party but [instead] for the community, trying to make my experience as a lawyer, as a social activist, useful.

In political terms, communities are more open than political parties. They are part of larger political projects of the sort of city we want to live in: an open city, diverse city, equal city, antiracist city, feminist city. Maybe now I am a city councillor . . . [but] I am [simultaneously] working in social movements, in the streets, in other realms. I don't think that there is a hierarchy of politics, where social movements are below and institutional politics are at the top. We can change how we work, from one [realm] to another.

14

Insurgent Budgeting

HOW MIGHT BUDGET lines of desire become routine rather than surreptitious exceptions to the rule? Justice-oriented policy changes are often labeled as either reformist—a band-aid solution at best, a farce at worst—or revolutionary, with little wiggle room in between. Accordingly, campaigns in invited spaces are frequently dismissed as expedient and too vulnerable to co-optation; those in invented spaces are often dismissed as too radical and unrealistic. But environmental psychologists and urban scholars Claire Cahen, Jakob Schneider, and Susan Saegert caution against "dichotomised accounts of social movements that oppose losses to victories, co-optation to resistance, and movements to institutions." In real life, the most successful campaigns that they examined moved iteratively between invited and invented spaces, engaging in "situated and dynamic" insurgent practices.[1] Likewise, political scientists Adrian Bua and Sonia Bussu argue that in a model of democracy-driven governance, grassroots participants "seek to gain leverage over the power of the state, within and against it."[2]

Research shows that PB can play a pivotal role in helping citizens to enact insurgent practices and different ecologies of citizenship in public budgets. As I discussed earlier in this book, PBNYC engaged citizens even when they had never worked with others on community issues before, and even when they did not hold formal nation-state citizenship or voting rights.[3] Once engaged, however, such citizens do not stay contained within PB invited spaces, even when (or especially if) the process feels quite limited. They also become more likely to vote, attempt to hold mayors and city council members accountable through town hall meetings and other invited spaces, and engage in invented spaces like mutual aid organizations and community safety programs.[4] They engage different spaces not as mutually exclusive but rather in concert, and not in competition or animus but instead in solidarity with other citizens.[5]

Before large-scale, structural changes are put into place, what is to be done in the meantime? Before ecosystems of meaningful participation become real and routine, and before well-meaning city bureaucrats engage in a technodemocracy rather than a technobureaucracy, insurgent practices are crucial to struggles for budget justice.

Solidarities are not formed in a vacuum, nor in parallel with state policies. They represent grassroots politics, always in relation to the state. Insurgent budgeting thus involves engaging and sometimes morphing existing invited spaces like PB, in order to engage in policy-oriented tactical urbanisms and enact budget lines of desire. Citizens then take policy ideas as well as dynamics between citizens from invented spaces like mutual aid and sneak them into invited governmental policy.

So how might communities judge which campaigns and actions make meaningful progress toward budget justice? When do actions constitute politics from below, as opposed to the top (or middle) of the totem pole? Will they be recognizably insurgent? These questions animate my thinking on budget justice in less-than-ideal circumstances and real-life systems of local governance, so different from those in textbooks. After all, as I noted earlier, not all budget lines of desire or tactical urbanisms are justice oriented. Given the amount of work to be done, I also wonder about risking burnout and where to focus precious resources.

I am particularly intrigued by the potential of *nonreformist reforms*, a term coined by theorist André Gorz to denote those "conceived, not in terms of what is possible within the framework of a given system and administration, but in view of what should be made possible in terms of human needs and demands."[6] Sometimes called structural, transformative, or abolitionist reforms, nonreformist reforms build "the capacity to cumulatively transform the existing system."[7]

While there are no surefire protocols for radical practice, there are nonnegotiables and strategic questions to keep in mind. In this chapter, I gather lessons from earlier chapters to present key criteria for identifying nonreformist reforms in public budgets.

———

Insurgent budgeting can only take place when citizens recognize that no matter how frustrating the bureaucracy is, it is not as immutable as it might appear. As Gilmore states, "The state is a contradictory object and subject of struggle.... The state does not think and do. People in various configurations of power (including from below) enliven states to think and do."[8]

Because mainstream discourse is dominated by talk of governmental waste and the *need* for austerity, it might be hard for average citizens to get behind-the-scenes looks at what people in government bureaucracies think and do. After learning about an unofficial social media account based in New York that posts anonymous testimonies by city workers, I saw that many of the posts center on budget cuts. One, for example, underscores the consequences of chronic understaffing:

> HPD [Housing Preservation and Development].... City hall continually tells us to lie to elected officials and the public about service delivery and how reduced staffing, hiring freezes, [and] merit increase freezes do not affect it.... It is affecting everything.... [H]undreds of units of housing cannot move forward because we do not have anyone to move them forward and they sit in the pipeline for years in the middle of a housing crisis. I am doing the work of at least three people.... My salary would qualify me for the low-income housing my own agency supplies.

Another post read,

> Anon please. HRA APS [Human Resources Administration Adult Protective Services, which provides services for physically and/or mentally impaired adults] ... no hybrid as promised, no O/T [overtime], no new hires. Management hardly around.

210 BUDGET JUSTICE

Although I am unable to fact-check these posts, they corroborate testimonies I have been able to verify. They feel like the sort of counter-public fugitive spaces that both citizens and state workers need in order to compare notes, understand their own experiences, and mobilize for change.

———

Testimonies like these can feel demoralizing. They can make trenchant critiques of public policies and the state all the more searing. To some, they can be signs to give up on budget justice, hunker down, and attempt to protect one's own. But they can also feed solidarities and perseverance. They serve as reminders to keep all spaces—especially invited ones as well as invented ones—as sites of contestation and struggle.

I underline this because when city services are being cut to the bone or appear to be in disarray, collective actions in invented spaces are not only necessary but feel particularly alluring too—as in, *Finally, getting something done on the community's terms, without red tape.* Radical formations in invented spaces attempt to elide state constraints; this is especially important in many experiments focused on the criminal justice system so as to try to make sure that they do not resort to supporting compromise policies—like body cameras and social work services performed by police officers—simply because those are familiar and most easily attainable. Many community safety groups object to such policies because they can legitimize the police force as an institution without actually reducing police violence.[9] Some groups might view any engagement with government as inevitably co-opting and corrupting.[10]

Cooperative practices in invented spaces also help communities to contest *how* states implement existing services, so as to practice new racial and class solidarities. For instance, reliance on mutual aid and crowdfunding can give people deemed "undeserving" or ineligible by elected officials—like those using drugs, people with previous convictions, or a member of the working poor, making above the poverty line of $30,000 for a family of four in 2023—access to emergency provisions they could not get otherwise. Indeed, legal scholar Dean Spade argues that mutual aid is a political project because it works to meet immediate needs *while refusing* typical criteria for who does and does not deserve help.[11] Without the latter, and without attendant mobilization, different mutual aid and solidarity efforts can resemble noblesse oblige volunteerism, reifying existing social hierarchies, and potentially stigmatizing whoever needs help.

This particular sort of communitarian reliance on resources from invented spaces can ironically strengthen austerity too. Viewed uncritically, some of the antistate rhetoric used in some invented spaces can echo rhetoric used by neoliberal politicians. For example, in his encouragement of a more compassionate conservatism, George H. W. Bush called for "a thousand points of light"—volunteers and private nonprofit organizations, especially faith-based ones—to perform social services. He contended that a reliance on the private and nonprofit sectors would ensure that these services better reflect specific communities. Politicians have also weaponized this reasoning to justify continual budget cuts to public programming.

It is not surprising, then, that many mutual aid and solidarity economy collectives with trenchant critiques of current state formations as well as policies nevertheless work with specific state representatives or entities on a case-by-case basis.[12]

———

Nonreformist reforms are notoriously difficult to achieve. But quite a few activists have carefully articulated helpful criteria for nonreformist reforms in their respective domains of struggle. Spade, for instance, asks four questions: *Does it provide material relief? Does it leave out an especially marginalized part of the affected group (e.g., people with criminal records or people without immigration status)? Does it legitimize or expand a system we are trying to dismantle? Does it mobilize the most affected for an ongoing struggle?*[13] One question I particularly like, often attributed to the organization Critical Resistance, is, *Will we have to undo this later?*[14]

Such criteria are tremendously helpful. They are practical while helping collectives to maintain a critical stance. The last question posed by

Critical Resistance, for example, could help activists fighting the construction of a new proposed prison decide whether an alliance with local homeowners will ultimately build solidarities and greater understanding of their cause, or fuel a not-in-my-backyard campaign, but make it more likely that the prison will be built elsewhere—probably in a less-resourced community.

Scholars and activists working on issues of mass incarceration and toward prison abolition in particular have long grappled with the usefulness of nonreformist reforms. Gilmore calls for "changes that, at the end of the day, unravel rather than widen the net of social control through criminalization."[15] Historian Garrett Felber writes, "Examples of nonreformist reforms [in the area of policing and prisons] include, but are not limited to: abolishing solitary confinement and capital punishment; moratoriums on prison construction or expansion; freeing survivors of physical and sexual violence, the elderly, infirm, juveniles, and all political prisoners; sentencing reform; ending cash bail; abolishing electronic monitoring, broken windows policing, and the criminalization of poverty; and a federal jobs and homes guarantee for the formerly incarcerated."[16]

What might such proposed changes look like in the area of public budgets? Pondering this question, I realized that much of my work over the past decade has involved attempts to trace the hidden connections between various, seemingly disparate parts of the net of budget opacity and austerity so that I could one day find a frayed strand to unravel.

Here I present six criteria for identifying nonreformist reforms (and by extension, insurgent practices) in public budgets:

1. Does the proposed action, project, or policy meet a need or improve material conditions for the most vulnerable (such as those highlighted using intersectionality as method), without creating stigma along the way?
2. Does it give everyday citizens spaces for meaningful participation, including deliberation, mobilization, and experimentation?
3. Does it enact epistemic justice—taking seriously and building/acting on citizens' ways of knowing, especially relying on local knowledge alongside universal technical knowledge?

4. Does it build solidarities between residents—not as citizen-consumers ruled by market logics like competition, but as citizen-neighbors with a right to the city?
5. Does this extend an existing policy or attempt to change it with a justice orientation?
6. Does it make a demand of public resources and state power? Is it maneuvered in specific ways so that the government cannot quash, condescendingly humor or indulge, or ignore this effort?

Roughly, the first two questions correspond to those related to spaces for democratic decision-making and organization, which I frame as an ecosystem of participation. The third and fourth questions focus on tensions within an ecology of citizenship. The last two questions bring together the political and policy contexts, means and ends, to highlight whether and how insurgent practice might take place.

———

Going back to PBNYC-funded projects, I thought about how I could place them on two axes: an x-axis centered on a spectrum ranging from reformist/incremental change to transformational/radical change, and a y-axis focused on the spectrum ranging from a status quo or retrograde orientation to an equity- and justice-oriented one. I added some non-PB-funded collective actions, like gated communities and squatting movements, to the radical end of the spectrum. My aim is not to judge exactly how radical or justice-oriented any specific project might be but instead to think through the criteria for nonreformist reforms presented above.

In this matrix, the top-left quadrant denotes projects that largely mirror existing city agency priorities, and the right column displays projects not currently prioritized or funded by city agencies. I am most interested in the bubble in the top-right quadrant, which consists of projects that are currently publicly funded, but probably would not have received public funds without PB. This bubble represents a sort of critical *and* practical sweet spot of meaningful nonreformist reforms for budget justice.

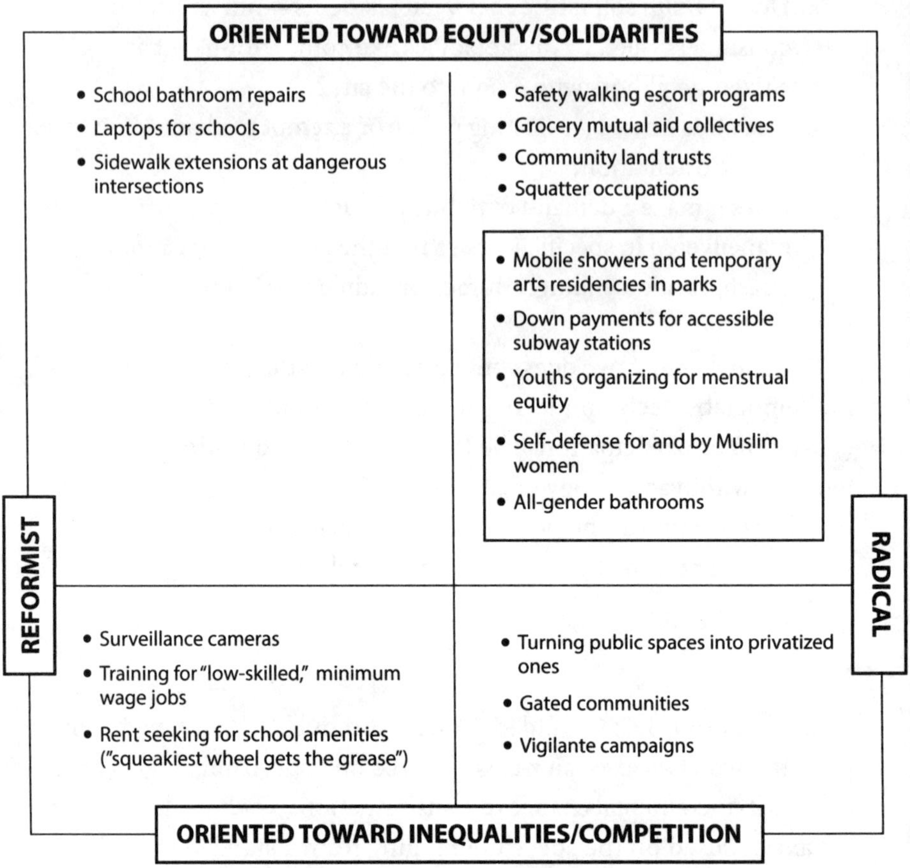

ORIENTED TOWARD EQUITY/SOLIDARITIES

REFORMIST

- School bathroom repairs
- Laptops for schools
- Sidewalk extensions at dangerous intersections

- Safety walking escort programs
- Grocery mutual aid collectives
- Community land trusts
- Squatter occupations

- Mobile showers and temporary arts residencies in parks
- Down payments for accessible subway stations
- Youths organizing for menstrual equity
- Self-defense for and by Muslim women
- All-gender bathrooms

- Surveillance cameras
- Training for "low-skilled," minimum wage jobs
- Rent seeking for school amenities ("squeakiest wheel gets the grease")

- Turning public spaces into privatized ones
- Gated communities
- Vigilante campaigns

RADICAL

ORIENTED TOWARD INEQUALITIES/COMPETITION

FIGURE 5. Budget Justice Matrix. A matrix for nonreformist reforms for budget justice.

I wonder what this quickly drawn matrix would look like if New York expanded PB to include just half of the $740 million New York police officers received in overtime payments for the 2023 fiscal year. That would be roughly the same amount that the NYPD spent beyond its allocated budget.[17] Even in that scenario, without changes in budget agency allocations, PB in New York would expand almost tenfold. What sorts of community safety programs, carefully and painstakingly developed by the Department of Health, would finally get widespread implementation? How many more subway stations would become accessible? How many worker cooperatives or community land trusts could receive seed funding, leading to further ripple effects?

I imagine what this matrix might look like if the sorts of spillover effects I noted earlier were taken more seriously, and thoughtfully woven into citizens' *and* bureaucrats' tactics as well as strategies for city making. What sorts of programs could then become routine, without concerted campaigns?

What might insurgent budgeting for community safety look like? Its framing might resemble the broader, more robust and holistic visions of community safety that I heard about from PBNYC participants in chapter 8, without getting whittled down to solely consist of surveillance cameras. It might include trials of innovative projects born in invented spaces, like the SafeWalks program I mentioned in chapter 12, articulated as the sort of budget line of desire I discussed in chapter 13.

And it would likely involve multiple rounds of contestations and deliberations across the entire ecosystem of political participation— elections, protests, invited spaces like task forces and hearings, and invented ones such as their own oppositional collectives.

For example, I learned that as one response to the 2020 uprisings, New York launched a nonpolice response program called the Behavioral Health Emergency Assistance Response Division (B-HEARD) to address mental health crises in 2021.[18] Such response systems are direly needed. New York City's 911 hotline alone receives two hundred thousand mental health crises calls a year, averaging one every three minutes or so. Meanwhile, some analyses estimate that nationwide, at least one-quarter of all fatal law enforcement encounters involve someone with a serious mental illness.[19]

But B-HEARD currently operates only in certain parts of the city and during certain hours of the day. Worse, many calls related to mental health still get directed to the police, so only 40 percent of such calls receive a response from B-HEARD.[20]

In response, a grassroots coalition called Correct Crisis Intervention Today-NYC (CCIT-NYC) protested the program's implementation. The coalition asked that B-HEARD be expanded, funded, and linked to 988 (the national suicide and crisis hotline launched in 2022) rather

216 BUDGET JUSTICE

than 911.[21] It also insisted that peer advocates with lived mental health crisis experience be sent alongside medical technicians to respond to calls. Further, CCIT-NYC demanded an oversight board consisting of 51 percent peers along with "peer involvement in all aspects of planning/ implementation/oversight as peers must have a say in the policies that affect them and must have a seat at the table—nothing about us, without us."[22] CCIT-NYC is currently seeking money from the city to pilot *its* program.

Could B-HEARD be a nonreformist reform for community safety? I noted that separately, Communities United for Police Reform (a grassroots coalition of two dozen core member organizations and over a hundred partner organizations) explicitly demands that NYPD officers be removed from mental health teams.[23] And I appreciated CCIT-NYC's insistence that all public programs—even ones as well-intentioned as a fully funded B-HEARD—need ongoing democratic accountability and epistemic justice to extend collective care.

I imagine a budget justice matrix shifting over time. Items in the lower-left quadrant decrease with each annual budget cycle, and maybe, as citizens increasingly connect as neighbors rather than consumers, some items in the lower-right quadrant will start to disappear as well. Slowly, items in the upper-right quadrant become more likely to appear in the sweet spot bubble of nonreformist reforms. Every once in a while, one of these nonreformist reforms sets a precedent, and thus eventually, it becomes policy.

———

When they fulfill the six criteria, public budget nonreformist reforms achieve the larger, fundamental practices for budget justice that I articulated in part I of this book: they essentially flip the gaze on public budgets, forcefully assert public budgets as moral documents with critical consequences, enact grassroots politics to hold governments accountable, and envision a right-to-the-city budget. They also articulate divest-invest formulations for the budgets needed to help communities thrive. These practices acknowledge that there are no just ends without just means.

Using intersectionality as method and targeted universalism—as opposed to recipients' deservingness—as foundational principles in public budgets helps citizens to shift their gaze from each other to state policies. In a context where state and corporate entities weaponize talk of transparency to justify surveillance programs, flipping the gaze insists on budget transparency for institutions along with a modicum of privacy for everyday citizens.

Taking after what writer and philosopher Édouard Glissant calls a "right to opacity," citizen-neighbors might imagine accessing the opportunities as well as resources they need to learn, play, work, and thrive in everyday life in the city—without having to self-consciously humblebrag about accomplishments or divulge the scars of suffering many would prefer to stay private. In my research, city residents repeatedly complained about how they usually have to "prove" themselves and their needs for even small grants or jobs; they noted that their PB work was partly motivated by the thought of helping others avoid such frequently humiliating experiences.

In invited spaces of participation vulnerable to governmentalities and respectability politics, epistemic justice is crucial to dreaming not just bigger but differently too. Processes like PB are in large part contestations over ways of knowing; no "participatory" process that ultimately deems technical, official expertise as above lived experience will truly address community needs.

When the state and citizenry are framed as mutually constitutive rather than oppositional, it becomes possible to imagine social change through provisional alliances. When everyday citizens are able to deliberate and collaborate in both invited and invented spaces, they can analyze public budgets critically and engage in different modes of organizing, building solidarities along the way. They can even start to experiment, articulate budget lines of desire, and engage in policy-oriented tactical urbanisms.

In this way, communities can help shape the rules of democratic institutions, not just participate in them, and reshape the criteria by which public policies and projects are funded. The animating questions then shift from those of deservingness to those of power.

218 BUDGET JUSTICE

In these practices of everyday democracy, people focus less on the winners and losers at the ballot box, and more on working with others. They nurture counterhegemonic connections in what feels like overwhelming isolation, austerity, and opacity.

Nonreformist reforms are simultaneously practical and utopian manifestations of everyday democracy, practiced with generosity and rigor. If citizens did not quite break some protocols for the PBNYC ones, perhaps they tiptoed around them for a righteous cause. Because such reforms are often the result of under-the-radar collective actions, they typically remain underrecognized triumphs.

Nonreformist reforms are culminations of community efforts to flip the gaze, reflect on our histories of inequities, demand a right-to-the-city budget, articulate their needs with the most vulnerable in mind through invited spaces like PB, move between invited spaces such as PB along with invented ones like mutual aid collectives and social movements in an ecosystem of participation, draw on multiple ways of knowing for a technodemocracy, articulate and enact new budget lines of desire, engage in tactical urbanisms to implement what they need using public funds, and build new provisional solidarities and vocabularies for lucid dreams of a different, better city. They are stepping stones to budget justice.

Epilogue

TWO YEARS AFTER my child entered New York's public school system, I felt less bewildered when I heard about proposed city budget cuts in the news. The numbers felt a bit more legible to me because I now knew how to access school-level budgets, which felt more humanly scaled.

I also understood that the numbers were mutable. Although the city was not awash in money, I knew that budget revenue numbers were not set in stone either; they reflected uncertain forecasts regarding school enrollments, business taxes, and stock markets. Further, sufficient public pressure could convince elected officials to roll back some cuts.

And as time passed, the moment-specific details faded. This reminded me to focus less on the current administration and more on the structural injustices that make budget crises perennial.

Meanwhile, in my city council district's PB process, the latest ballot included a project for my child's school, asking for air conditioners to help prevent overheating and asthma attacks among students. I noticed that the ballot had items for other schools too—fixing broken toilets and bathroom sinks.

On social media, I saw posts declaring, "Participatory budgeting is the worst," and, "Every year participatory budgeting makes me die a little inside."[1] Transportation blogger Ben Kabak wrote, "This isn't . . . 'fun.' . . . This is a reminder that one of the richest cities in the world is nickel-and-diming itself out of a bunch of cheap infrastructure upgrades it should be doing as a matter of course."[2]

220   BUDGET JUSTICE

Also meanwhile, several of my child's friends transferred to other schools. There were consequences not just for my child but for her school as well. Her principal noted that the school's budget is tied to enrolled students rather than programs. Classes are not guaranteed sufficient funding when students leave.

Indeed, for exactly such reasons, one neighbor fretted over her family's decision to transfer from the neighborhood public school to a charter one, where every classroom had two teachers instead of one. At the same time, she noticed that her child, who had recently been diagnosed with a learning disability, benefited from the additional attention she received in her new class.

In a local newsletter, I saw that my child's school's test scores had fallen in the past year. Though I knew better than to read too much into a single statistic with little context, it was hard to not worry or default to parent-consumer instincts. Several times a week, I received emails advertising charter or private schools touting bright futures and academic success.

And like other children her age, my now-six-year-old peppers me with incessant questions. Yesterday, she asked why I did not give money to the family members sitting on the sidewalk outside the grocery store, when they clearly lacked a home. And why did I give disapproving looks to those teenagers snickering "ching ching chong chong" at us? That could have escalated the situation since, as my kid commented, "One of them looks like they're losing control." I lamented the fact that in the heat of the moment, I wasn't able to respond to desperate poverty or racist taunts in more productive ways.

I was also curious about my kid's thoughts. How would she want the city to address poverty and the housing crisis? How would she define community safety?

And I reflected on the sorts of childhood experiences I described in the prologue. I hadn't paid much attention to them growing up, but looking back, they profoundly shaped my orientations toward budgets, politics, and the possibility of solidarities. As activists and writers Leah Hunt-Hendrix and Astra Taylor note, "Solidarity, in this transformative sense, isn't a feeling, affect, or fuzzy sense of connection; it is a form of power rooted in the acknowledgment that our lives are materially inter-twined."[3] What will my child's solidarities look like?

I need to not only develop but also practice better responses to such everyday questions—working toward meaningful, collective alterna-tives in, say, affordable housing and community safety that feel routine, as immediate and internalized a reaction as steeling myself and walking with eyes looking straight ahead, trying to "mind my own business," as I was trained to. As poet and scholar Éireann Lorsung writes, "There is no outside to it, the act of looking / or of looking away that makes an entire life. . . . [W]e are here in the interwar period (every period is an interwar period)."[4]

My core work involves more than voting for the best political candi-date or showing up for rallies. It revolves around the *meanwhiles* of everyday democracy, thinking out loud together and engaging in col-lective actions *between* elections and crises.

Personally, this currently entails poring over governmental docu-ments to analyze inequalities, in order to get a better sense of how city budgets operate as moral documents. It also includes connecting New York activists with counterparts in other cities in a learning exchange for the People's Plan NYC, a local grassroots coalition working toward a democratic people's budget in the city.[5] And it involves sharing stories and evidence about more inspiring PB processes in neighboring dis-tricts, so that more meaningful PB is not a far-fetched idea.

My work encompasses practices completely unrelated to my training too, like co-organizing after-school pickups (basically, the urban version of carpooling) or thinking through the best ways to contribute to, say, the local food cooperative. Some of these initiatives are solely local; others are networked with grassroots groups around the country or the world. My efforts change with the possibilities in the ecosystem of par-ticipation around me, as well as my evolving motivations and experi-ences as a citizen-neighbor.

The spaces between the formal chambers of power and moments between elections are not sideshows to me. They are the main attrac-tion, where citizens can collectively make a difference, and while the initial impact of a budget line of desire may not feel as grand as that of a presidential election, it is real. Cumulatively, these democratic practices for budget justice can be formidable.

When local struggles feel all-consuming and insurmountable, I find it helpful to consider the often similar ways in which budget injustice is felt and enacted around the world, and feel inspired not only by other communities' successes, but also their perseverance in hard times. I think about my parting questions to the thinker-practitioners I interviewed in this book's interludes: What keeps you going? What is to be done?

In the preceding chapters, I concentrated on the challenges, lessons, and implications for budget justice. Here I end with an exhortation of possibilities. First, by focusing on creating change at the city level, movements for budget justice can achieve impressive scale and build power. Second, by directly engaging the public along with building infrastructures of collective care and action, movements for budget justice can make their power durable. Budget justice is not only necessary for communities to thrive; it is eminently possible.

———

In *Black Reconstruction in America*, Du Bois articulated that the true abolition of slavery did not happen with the Emancipation Proclamation. The economic exploitation and racialized violence of slavery would live on through Jim Crow and other instantiations of budget injustice as long as the United States lacked what he called abolition democracy. He asked, "If all labor, black as well as white, became free, were given schools and the right to vote, what control could or should be set to the power and action of these laborers?"[6] The formal absence of institutions like slavery does not imply the absence of their shadows and power, and more pointedly, the presence of their replacements.

Legal scholar Bernard Harcourt asserts that the seedlings of a more just world already exist, especially via solidarity economy initiatives to foster the sorts of citizen-neighbor practices I examined in my chapters on ecologies of citizenship. Building partly on Du Bois's notion of abolition democracy, Harcourt argues that harnessing, deepening, and compounding initiatives from credit unions to worker cooperatives can forward what he dubs "cooperation democracy."[7]

Still, a persistent challenge to budget justice lies in building solidarities across geographies. As Du Bois wrote in 1935, the work of abolition democracy cannot be contained in the legal or electoral order of the United States, or any single nation-state. It is international.

> Immediately in Africa, a black back runs red with the blood of the lash; in India, a brown girl is raped; in China, a coolie starves; in Alabama, seven darkies are more than lynched; while in London, the white limbs of a prostitute are hung with jewels and silk. Flames of jealous murder sweep the earth, while brains of little children smear the hills.[8]

And if budget injustice is transnational, then public responses to such injustices must be as well.

I think of how many of New York City's PB ballot items reflect global issues that deserve worldwide as well as local responses. Projects aiming to provide immigrant New Yorkers and asylum seekers with basic supplies, for instance, can sidestep the fact that many people are fleeing armed conflict, persecution, and poverty that is sometimes shaped or even driven by US policy.

And at a small housing workshop I attended over Zoom, activists from New York, Cape Town, Rio de Janeiro, Lisbon, and elsewhere became momentarily speechless—visibly so, even through computer screens—when they realized that they were all fighting the Blackstone investment firm as a landlord in their respective cities.[9]

Many grassroots groups already articulate trenchant critiques of global systems of budget injustice through their local campaigns. Members of Okinawan Women Act Against Military Violence, for example, are Japanese citizens, but they also live the consequences of Japanese and US imperialism, including a long history of sexual assaults by members of the US military stationed there. Through a network called Women for Genuine Security, they work in solidarity with groups in the Philippines, Puerto Rico, and elsewhere to "strategize for economic planning that meets people's needs, especially women and children."[10]

224 BUDGET JUSTICE

And through localized community safety campaigns, they fuse decolonial, antiracist, and feminist framings. In doing so, they "'queer' the nation," as Black studies scholar George Lipsitz writes, "not because they take an explicit position on the rights of gays and lesbians, but because they interrupt and contest the narrative of patriarchal protection upon which the nation-state so often rests."[11]

Such networks show how different cities' struggles against budget injustice are already interconnected internationally, and they model solidarities and self-determination without resorting to nationalism (or other forms of us-versus-them thinking).[12] They reveal how the logics of empire are felt at the local level, and how new democratic experiments and politics incubated in cities can, when networked, reverberate nationwide and worldwide.

———

Besides, public policies and social movement struggles for budget justice cannot be scaled up like sneakers in a fast fashion supply chain, enlisting more factories and distribution networks to meet demand. Nor should they necessarily scale up to the nation-state level when in many contexts, national and federal elections as well as politics arguably contain many of the rotting roots of the current democratic crises, such as rising authoritarianism, loss of public trust, and polarization.

In the framing of ecosystems of participation and ecologies of citizenship I develop in this book, it is better for movements for budget justice to spread through the grass roots, than to solely aspire to congressional or parliamentary halls of power.

This framing—of looking toward the city level as the appropriate one to aim for in terms of socially just public policies—is evidenced by growing global movements of what some scholars call radical or new municipalism. The sanctuary cities movement in the United States, for example, asked city governments to welcome immigrants and asylum seekers, and refuse to carry out deportation orders by federal Immigration and Customs Enforcement. Newer iterations, like that nurtured

EPILOGUE 225

by organizations such as the Solidarity Research Center based in Los Angeles, focus on gaining "democratic control of cities and towns" while "reclaiming the right to the city."[13] The fearless cities movement spearheaded by Barcelona in 2017 likewise revolves around cities as crucial sites of policy contestation and movement building, "introducing novel forms of PB, sortition chambers, associative democracy, public-commons partnerships and techno-democracy."[14] Less formally, many policy innovations relevant to budget justice—like minimum wage legislation—spread across cities before scaling to state or provincial levels.

I used to think of municipalist networks as land-based archipelagoes—havens with social services, cultural spaces, infrastructure, and density to allow diverse peoples to thrive. But examining the dynamics of budget justice, and practices across seemingly siloed invited and invented spaces, has made me better appreciate the permeability and mutability of city borders, despite their violence. Every border wall has its foundation, top, cracks, and formal gates.

And framing cities as a protective archipelago unfairly and inaccurately dismisses the spaces between cities as inevitably treacherous waters. Paying attention to insurgent budgeting has refocused my attention to the less visible connections between seemingly distinct spaces, like the rhizomatic networks of food connecting seemingly unrelated mushroom colonies sprouting up far from each other on the forest floor. Such infrastructures of collective care cross boundaries like people do, and like capital does.

Indeed, the ecologies of citizenship framing I use in this book builds partly on the premise that, as poet John Donne wrote, "No man," no person, "is an island."[15] Nor cities.

Paying attention to the *spaces between* (both within a city and between cities) is strategic. Often this is where the real action is—where struggles for budget justice might not just scale sideways but spark multiplier effects too.

I suspect that just as some of PBNYC's most significant impacts lay in its spillover effects (like compelling city agencies to shift priorities in

226 BUDGET JUSTICE

their much larger, *non*-PB budgets), democratic experiments and policies for budget justice will have greater effects than they first seem to, and in nonlinear ways.

Perhaps they will elicit ripple effects like a pebble in water. Research shows that cities with greater percentages of unionized workers have higher wages for *everyone* there, partly because wage standards in unionized workplaces ripple to nonunionized ones as well.

Or perhaps a campaign for budget justice will elicit snowball effects instead—like a protest by a single street vendor in Tunis, prompting hundreds and then thousands of others during the Arab Spring to call for democratic reforms and sustainable livelihoods.

Or perhaps they can even elicit something akin to a butterfly effect, when the flutter of a butterfly in one part of the world might eventually, with the right wind and climate conditions, cause a storm in another. When I reflected on PB traveling from Porto Alegre to Chicago and New York, then spreading around the United States, this claim felt like a laughable stretch. PB's effects appear to be far-reaching but diffuse, and sometimes even "the worst."

But when I reflect on PB in the context of larger ecosystems of participation, I am forced to reconsider how, around the country, different communities are reinvigorating PB to meet the post-2020 political moment in potentially redemptive, radical, and rigorous ways. The murder of Floyd brought millions of people in the United States and beyond to protest police brutality, and the COVID-19 pandemic mobilized neighbors from around the world to organize themselves in thousands of mutual aid collectives, sometimes sending masks and protective equipment halfway around the globe. Since 2020, these different movements for budget justice have continued to ebb and flow, sometimes ending or splitting into factions, but sometimes combining and gathering force as people's budgets campaigns and coalitions.

So I revisit my butterfly analogy. I can't imagine the welcome storm of budget justice as the effect of one butterfly, but I could imagine it as the effect of a hundred—especially given that sometimes, as in 2020, the surrounding winds gather and change. Porto Alegre's PB process is just one butterfly, but PB has spread to thousands of cities around the world. And in many cities, PB is just one democratic experiment among many for budget justice—alongside people's movement assemblies, mutual aid groups, coordinated antieviction and affordable housing collectives, and so many other initiatives. Given diverse democratic struggles and experiments happening at the same time, and given global networks of activists and policymakers working in solidarity, one could imagine that the storm of budget justice is still gathering force, and requires thousands of butterfly-like struggles to poise and flutter their wings.

Whether rippling, snowballing, or butterflying, multiplier effects depend on the ecosystem of participation at hand. By scaling sideways across cities, budget justice campaigns can better weave such multiplier effects into their strategizing and ecologies of transnational citizenship.

———

PB's diffusion from a policy that dramatically reduced poverty and infant mortality in Porto Alegre to an exercise dubbed "the worst" in my New York City neighborhood serves as a reminder and rejoinder, yet again, that no foolproof blueprint exists for budget justice. But even as my heart sank, even the social media post that "participatory budgeting is the worst" reflects a righteous refusal of the status quo, and to instead reach for something better. This also confirmed my suspicions that even "the best" democratic institutions are only as good as their current practice.

Because scaling sideways takes time, and because democratic practice never ends, it is imperative that struggles for budget justice be ready for the long haul. This means that the three points of analysis and practice at the heart of this book—to bear witness to budgets as moral documents, traverse multiple political spaces in ecosystems of participation, and cooperate on new ways to adjudicate public resources through ecologies of citizenship—are imperative to not only win campaigns and build new institutions of accountability, but also reap intermediary rewards and successes, build camaraderie, and lend a sense of dignity in the meantime . . . just enough for citizens to keep going.

By scaling sideways rather than up, experiments in and struggles for budget justice can continue to serve as experimental and fertile fields, schools, and laboratories of democracy. When citizens get into the muck of democracy themselves rather than leaving deep participation to professional lobbyists or campaigners—whether through PB, an antieviction stoop watch, a worker cooperative, another activity, or all of the above—and when they can reject logics of competition in favor of cooperation, they become better equipped to protect themselves from inevitable burnout, backlash from countermovements, disinformation, and infighting.

By practicing grassroots politics and solidarities, citizen-neighbors shift from serving as competing constituencies or voting blocs to become a new sort of public, more capable of articulating policies for the good of the public and pressing the provision of public goods, even after mass protests like those in 2020 have waned.

———

I turn back to my budget justice as democratic practice, and democratic practice as collective play, as in music or sports: practice does not quite make perfect because the conditions and teammates or bandmates will change, but practice certainly makes better. Every drill—whether in playing musical scales or passing a ball—counts. These practices must be built with care, but are much more flexible than, say, elections, with their laws and calendars. They are the political equivalents of pickup basketball games and drum circles in the park.

This sort of democratic work is also sustenance. It feels less lonely than attempting to navigate the affordability crisis on my own and less dispiriting than attending to the last crisis. With an ever-changing cast of citizen-neighbors from around the world as teammates, I try to keep my democratic knees bent and my feet shoulder-width apart on the ground, contingencies articulated. Willing to go out on a limb, to try something new, to engage in conjecture. Knowing that political conditions will never be perfect, I practice the political equivalents of musical scales and ball dribbles in anticipation of the next cycle, the next big performance, the next match, to have the strategy, collective strength,

EPILOGUE   229

flexibility, and endurance to meet the conditions at hand, primed for conjuncture, an opportune moment in critical times.

————

In what she calls "transboundary self-determination," legal scholar Harum Mukhayer writes of communities riven through by the nation-states of borders. In these communities, residents regularly cross national borders in order to attend school, go to work, or go shopping. They live in this way despite the fact that their rights to do so are not technically enshrined in international law, but instead enacted as if they are. Their daily commutes are, to me, an international expression of policy lines of desire.

Likewise, citizens struggling to enact a right to the city and achieve budget justice must sharpen their analyses, their collaborations and generative conflicts, their direct actions, and their modes of holding government and each other accountable. In other words, to make budget justice real, citizens must first delineate and prove possible alternative ways of engaging in urban governance, rendering and enacting *the city as if.*

ACKNOWLEDGMENTS

DEMOCRATIC PRACTICE is not just the subject of this book; *Budget Justice* was born out of collective thinking and action. I hope that this book serves as an invitation to continue the conversations that have nurtured me so much.

The urgent and incisive questions of those on the ground, doing the grunt work of democratic politics on a daily basis, galvanized me to write this book. I learned so much from those I met through the New York participatory budgeting process, especially Josh Lerner, Erin Markman, Caron Atlas, Alexa Kasdan, and Melissa Appleton. I want to thank those at the New York City Participatory Budgeting Steering Committee and Advisory Council, Community Voices Heard, New York City Council, Civic Engagement Commission, district 39 committee, and dozens of grassroots organizers who, every single day, under difficult conditions, work to make local policies more just and policy-making more democratic. Thank you to Carolin Hagelskamp, David Schleifer, Shahana Hanif, and Sabina Unni for our writing collaborations on the New York process, and to everyone on the Participatory Budgeting New York City research board (especially H. Jacob Carlson, Isaac Jabola-Carolus, Ron Hayduk, Carolina Johnson, Sonya Reynolds, and Rachel Swaner) for our discussions on and joint efforts in critical participatory action research. I feel incredibly lucky to be working with Zara Nasir with the People's Plan and Kesi Foster, who both seem to possess inimitably analytic bifocals, always seeing the long game as well as urgent needs.

Over time, this work connected me with practitioners and scholars around the country and the world. I am grateful for the critical insights of current as well as former staff and research boards at the Participatory

232   ACKNOWLEDGMENTS

Budgeting Project and People Powered: Global Hub for Participatory Democracy.

I have had the fortune to present parts of this project in a number of forums, and benefit from the questions and feedback of event organizers and others in attendance at the Harvard Kennedy School Ash Center for Democratic Governance and Innovation Seminar (with special thanks to Ashley Nickels, Archon Fung, Peter Levine, and Christopher Ojeda), City University of New York (CUNY) Graduate Center Political Theory Workshop (with special thanks to Mette Christiansen and Michael Villanova), International Observatory on Participatory Democracy, AGITATE! Unsettling Knowledges workshop at the University of Minnesota, Sasha Seminar for Human Concerns at Wesleyan University, American Political Science Association Institute for Civically Engaged Research at Tufts University, New Taipei City Legislative Yuan, University of Colorado at Boulder, Urban Affairs Association, Interpretive Policy Analysis, International Sociological Association, and Society for the Advancement of Socio-economics. Helena Najm, George Nakkas, and Amala Vattappally provided invaluable research assistance.

This work also benefited from feedback from my writing group focused on organizations and collective action, consisting of Katherine Chen, Howard Lune, James Mandiberg, and Jacqueline Olvera; Deb Chasman, Matt Lord, and Hannah Liberman at the *Boston Review*, and Emily Cooke at the *New Republic*; and Althea Wasow and Ramsey Mc-Glazer of the Abolition as Form and Practice working group. My heartfelt thanks go to Alisa Algava, Sarah Atwood, Maddy Fox, Ingrid Haftel, Erika Iverson, Krystal Languell, Tina Law, Noelle Mapes, Ann Brian Murphy, and Sam Stein, who provided feedback on substantial portions or the entirety of the manuscript.

I am grateful for the intellect and camaraderie of so many at Brooklyn College and the Graduate Center at CUNY, URBAN Research Network, and beyond: Dayna Cunningham, Michelle Fine, Ruth Wilson Gilmore, Cindi Katz, Ben Lerner, Lize Mogel, Richa Nagar, Alissa Quart, Mary Taylor, Jeanne Theoharis, J. Phillip Thompson, and Mark

Ungar. Whether through invitations to think out loud in vulnerable ways, regular check-ins, or singular conversations, your wisdom and encouragement carried me through and broadened my thinking on radical imaginaries. My colleagues and students at CUNY have taught me a lot about the role that public institutions must play in the making of truly just cities, for which I am thankful.

My parent-scholar writing group, especially Kendra Sullivan, Caroline Loomis, and Bonnie Ip, got me through by providing unparalleled understanding and problem-solving on an almost weekly basis. I am grateful for conversations on parent-citizen subjectivities, of trying to be decent parents of growing, spirited, decent kid citizens of the world, with Mirene Arsanios, Annie Baker, Farnoosh Hashemian, Henry Lam, and Brynn Wallace. Thank you to Diane Wong and Wah-Ming Chang for our collaborations during the pandemic, which informed my thinking on Asian American subjectivities.

I am indebted to Stephanie Steiker, my agent, and Bridget Flannery-McCoy, my editor at Princeton University Press and now Grove/Atlantic, for championing this book from inception to fruition. At Princeton, thanks also to Alena Chekanov, Eric Crahan, Theresa Liu, and Dave McBride. This book also benefited greatly from Cindy Milstein's copyedits. Thank you to the three readers of the book manuscript, whose insightful suggestions galvanized me to improve this manuscript in substantive ways and get to the finish line.

My gratitude goes to Sara Miller McCune and the SAGE Foundation, whose support of the Gittell Collective at the CUNY Graduate Center enabled me to practice public scholarship and participatory research in newly generative ways. This research was made possible in part with funding from the American Academy in Berlin, Economic Hardship Reporting Project, Tow Foundation, CUNY Graduate Center Advanced Research Collaborative, and PSC-CUNY Research Grants.

Hundreds of unnamed community organizers, activists, civil servants, and neighbors shared their time, creative energies, and critical reflections on their political experiences, for which I feel immensely honored and grateful.

234 ACKNOWLEDGMENTS

Earlier and different iterations of portions of the book appear in the *Boston Review, New Republic, New Political Science,* and *Nonprofit and Voluntary Sector Quarterly.*

This book, with all of its limitations that remain mine alone, would not have been possible without each person listed here. Some of you have supported me in so many different ways that I could have listed your name again and again. Still, this list is only a beginning. To those whom I have failed to mention, I am sorry, and remain deeply grateful for your insights and our encounters.

I am profoundly thankful for the love and support of my family, Alex Su, Caleb Su, Ellen Blinder, and Russell Blinder. Of Althea, with your fierce intelligence and care. Of my mother, Christina Su, who has passed but still serves as a foundational example of what it means to act selflessly, with conviction and dignity, every day. And of my partner, Justin Blinder, who remains my most resolute ally, and my child, Åstra, who continually enables me to see the world anew. I am so lucky to get to be with you in this project called life.

NOTES

Prologue: Linchpins of Solidarities

1. Lisa Lowe, *Immigrant Acts: On Asian American Cultural Politics* (Duke University Press, 1996).

2. Here I capitalize "White" to underscore that it not a racially neutral term; Whiteness as a racial identity is as much of a political project as Blackness, Asian Americanness, and other social constructs. I am grateful for the discussion in Nell Irvin Painter, "Why 'White' Should Be Capitalized, Too," *Washington Post*, July 22, 2020, sec. Opinion, https://www.washingtonpost.com/opinions/2020/07/22/why-white-should-be-capitalized/.

3. Claire Jean Kim, "The Racial Triangulation of Asian Americans," *Politics & Society* 27, no. 1 (1999): 105–38.

4. Wen Liu, *Feeling Asian American: Racial Flexibility between Assimilation and Oppression* (University of Illinois Press, 2024); Edward Wyatt, "At Ground Zero, a New Divide; Some of 9/11's Neediest Get the Least Government Aid," *New York Times*, June 5, 2002, sec. New York, https://www.nytimes.com/2002/06/05/nyregion/at-ground-zero-a-new-divide-some-of-9-11-s-neediest-get-the-least-government-aid.html; Eveline Chao, "The Forgotten Neighborhood: How New York's Chinatown Survived 9/11 to Face a New Crisis," *Guardian*, September 5, 2021, sec. US News, https://www.theguardian.com/us-news/2021/sep/05/new-york-chinatown-11-september-covid-19-crisis.

5. Rob Nixon, *Slow Violence and the Environmentalism of the Poor* (Harvard University Press, 2011).

6. Rebecca Klar, "Navajo Nation Reports More Coronavirus Cases per Capita than Any US State," *Hill*, May 11, 2020, https://thehill.com/policy/healthcare/497091-navajo-nation-has-more-coronavirus-cases-per-capita-than-any-us-state/.

7. Donovan Quintero, "The COVID-19 Outbreak in the Navajo Nation," *American Indian Magazine*, 2021, https://www.americanindianmagazine.org/story/the-covid-19-outbreak-in-the-navajo-nation.

8. Ruth Wilson Gilmore, *Golden Gulag: Prisons, Surplus, Crisis, and Opposition in Globalizing California* (University of California Press, 2007), 28.

9. Katie Rogers, Lara Jakes, and Ana Swanson, "Trump Defends Using 'Chinese Virus' Label, Ignoring Growing Criticism," *New York Times*, March 18, 2020.

10. A 2017 Urban Institute report cites that noncitizen Asian immigrant women account for 87 percent of arrests for unlicensed massage, partly because many find licenses prohibitively difficult to obtain.

11. Quoted in Eithne Luibhéid, *Entry Denied: Controlling Sexuality at the Border* (University of Minnesota Press, 2002), 37.

NOTES TO INTRODUCTION

Introduction: Budgeting Justice

1. Larry Buchanan, Quoctrung Bui, and Jugal K. Patel, "Black Lives Matter May Be the Largest Movement in U.S. History," *New York Times*, July 3, 2020, https://www.nytimes.com/interactive/2020/07/03/us/george-floyd-protests-crowd-size.html.

2. Quoted in Stefanos Chen, "New York's Millionaire Class Is Growing. Other People Are Leaving," *New York Times*, December 5, 2023, sec. New York, https://www.nytimes.com/2023/12/05/nyregion/nyc-working-class-tax-rich.html.

3. Eliza Shapiro, Asmaa Elkeurti, and Maansi Srivastava, "How Soaring Child Care Costs Are Crushing New Yorkers," *New York Times*, September 11, 2023, sec. New York, https://www.nytimes.com/2023/09/11/nyregion/child-care-nyc.html.

4. New York City Comptroller Brad Lander et al., *New York by the Numbers: Monthly Economic and Fiscal Outlook*, January 15, 2025, https://comptroller.nyc.gov/newsroom/newsletter/new-york-by-the-numbers-monthly-economic-and-fiscal-outlook-no-97-january-15-2025/.

5. Molly Dickens and Lucy Hutner, "What the Child Care Crisis Does to Parents," *New York Times*, January 16, 2024, sec. Opinion, https://www.nytimes.com/2024/01/16/opinion/child-care-parenting-stress.html.

6. Editorial Staff, "This Is How Much Child Care Costs in 2024," *Care*, January 17, 2024, https://www.care.com/c/how-much-does-child-care-cost/.

7. Brooke Reilly, "Loss of Federal Funding Raises Concerns for Some Child Care Centers," Spectrum News 1, October 5, 2023, https://spectrumlocalnews.com/nys/central-ny/news/2023/10/05/expiration-of-federal-funds-threatens-child-care-centers.

8. Chen, "New York's Millionaire Class Is Growing."

9. Emily Eisner and Andrew Perry, *Who Is Leaving New York State?* (Fiscal Policy Institute, 2023), https://fiscalpolicy.org/wp-content/uploads/2023/12/FPI-Who-is-Leaving-Full-Report-Dec-2023.pdf.

10. As discussed in Matthias Lecoq, "The Right to the City: An Emancipating Concept?," trans. Oliver Waine, *Metropolitics*, March 7, 2020, https://metropolitics.org/The-Right-to-the-City-An-Emancipating-Concept.html.

11. Samar Khurshid, "Effort to 'Defund the NYPD' Appears Stalled Ahead of De Blasio's Final Budget," *Gotham Gazette*, August 6, 2021, https://www.gothamgazette.com/city/10549-defund-the-nypd-stalled-de-blasio-final-budget-gun-violence.

12. New York City Council, "Speaker Corey Johnson, Finance Committee Chair Daniel Dromm, and Capital Budget Subcommittee Chair Vanessa Gibson Announce Agreement on FY 2021 Budget," June 20, 2020, https://council.nyc.gov/press/2020/06/30/1999/.

13. Among other works that use the same analogy, see Josh Lerner, "From Waves to Ecosystems: The Next Stage of Democratic Innovation," University of Delaware, Stavros Niarchos Foundation Initiative, 2024, https://udspace.udel.edu/items/95bf3dbb-9990-483c-9040-197f42060df1; Hans Asenbaum, "Beyond Deliberative Systems: Pluralizing the Debate," *Democratic Theory* 9, no. 1 (2022): 87–98.

14. Lichens are conventionally called a species, but they are actually colonies (neighborhoods?) of two or three species of different ancestral lineages living together. Here I draw inspiration from Anna Lowenhaupt Tsing, *The Mushroom at the End of the World: On the Possibility of Life in Capitalist Ruins* (Princeton University Press, 2021).

NOTES TO CHAPTER 1   237

15. Stephanie McNulty, "Embedded Exclusions: Exploring Gender Equality in Peru's Participatory Democratic Framework," *Global Discourse* 8, no. 3 (2018): 532–49; Brian Wampler, Stephanie McNulty, and Michael Touchton, *Participatory Budgeting in Global Perspective* (Oxford University Press, 2021).

16. Alexa Kasdan and Erin Markman, *A People's Budget: Cycle 4: Key Research Findings* (Urban Justice Center Community Development Project, 2015).

17. Carolina Johnson, H. Jacob Carlson, and Sonya Reynolds, "Testing the Participation Hypothesis: Evidence from Participatory Budgeting," *Political Behavior* (2021): 1–30.

18. Gianpaolo Baiocchi and Ernesto Ganuza, "Participatory Budgeting as if Emancipation Mattered," *Politics & Society* 42, no. 1 (2014): 29–50; Jamie Peck and Nik Theodore, *Fast Policy* (University of Minnesota Press, 2015).

19. Stuart Hall, "Race, Articulation, and Societies Structured in Dominance," in *Black British Cultural Studies*, ed. Houston A. Baker, Manthia Diawara, and Ruth H. Lindeborg (University of Chicago Press, 1996), 55.

20. William Edward Burghardt Du Bois, *Black Reconstruction in America: Toward a History of the Part Which Black Folk Played in the Attempt to Reconstruct Democracy in America, 1860–1880* (Free Press, 1998).

21. Harsha Walia, *Undoing Border Imperialism* (AK Press, 2013), 249.

Chapter 1: Moral Documents

1. "Testimony of New York City Comptroller Brad Lander to the New York City Council Committee on Education on Resolution 283-2022 to Immediately Reverse DOE Reductions to School Budgets for FY 2023," New York City Comptroller Brad Lander, August 22, 2022, https:// comptroller.nyc.gov/newsroom/testimony-of-new-york-city-comptroller-brad-lander-to-the -new-york-city-council-committee-on-education-on-resolution-283-2022-to-immediately -reverse-doe-reductions-to-school-budgets-for-fy-2023/.

2. Jessica Gould, "NYC Schools Are Facing Larger Cuts than Adams Administration Detailed," *Gothamist*, July 7, 2022, https://gothamist.com/news/nyc-schools-are-facing-larger-cuts -than-adams-administration-detailed.

3. Alex Zimmerman, "Eric Adams Is Facing Pressure to Reverse NYC School Budget Cuts. Should He?," *Chalkbeat*, August 4, 2022, https://www.chalkbeat.org/newyork/2022/8/4 /23292221/eric-adams-nyc-school-budget-cuts-explainer/.

4. Gould, "NYC Schools Are Facing Larger Cuts."

5. Shantel Destra, "How One Brooklyn School Is Coping with Coming Budget Cuts— Painfully," *City*, June 26, 2022, https://www.thecity.nyc/2022/06/26/brooklyn-middle-school -budget-cuts/.

6. Samar Khurshid, "Mayor Adams and City Council Announce Deal on $101 Billion NYC Budget," *Gotham Gazette*, June 10, 2022, https://www.gothamgazette.com/city/11376-mayor -adams-council-speaker-adams-nyc-budget-deal-fy23.

7. "Testimony of New York City Comptroller Brad Lander."

8. Alex Zimmerman, "NYC School Bus Delays Reach Highest Level in Five Years, City Council Analysis Shows," *Chalkbeat*, November 21, 2022, https://www.chalkbeat.org/newyork /2022/11/21/23472253/nyc-school-bus-delay/.

238   NOTES TO CHAPTER 1

9. Liz Donovan and Fazil Khan, "The Pandemic Robbed Thousands of NYC Children of Parents. Many Aren't Getting the Help They Need," THE CITY, January 26, 2023, https://www.thecity.nyc/2023/01/26/thousands-nyc-children-whose-parent-died-from-covid-need-help/.

10. "A How-To Guide for Making Sense of Your City's Budget," Strong Towns, July 29, 2020, https://www.strongtowns.org/journal/2020/7/23/a-how-to-guide-for-making-sense-of-your-citys-budget.

11. Steve Hendershot, "The Making of Chicago's Fiscal Mess," University of Chicago Center for Effective Government, March 6, 2023, https://effectivegov.uchicago.edu/news/the-making-of-chicagos-fiscal-mess.

12. Fresnoland, "Fresno's Budget Subcommittee Doesn't Meet in Public. It's a 'Major Problem,' Legal Experts Say," GVWire, August 4, 2023, https://gvwire.com/2023/08/24/fresnos-budget-subcommittee-doesnt-meet-in-public-its-a-major-problem-legal-experts-say/.

13. Leonard Burman and Elaine Maag, "The Effect of the 2001 Tax Cut on Low- and Middle-Income Families and Children," Urban Institute, April 29, 2002, https://www.urban.org/research/publication/effect-2001-tax-cut-low-and-middle-income-families-and-children.

14. Jamie Peck, "Austerity Urbanism: American Cities under Extreme Economy," City 16, no. 6 (December 2012): 629, https://doi.org/10.1080/13604813.2012.734071.

15. See the dataset at "Open Book State Contracts, New York," Office of the State Comptroller, n.d., https://wwe2.osc.state.ny.us/transparency/contracts/contractsearch.cfm; "Testimony to the CUNY Board of Trustees in Opposition to the Resolution to Approve a Contract with Turnitin for Plagiarism Detection Software, December 14th, 2020 Meeting," CUNY Academic Works, December 3, 2020, https://academicworks.cuny.edu/gc_pubs/670/.

16. "Testimony to the CUNY Board of Trustees," 1.

17. "Testimony of New York City Comptroller Brad Lander on NYC's FY 2024 Preliminary Budget and FY 2023–2027 Financial Plan," New York City Comptroller Brad Lander, March 6, 2023, https://comptroller.nyc.gov/newsroom/testimony-of-new-york-city-comptroller-brad-lander-on-nycs-fy-2024-preliminary-budget-and-fy-2023-2027-financial-plan/.

18. "Statement from NYC Comptroller Brad Lander on the FY25 Adopted Budget," New York City Comptroller Brad Lander, June 28, 2024, https://comptroller.nyc.gov/newsroom/statement-from-nyc-comptroller-brad-lander-on-the-fy25-adopted-budget/.

19. Kim Phillips-Fein, Fear City: New York's Fiscal Crisis and the Rise of Austerity Politics (Metropolitan Books, 2017), 28.

20. For popular coverage of relevant research, see, for example, Libby Nelson, "The Biggest Benefit of Pre-K Might Not Be Education," Vox, July 30, 2014, https://www.vox.com/2014/7/30/5952739/the-research-on-how-pre-k-could-reduce-crime; Julien Lafortune, Understanding the Effects of School Funding (Public Policy Institute of California, May 2022), https://www.ppic.org/publication/understanding-the-effects-of-school-funding/.

21. Here, care ("first-aid") is conflated with policing ("pistols") and "budget cuts," to awful effect. In my mind, "more casual more indifference" echoes not only "mere casualties" but also "causal inference" from statistical models. Zoë Hitzig, Mezzanine: Poems (HarperCollins, 2020), 37.

Chapter 2: Flip the Gaze

1. Hunter Walker, "Mayor Bloomberg: 'I Have My Own Army,'" *New York Observer*, November 30, 2011, https://observer.com/2011/11/mayor-bloomberg-i-have-my-own-army-11-30-11/.

2. Public Service Project, "The Morris Justice Project: A Summary of Our Findings," 2013, https://morrisjustice.org/reports/.

3. Kim Phillips-Fein, *Fear City: New York's Fiscal Crisis and the Rise of Austerity Politics* (Metropolitan Books, 2017), 28; Corey Kilgannon, "N.Y.P.D. Anti-Crime Units Stopping People Illegally, Report Shows," *New York Times*, June 5, 2023, https://www.nytimes.com/2023/06/05/nyregion/nypd-anti-crime-units-training-tactics.html.

4. Guilherme Guerreiro, "Counting Cash in the City Controller Contest," *Crosstown LA*, November 7, 2022, https://xtown.la/2022/11/07/city-controller-fundraising-los-angeles-kenneth-mejia-paul-koretz/.

5. Kenneth Mejia (@kennethmejiaLA), "WHAT?!?! Where did this billboard come from telling all of Los Angeles where our budget priorities are?! ...," Twitter, August 23, 2022, https://x.com/kennethmejiaLA/status/1562122364006981637.

6. Mejia, "WHAT?!?! Where did this billboard come from ... "

7. Florence C. Sharp, Frances H. Carpenter, and Robert F. Sharp. "Popular Financial Reports for Citizens," *CPA Journal* 68, no. 3 (1998): 34.

8. "January 2023 Financial Plan, Fiscal Years 2023–2027," NYC Mayor's Office of Management and Budget, January 2023, https://www.nyc.gov/site/omb/publications/finplan01-23.page.

9. Rachel Bardin and Charles Brecher, "A PEG by Any Other Name Would Smell as Sweet," Citizens Budget Commission, April 19, 2015, https://cbcny.org/research/peg-any-other-name-would-smell-sweet.

10. *The City of New York Preliminary Budget Fiscal Year 2024: Expense Revenue Contract* (Mayor's Office of Management and Budget, n.d.), 15E, https://www.nyc.gov/assets/omb/downloads/pdf/perc1-23.pdf.

11. *The City of New York Preliminary Budget Fiscal Year 2024*, 149E.

12. *The City of New York Preliminary Budget Fiscal Year 2024*, 29E.

13. Safiya Umoja Noble, *Algorithms of Oppression: How Search Engines Reinforce Racism* (NYU Press, 2018), https://nyupress.org/9781479837243/algorithms-of-oppression/.

14. Samar Khurshid, "New Analysis Details Just How Late and Over-Budget City Infrastructure Projects Run," *Gotham Gazette*, September 14, 2021, https://www.gothamgazette.com/city/10760-new-york-city-infrastructure-projects-late-over-budget.

15. Paulina Cachero, "Student Debt Is Up 2,807% since Supreme Court Justices Graduated," *Bloomberg Law*, January 3, 2023, https://news.bloomberglaw.com/us-law-week/student-debt-is-up-2-807-since-supreme-court-justices-graduated.

16. For a glimpse at popular debates, see news stories such as Jeff Stein, "Biden Student Debt Plan Fuels Broader Debate over Forgiving Borrowers," *Washington Post*, August 31, 2022, https://www.washingtonpost.com/us-policy/2022/08/31/student-debt-biden-forgiveness/.

17. Cassidy McCants, "Comparing the Costs of Generations," *Consumer Affairs*, June 1, 2023, https://www.consumeraffairs.com/finance/comparing-the-costs-of-generations.html.

240 NOTES TO CHAPTER 3

18. In *Discipline and Punish*, Foucault asks why he aims to write a history of modern prisons: "Simply because I am interested in the past? No, if one means by that writing a history of the past in terms of the present. Yes, if one means writing the history of the present." Michel Foucault, *Discipline and Punish: The Birth of the Prison* (Pantheon, 1977), 31.

19. Brad Plumer and Nadja Popovich, "How Decades of Racist Housing Policy Left Neighborhoods Sweltering," *New York Times*, August 24, 2020, https://www.nytimes.com/interactive/2020/08/24/climate/racism-redlining-cities-global-warming.html.

20. Richard Rothstein, *The Color of Law: A Forgotten History of How Our Government Segregated America* (Liveright Publishing Corporation, 2017); Adam Paul Susaneck, "Segregation by Design," Segregation by Design, n.d., https://www.segregationbydesign.com/.

21. Plumer and Popovich, "How Decades of Racist Housing Policy Left Neighborhoods Sweltering."

22. K-Sue Park, "Race, Innovation, and Financial Growth: The Example of Foreclosure," in *Histories of Racial Capitalism*, ed. Justin Leroy and Destin Jenkins (Columbia University Press, 2021), 31, 40, https://doi.org/10.7312/jenk19074-003.

23. Claire Schwartz, *Civil Service* (Graywolf Press, 2022), 27.

Chapter 3: Follow the Money

1. Juita-Elena Yusuf, Meagan M. Jordan, Katharine A. Neill, and Merl Hackbart, "For the People: Popular Financial Reporting Practices of Local Governments," *Public Budgeting & Finance* 33, no. 1 (2013): 95–113. I thank Ellen Haustein profusely for pointing me to especially helpful articles in this literature.

2. Checkbook NYC, accessed November 29, 2024, www.checkbooknyc.com.

3. "NYC Funds Tracker," FPWA, accessed October 9, 2024, https://www.fpwa.org/nycfundstracker/.

4. *2021–22 Budget Summary* (City of Los Angeles, June 2, 2021), 5, https://cao.lacity.gov/budget/summary/2021-22BudgetSummaryBooklet.pdf.

5. *City of Los Angeles FY 22–23 Proposed Budget* (City of Los Angeles, April 2022), https://cao.lacity.gov/budget22-23/2022-23Proposed_Budget.pdf.

6. "Measuring NYC Government Performance," Office of the New York City Comptroller Brad Lander, accessed October 9, 2024, https://comptroller.nyc.gov/services/for-the-public/measuring-nyc-government-performance/agencies/.

7. Sergio Hernandez, "Looking Up an NYPD Officer's Discipline Record? Many Are There One Day, Gone the Next," *ProPublica*, May 9, 2024, https://www.propublica.org/article/nypd-police-displicine-records-database-accountability-misconduct.

8. Derek Willis, Eric Umansky, and Moiz Syed, "The NYPD Files: Search Thousands of Civilian Complaints against New York City Police Officers," *ProPublica*, July 26, 2020, https://projects.propublica.org/nypd-ccrb/. Another such database is 50-a.org, a website without public authorship or attribution information, but with clear source codes, named after the 1976 New York Civil Rights Law that concealed police disciplinary records from the public. This was repealed by Governor Andrew Cuomo in 2020.

NOTES TO CHAPTER 3   241

9. See, for example, Robert Steuteville, "The Value of Walkability and Walk Score Inaccuracies," *Congress for the New Urbanism*, September 16, 2016, https://www.cnu.org/publicsquare/2016/09/19/value-walkability-and-walk-score-inaccuracies.

10. "Fiscally Standardized Cities," Lincoln Institute on Land Policy, n.d., https://www.lincolninst.edu/research-data/data-toolkits/fiscally-standardized-cities.

11. Emily Badger and Quoctrung Bui, "Cities Grew Safer. Police Budgets Kept Growing," *New York Times*, June 12, 2020, https://www.nytimes.com/interactive/2020/06/12/upshot/cities-grew-safer-police-budgets-kept-growing.html.

12. John Gramlich, "What the Data Says about Crime in the U.S.," Pew Research Center, April 24, 2024, https://www.pewresearch.org/short-reads/2024/04/24/what-the-data-says-about-crime-in-the-us/.

13. Ruth Wilson Gilmore, *Golden Gulag: Prisons, Surplus, Crisis, and Opposition in Globalizing California* (University of California Press, 2007), 20.

14. Ellora Derenoncourt (@EDerenoncourt), "My study of northern backlash against the Great Migration has no policy prescription, but it has a smoking gun. Police are the only public investment to increase in metro areas w/ more black migration. Good faith pursuit of racial justice starts by questioning this institution," Twitter, May 30, 2020, https://twitter.com/ederenoncourt/status/1266741876897583105; Ellora Derenoncourt, "Can You Move to Opportunity? Evidence from the Great Migration," *American Economic Review* 112, no. 2 (February 2022): 369–408, https://doi.org/10.1257/aer.20200002.

15. Elizabeth Hinton, *From the War on Poverty to the War on Crime: The Making of Mass Incarceration in America* (Harvard University Press, 2017), 70.

16. Mapping Police Violence, accessed October 9, 2024, https://mappingpoliceviolence.us.

17. Peter Marcuse, "The Targeted Crisis: On the Ideology of the Urban Fiscal Crisis and Its Causes," *International Journal of Urban and Regional Research* 5, no. 3 (1981): 339.

18. Benjamin Holtzman, *The Long Crisis: New York City and the Path to Neoliberalism* (Oxford University Press, 2021).

19. Kim Phillips-Fein, *Fear City: New York's Fiscal Crisis and the Rise of Austerity Politics* (Metropolitan Books, 2017), 161, 67–68, 147.

20. Phillips-Fein, *Fear City*, 182.

21. Phillips-Fein, *Fear City*, 313.

22. For a primer on federal revenue sharing in the United States, see Mary Schulz, "State and Local Fiscal Assistance Act of 1972," Michigan State University, May 4, 2021, https://www.canr.msu.edu/news/state-and-local-fiscal-assistance-act-of-1972.

23. "Researchers: Flint's Fertility Rates Fell, Fetal Death Rates Climbed during Water Crisis," Internet Archive, September 20, 2017, https://web.archive.org/web/20170921000219/http://www.abc12.com/content/news/Researchers-Flints-fertility-rates-fell-fetal-death-rates-climbed-during-water-crisis-446109953.html.

24. Laura Pulido, "Flint, Environmental Racism, and Racial Capitalism," *Capitalism Nature Socialism* 27, no. 3 (July 2, 2016): 2, https://doi.org/10.1080/10455752.2016.1213013.

25. "NYC Comptroller Audit Exposes Major Management Gaps in Intensive Mobile Treatment (IMT) for New Yorkers with Severe Mental Health Challenges," Office of the New York City Comptroller Brad Lander, February 7, 2024, https://comptroller.nyc.gov/newsroom/nyc

-comptroller-audit-exposes-major-management-gaps-in-intensive-mobile-treatment-imt-for-new-yorkers-with-severe-mental-health-challenges/.

26. Megan Rose Dickey, "San Francisco's School District Budget Crisis," *Axios San Francisco*, May 9, 2024, https://www.axios.com/local/san-francisco/2024/05/09/sf-school-board-budget-crisis.

27. Allyson Aleksey, "SFUSD Finds an $8.8 Million Solution to a $13.7 Million Problem," *San Francisco Examiner*, December 13, 2022, https://www.sfexaminer.com/news/sfusd-finds-an-8-8-million-solution-to-a-13-7-million-problem/article_5712fe68-7b1a-11ed-85cf-9f589593035a.html.

28. "San Francisco Unified School District Set to Scrap Old Payroll System after Numerous Issues," *CBS News*, March 4, 2024, https://www.cbsnews.com/sanfrancisco/news/sfusd-school-district-scraps-empowersf-payroll-system-numerous-issues/.

29. Michael H. Fine, *Fiscal Health Risk Analysis for the San Francisco County Office of Education* (Fiscal Crisis and Management Assistance Team, April 26, 2024), https://go.boarddocs.com/ca/sfusd/Board.nsf/files/D4Q3CF06352F/$file/San%20Francisco%20COE%20FHRA%20final%20report.pdf.

30. James E. Alt, David Dreyer Lassen, and David Skilling, "Fiscal Transparency, Gubernatorial Approval, and the Scale of Government: Evidence from the States," *State Politics & Policy Quarterly* 2, no. 3 (2002): 230–50.

31. Rae Armantrout, *Money Shot* (Wesleyan University Press, 2012), 73.

32. Phillips-Fein, *Fear City*, 139.

33. Phillips-Fein, *Fear City*, 139.

34. Abraham Maslow, *The Psychology of Science: A Reconnaisance* (Harper & Row, 1966), 15–16.

Chapter 4: Austerity for Profit

1. J. E. Stiglitz, *Globalization and Its Discontents* (W. W. Norton, 2002). The country was not dealing with inflation; its macroeconomic indicators were all sound. But still, the IMF wanted the country to deregulate its financial markets in ways originally designed to control inflation, and objected to Ethiopia paying off other loans early and saving on interest. In terms of governance, the IMF is supposed to represent all of its member countries, but traditionally, the director has always been a European citizen, while the World Bank has historically been led by a US citizen. Countries in the Global South continue to resist not only such one-size-fits-all policies but also the deeply undemocratic ways in which they unfurled in the first place. The so-called antiglobalization protests prominent in the 1990s and early 2000s demanded a debt jubilee.

2. Allyson Aleksey, "SFUSD Finds an $8.8 Million Solution to a $13.7 Million Problem," *San Francisco Examiner*, December 13, 2022, https://www.sfexaminer.com/news/sfusd-finds-an-8-8-million-solution-to-a-13-7-million-problem/article_5712fe68-7b1a-11ed-85cf-9f589593035a.html; Lena Afridi, "People over Police—New York City Needs Budget Equity," ANHD, June 4, 2020, https://anhd.org/blog/people-over-police-new-york-city-needs-budget-equity.

3. "NYPD Overspending on Overtime Grew Dramatically in Recent Years," New York City Comptroller Brad Lander, March 20, 2023, https://comptroller.nyc.gov/newsroom/nypd-overspending-on-overtime-grew-dramatically-in-recent-years/.

NOTES TO CHAPTER 4   243

4. Emma G. Fitzsimmons, "3-K for All? Adams Retreats from Expanding N.Y.C. Preschool Program," *New York Times*, September 22, 2022, https://www.nytimes.com/2022/09/22/nyregion/prekindergarten-adams-nyc-3k.html.

5. Libby Nelson, "The Biggest Benefit of Pre-K Might Not Be Education," *Vox*, July 30, 2014, https://www.vox.com/2014/7/30/5952739/the-research-on-how-pre-k-could-reduce-crime.

6. Shelli B. Rossman, Janeen Buck Willison, Kamala Mallik-Kane, KiDeuk Kim, Sara Debus-Sherrill, and P. Mitchell Downey, *Criminal Justice Interventions for Offenders with Mental Illness: Evaluation of Mental Health Courts in Bronx and Brooklyn, New York* (National Institute of Justice, 2012), https://www.urban.org/sites/default/files/publication/25576/412603-Criminal-Justice-Interventions-for-Offenders-With-Mental-Illness-Evaluation-of-Mental-Health-Courts-in-Bronx-and-Brooklyn-New-York.PDF.

7. Dana Rubinstein, "Security Robots. DigiDog. GPS Launchers. Welcome to New York," *New York Times*, April 11, 2023, sec. New York, https://www.nytimes.com/2023/04/11/nyregion/nypd-digidog-robot-crime.html.

8. Naomi Murakawa, "Freedom Is a Place: Celebrating the Scholarship, Writing, and Organizing of Ruth Wilson Gilmore," People's Forum NYC, YouTube, November 11, 2022, https://www.youtube.com/watch?v=JCylQyXIocU.

9. Ruth Wilson Gilmore, "What Is to Be Done?," *American Quarterly* 63, no. 2 (June 2011): 245–65; Ronald Reagan, "Inaugural Address 1981," Ronald Reagan Presidential Library and Museum, January 20, 1981, https://www.reaganlibrary.gov/archives/speech/inaugural-address-1981.

10. Jackie Wang, *Carceral Capitalism* (Semiotext(e), 2018), 76; Joshua Page and Joe Soss, "Criminal Justice as Racialized Resource Extraction," *Institute for Research on Poverty* 38, no. 2 (November 2022): 8.

11. Reginald Dwayne Betts, *Felon* (W. W. Norton, 2019), 78, 80. Here, I lineate Betts's poem with line breaks in lieu of redactions.

12. "Mayor: 'It Is Just Not Practical This Year,'" ESPN, January 7, 2002, https://www.espn.com/mlb/news/2002/0107/1307152.html; Stefan C. Friedman, "End to Corp. Welfare Is News to Biz," *New York Post*, October 22, 2003, https://nypost.com/2003/10/22/end-to-corp-welfare-is-news-to-biz/.

13. Jim Dwyer, "A New Yankee Stadium, the Same Old Politics," *New York Times*, January 13, 2009, https://www.nytimes.com/2009/01/14/nyregion/14about.html; Ken Dilanian, "Michael Bloomberg Loved to Give Fellow Billionaires Taxpayer Dollars for Sports," *Washington Examiner*, November 19, 2019, https://www.washingtonexaminer.com/opinion/19681/michael-bloomberg-loved-to-give-fellow-billionaires-taxpayer-dollars-for-sports/.

14. Dana Rubinstein, "Madison Square Garden Wants to Stay Put Forever. It May Not Be So Easy," *New York Times*, February 2, 2023, https://www.nytimes.com/2023/01/31/nyregion/madison-square-garden-permit-dolan.html.

15. J. C. Bradbury, "So, Your City Wants to Build a Sports Stadium?," *Global Sport Matters*, June 15, 2022, https://globalsportmatters.com/business/2022/06/15/so-your-city-wants-sports-stadium/.

16. Thomas Nocera, "Nashville Stadium Bond Sale Helps Set Public Subsidy Record," *Bond Buyer*, August 16, 2023, https://www.bondbuyer.com/news/nashville-stadium-bond-sale-helps

244 NOTES TO CHAPTER 4

-set-public-subsidy-record; Luis Ferré-Sadurní, "Buffalo Bills Strike Deal for Taxpayer-Funded $1.4 Billion Stadium," *New York Times*, March 22, 2022, https://www.nytimes.com/2022/03/28 /nyregion/buffalo-bills-stadium-deal.html.

17. Kim Phillips-Fein, *Fear City: New York's Fiscal Crisis and the Rise of Austerity Politics* (Metropolitan Books, 2017), 26.

18. David Brand, "NYC2036? How the 2012 Olympics Bid Reshaped New York City," *City Limits*, August 9, 2021, https://citylimits.org/2021/08/09/nyc2036-how-the-2012-olympics -bid-reshaped-new-york-city/; Bridget Fisher, Flávia Leite, and Rachel Weber, "Value Creation, Capture, and Destruction," *Journal of the American Planning Association* 89, no. 1 (n.d.): 134–45, https://doi.org/10.1080/01944363.2022.2026808.

19. Darren Sands, "Opinions Harden over Atlantic Yards Housing," *City Limits*, February 15, 2012, https://citylimits.org/2012/02/15/opinions-harden-over-atlantic-yards-housing/.

20. Ximena Del Cerro, "'We Need Accountability and Affordability': 20 Years Later, Coalition Denounces Lack of Results on Atlantic Yards Ahead of Rights Auction," *Brooklyn Paper*, December 19, 2023, https://www.brooklynpaper.com/atlantic-yards-20-year-anniversary -auction/.

21. Norman Oder, "The Times Low-Balls the Total Subsidies and Tax Breaks for Atlantic Yards," *Atlantic Yards Report* (blog), February 7, 2002, https://atlanticyardsreport.blogspot.com /2009/07/times-low-balls-total-subsidies-and-tax.html.

22. Benjamin Holtzman, *The Long Crisis: New York City and the Path to Neoliberalism* (Oxford University Press, 2021), 197.

23. Holtzman, *The Long Crisis*, 189.

24. Holtzman, *The Long Crisis*, 189–90.

25. Samuel Stein, "The Housing Crisis and the Rise of the Real Estate State," *New Labor Forum* 28, no. 3 (September 2019): 52–60, https://doi.org/10.1177/1095796019864098.

26. Kriston Capps, "Where New York City's Affordable Housing Push Fell Short," *Bloomberg*, December 16, 2021, https://www.bloomberg.com/news/articles/2021-12-16/why -mandatory-inclusionary-housing-flopped-in-nyc.

27. Derek Thompson, "Why Manhattan's Skyscrapers Are Empty," *Atlantic*, January 16, 2020, https://www.theatlantic.com/ideas/archive/2020/01/american-housing-has-gone-insane /605005/; Stefanos Chen, "One in Four of New York's New Luxury Apartments Is Unsold," *New York Times*, September 13, 2019, https://www.nytimes.com/2019/09/13/realestate/new -development-new-york.html.

28. Louise Story, "Stream of Foreign Wealth Flows to Elite New York Real Estate," *New York Times*, February 7, 2015, https://www.nytimes.com/2015/02/08/nyregion/stream-of-foreign -wealth-flows-to-time-warner-condos.html.

29. Julie Satow, "Why the Doorman Is Lonely," *New York Times*, January 15, 2015, https:// www.nytimes.com/2015/01/11/realestate/new-york-citys-emptiest-co-ops-and-condos.html.

30. Jasmine Cui, "Absentee Owners Are Crowding the Housing Market, Data Shows," *NBC News*, February 24, 2023, https://www.nbcnews.com/data-graphics/absentee-homeowners -crowding-housing-market-data-rcna69828.

31. David Wachsmuth and Alexander Weisler, "Airbnb and the Rent Gap: Gentrification through the Sharing Economy," *Environment and Planning A: Economy and Space* 50, no. 6 (September 2018): 1147–70, https://doi.org/10.1177/0308518X18778038; Rebecca Mead, "The

Airbnb Invasion of Barcelona," *New Yorker*, April 22, 2019, https://www.newyorker.com /magazine/2019/04/29/the-airbnb-invasion-of-barcelona.

32. Wachsmuth and Weisler, "Airbnb and the Rent Gap."

33. Michelle Fine and Jessica Ruglis, "Circuits and Consequences of Dispossession: The Racialized Realignment of the Public Sphere for US Youth," *Transforming Anthropology* 17, no. 1 (2009): 20–33.

34. Neil Brenner and Nik Theodore, "Cities and the Geographies of 'Actually Existing Neo-liberalism,'" *Antipode: A Radical Journal of Geography* 34, no. 3 (July 2002): 349–79, https://doi .org/10.1111/1467-8330.00246.

35. Erin Michaels, "The 'Structurally Adjusted' School: A Case from New York," *Critical Sociology* 47, no. 7–8 (n.d.): 1171–89, https://doi.org/10.1177/0896920521995535.

36. Michaels, "The 'Structurally Adjusted' School."

37. Gaston Alonso, Noel S. Anderson, Celina Su, and Jeanne Theoharis, *Our Schools Suck: Students Talk Back to a Segregated Nation on the Failures of Urban Education* (NYU Press, 2009).

38. Abigail Kramer, "NYC Schools Handcuff and Haul Away Kids in Emotional Crisis," *ProPublica*, May 4, 2023, https://www.propublica.org/article/nyc-schools-students-police -emotional-crisis-nypd.

39. David Stovall calls it the prison-school nexus. Valerie Strauss, "Do #BlackLivesMatter in Schools? Why the Answer Is 'No,'" *Washington Post*, July 14, 2020, https://www.washingtonpost .com/education/2020/07/14/do-blacklivesmatter-schools-why-answer-is-no/; David Stovall, "Are We Ready for 'School' Abolition? Thoughts and Practices of Radical Imaginary in Education," special issue, *Taboo: The Journal of Culture and Education* 17, no. 1 (May 2018): 51–61, https://doi.org/10.31390/taboo.17.1.06.

40. Michael W. Apple, "Education, Markets, and an Audit Culture," *International Journal of Educational Policies* 1, no. 1 (2007): 8.

41. Samuel Stein, *Capital City: Gentrification and the Real Estate State* (Verso Books, 2019), 57.

42. Adam Willis, "Proposed Ballot Measure Wants Hopkins and Baltimore's Other Tax-Exempt Institutions to Pay Up," *Baltimore Buyer*, August 11, 2023.

43. Matthew Haag and Meredith Kolodner, "'The Untouchables': How Columbia and N.Y.U. Benefit from Huge Tax Breaks," *New York Times*, September 26, 2023, https://www.nytimes.com /2023/09/26/nyregion/columbia-university-property-tax-nyc.html.

44. Amira McKee, "Exceeding Previous Estimates, Columbia Is the Largest Private Land-owner in New York City, City Data Reveals," *Columbia Spectator*, April 20, 2023, https://www .columbiaspectator.com/city-news/2023/04/20/exceeding-previous-estimates-columbia-is -the-largest-private-landowner-in-new-york-city-city-data-reveals/; Haag and Kolodner, "'The Untouchables.'"

45. Matthew Haag and Meredith Kolodner, "Columbia and N.Y.U. Would Lose $327 Million in Tax Breaks under Proposal," *New York Times*, October 12, 2023, https://www.nytimes.com /2023/12/10/nyregion/columbia-nyu-property-tax-exemptions-legislation.html.

46. "History of BND," Bank of North Dakota, n.d., https://bnd.nd.gov/history-of-bnd/.

47. James Sanders Jr., "Senate Bill S1754," New York State Senate, 2023, https://www.nysenate .gov/legislation/bills/2023/S1754.

48. "Public Banks 101," Public Banking Institute, n.d., https://publicbankinginstitute.org /public-banks-101/.

246   NOTES TO CHAPTER 5

49. Louise Matsakis, "The Truth about Amazon, Food Stamps, and Tax Breaks," *Wired*, September 6, 2018, https://www.wired.com/story/truth-about-amazon-food-stamps-tax-breaks/; Martin Austermuhle, "Amazon Insists on Silence from Twenty HQ2 Finalists," WAMU 88.5, January 30, 2018, https://wamu.org/story/18/01/30/amazon-insists-silence-twenty-hq2-finalists/; Julie Creswell, "Cities' Offers for Amazon Base Are Secrets Even to Many City Leaders," *New York Times*, August 5, 2018, https://www.nytimes.com/2018/08/05/technology/amazon-headquarters-hq2.html.

50. Dennis Green, "The Professor Who Predicted Amazon Would Buy Whole Foods Says Only 2 Cities Have a Shot at HQ2," *Business Insider*, February 12, 2018, https://www.businessinsider.com/amazon-hq2-will-be-new-york-or-dc-scott-galloway-predicts-2018-2.

Chapter 5: A Right-to-the-City Budget

1. Peyton Whitney, "Number of Renters Burdened by Housing Costs Reached a Record High in 2021," Joint Center for Housing Studies of Harvard University, February 1, 2023, https://www.jchs.harvard.edu/blog/number-renters-burdened-housing-costs-reached-record-high-2021.

2. Oksana Mironova and Samuel Stein, "Our Fast Analysis of the 2021 New York City Housing and Vacancy Survey," Community Service Society, October 12, 2023, https://www.cssny.org/news/entry/our-fast-analysis-of-the-2021-new-york-city-housing-and-vacancy-survey.

3. Allison Brown and Annali Kristiansen, "Urban Policies and the Right to the City: Rights, Responsibilities and Citizenship," UNESCO, March 2009; Nadia Albuquerque and Manuel Correia Guedes, "Cities without Slums and the Right to the City: Slums in Subsaharan Africa," *Renewable Energy and Environmental Sustainability* 6, no. 24 (July 30, 2021): 1–14, https://doi.org/10.1051/rees/2021022.

4. "Right to the City," Right to the City, 2024, https://www.righttothecity.org/.

5. Christian Sowa, "Urban Citizenship: A Right to the City?," We Refugees, 2019, https://en.we-refugees-archive.org/chapters/urban-citizenship-a-right-to-the-city/.

6. James Holston, "Metropolitan Rebellions and the Politics of Commoning the City," *Anthropological Theory* 19, no. 1 (2019): 127.

7. Henri Lefebvre, *The Right to the City* [*Le Droit à ville*] (1968; repr., Anarchist Library, 1996), https://theanarchistlibrary.org/library/henri-lefebvre-right-to-the-city.

8. Mine Islar and Ezgi Irgil, "Grassroots Practices of Citizenship and Politicization in the Urban: The Case of Right to the City Initiatives in Barcelona," *Citizenship Studies* 22, no. 5 (July 4, 2018): 502, https://doi.org/10.1080/13621025.2018.1477919.

9. Lester Spence, "Vol. 8 No. 13," *Counterpublic Papers* (blog), April 10, 2024, https://lesters-newsletter-2ff539.beehiiv.com/p/counterpublic-papers-vol-8-no-13.

10. David Harvey, "The Right to the City," *New Left Review* 53 (September 2008): 23.

11. Peter Levine, *We Are the Ones We Have Been Waiting For: The Promise of Civic Renewal in America* (Oxford University Press, 2015).

12. Holston, "Metropolitan Rebellions"; Dean Spade, *Mutual Aid: Building Solidarity during This Crisis (and the Next)* (Verso Books, 2020).

13. Annika Agger, "Democratic Innovations in Municipal Planning: Potentials and Challenges of Place-Based Platforms for Deliberation between Politicians and Citizens," *Cities* 117

NOTES TO CHAPTER 5   247

(October 2021), https://doi.org/10.1016/j.cities.2021.103317; Hollie Russon Gilman, "Civic Innovation Is Flourishing in Cities Right Now," *Next City*, July 28, 2023; Abraham Maslow, *The Psychology of Science: A Reconnaisance* (New York: Harper & Row, 1966), 15–16, https://scholar.google.com/scholar?cluster=17162065919096658039&hl=en&as_sdt=0,33; James Holston and Arjun Appadurai, "Cities and Citizenship," *Globalization: Religion, Nature, and the Built Environment* 5 (2003): 286; Robert A. Beauregard and Anna Bounds, "Urban Citizenship," in *Democracy, Citizenship and the Global City*, ed. Engin F. Isin (Routledge, 2013), 243–56; Talja Blokland, Christine Hentschel, Andrej Holm, Henrik Lebuhn, and Talia Margalit, "Urban Citizenship and Right to the City: The Fragmentation of Claims," *International Journal of Urban and Regional Research* 39, no. 4 (2015): 655–65.

14. This is from a longer passage reading, "The only indispensable material factor in the generation of power is the living together of people. Only where men live so close together that the potentialities of action are always present can power remain with them, and the foundation of cities, which as city-states have remained paradigmatic for all Western political organisation, is indeed the most important material prerequisite for power." Hannah Arendt, *The Human Condition* (University of Chicago Press, 1958), 201.

15. Kim Phillips-Fein, *Fear City: New York's Fiscal Crisis and the Rise of Austerity Politics* (Metropolitan Books, 2017), 316.

16. Iris Marion Young, "City Life and Difference," in *People, Place and Space Reader*, ed. Jen Jack Gieseking, William Mangold, Cindi Katz, Setha Low, and Susan Saegert (Routledge, 2014), 249.

17. Young, "City Life and Difference."

18. I am not sure about the origins of this assertion, but a quick web search generated a number of instances, including a symposium on serendipity and the city as a field of inquiry at https://www.allthingsurban.net/events/281, as well as an interview in which the media scholar Ethan Zuckerman questions it at https://nextcity.org/urbanist-news/mits-ethan-zuckerman-on-digital-cosmopolitans-in-the-age-of-connection.

19. Edward Glaeser, "What a City Needs," *New Republic*, October 3, 2009, https://newrepublic.com/article/68989/what-city-needs; Emily Badger, "Cities Foster Serendipity. But Can They Do It When Workers Are at Home?," *New York Times*, October 20, 2023.

20. Not quoting exactly but inspired by Sowa, "Urban Citizenship."

21. Mark E. Dornauer and Robert Bryce, "Too Many Rural Americans Are Living in the Digital Dark. The Problem Demands a New Deal Solution," *Health Affairs*, October 28, 2020, https://www.healthaffairs.org/content/forefront/too-many-rural-americans-living-digital-dark-problem-demands-new-deal-solution.

22. Alexandre Apsan Frediani, Barbara Lipietz, and Julian Walker, "Reflections: Multiple Visions of the 'Right to the City,'" in *Urban Claims and the Right to the City: Grassroots Perspectives from Salvador da Bahia and London*, ed. Julian Walker, Marcos Bau Carvalho, and Ilinca Diaconescu (University College London, 2020), 106, https://muse.jhu.edu/pub/354/oa_edited_volume/chapter/2778340.

Interlude: An interview with Makani Themba

1. Makani Themba, "The Most Radical City on the Planet," *Boston Review*, April 29, 2019, https://www.bostonreview.net/articles/makani-themba-most-radical-city-planet/.

248 NOTES TO CHAPTER 6

2. Ajamu Nangwaya and Kali Akuno, *Jackson Rising: The Struggle for Economic Democracy and Black Self-Determination in Jackson, Mississippi* (Daraja Press, 2017).

3. "Statement by Administrator Regan on the Ongoing Water Crisis in Jackson, Mississippi," US Environmental Protection Agency, September 26, 2022, https://www.epa.gov/newsreleases /statement-administrator-regan-ongoing-water-crisis-jackson-mississippi.

4. "Water and Wastewater Systems," Cybersecurity & Infrastructure Security Agency, n.d., https://www.cisa.gov/topics/critical-infrastructure-security-and-resilience/critical-infrastruc ture-sectors/water-and-wastewater-sector; "The WATER Act: Restoring Federal Support for Clean Water Systems," Food & Water Watch, March 2022, https://www.foodandwaterwatch.org /2022/03/18/the-water-act-restoring-federal-support-for-clean-water-systems/.

5. Hadas Thier, "Jackson's Water System Is Broken by Design," *Nation*, February 22, 2023, https://www.thenation.com/article/society/jackson-mississippi-water-infrastructure/.

6. Alex Rozier, "Senate Passes Bill Putting Jackson Water under State Control, House to Vote Next," *Mississippi Today*, July 2, 2023, https://mississippitoday.org/2023/02/07/senate-passes -bill-placing-jackson-water-under-state-control/; Wicker Perlis, "Jackson Sales Tax Could Be Required to Be Used on Water and Sewer, Not Roads and Bridges," *Mississippi Clarion Ledger*, February 2, 2023, https://www.clarionledger.com/story/news/politics/2023/02/02 /infrastructure-sales-tax-changes-might-be-coming-in-jackson-ms/69867080007/.

7. Thier, "Jackson's Water System Is Broken by Design."

8. Quoted in Thier, "Jackson's Water System Is Broken by Design."

9. "The People Must Decide!," Jackson People's Assembly, n.d., https://jxnpeoplesassembly .org/.

10. Makani Themba-Nixon, "The City as Liberated Zone: The Promise of Jackson's People's Assemblies," in *Jackson Rising: The Struggle for Economic Democracy and Black Self-Determination in Jackson, Mississippi*, ed. Kali Akuno and Ajamu Nangwaya (Press Books, 2017).

11. Quoted in Thier, "Jackson's Water System Is Broken by Design."

12. Themba's brother, Robin D. G. Kelley, has written about his relationship with Boggs in remembrances such as this one: "Thinking Dialectically: What Grace Lee Boggs Taught Me," *Portside*, October 21, 2015, https://portside.org/2015-10-21/thinking-dialectically-what-grace -lee-boggs-taught-me.

13. "'Curing' What Truly Ails Us: Reflections on Movement Strategy in the Time of Coronavirus," *Higher Ground*, 2020, https://highergroundstrategies.net/curing-what-truly-ails-us/.

Chapter 6: No Taxation without Participation

1. Daniel Laurison and Ankit Rastogi, "Income Inequality in U.S. Voting: A Visualization," *Socius* 9 (February 21, 2023), https://doi.org/10.1177/23780231231154358.

2. Jackie Wang, *Carceral Capitalism* (Semiotext(e), 2018).

3. Harry J. Enten, "Will Your Vote Make a Difference? Understanding Our Election Interactive," *Guardian*, October 1, 2012, https://www.theguardian.com/world/2012/oct/01/election -interactive-vote-make-a-difference.

4. Sahil Kapur, "Scholar behind Viral 'Oligarchy' Study Tells You What It Means," *Talking Points Memo*, April 22, 2014, https://talkingpointsmemo.com/dc/princeton-scholar-demise-of -democracy-america-tpm-interview.

NOTES TO CHAPTER 6 249

5. "Public Trust in Government: 1958–2024," Pew Research Center, June 24, 2024, https://www.pewresearch.org/politics/2024/06/24/public-trust-in-government-1958-2024/.

6. "Voting Laws Roundup: June 2023," Brennan Center for Justice, June 14, 2023.

7. Matt DeRienzo, "How We Documented Inequity in Access to Voting," Center for Public Integrity, October 6, 2022, https://publicintegrity.org/politics/elections/who-counts/how-we-documented-inequity-in-access-to-voting/.

8. DeRienzo, "How We Documented Inequity in Access to Voting"; "Voting Laws Roundup."

9. For discussions of examples, see McCray Jones, "From 'Don't Say Gay' to 'Rainbowland,'" ACLU, July 4, 2023, https://www.aclu-wi.org/en/news/dont-say-gay-rainbowland; Kathrin F. Stanger-Hall and David W. Hall, "Abstinence-Only Education and Teen Pregnancy Rates: Why We Need Comprehensive Sex Education in the U.S.," *PLOS ONE* 6, no. 10 (October 14, 2011), https://doi.org/10.1371/journal.pone.0024658.

10. Quoted in Javier C. Hernández, "Schools Panel Is No Threat to the Mayor's Grip," *New York Times*, April 22, 2009, https://www.nytimes.com/2009/04/23/nyregion/23panel.html.

11. Reema Amin and Amy Zimmer, "Find Out How Much Your School's PTA Raises (or Doesn't)," *Chalkbeat*, December 2, 2019, https://www.chalkbeat.org/newyork/2019/12/2/21113658/find-out-how-much-your-school-s-pta-raises-or-doesn-t/; Editorial Board, "Why Shouldn't New York's Wealthiest P.T.A.s Share with Its Neediest Schools?," *New York Times*, January 12, 2020, https://www.nytimes.com/2020/01/12/opinion/new-york-pta.html.

12. Peter Levine, *We Are the Ones We Have Been Waiting For: The Promise of Civic Renewal in America* (Oxford University Press, 2015), 12, 191. See also, among others, Faranak Miraftab and Shana Wills, "Insurgency and Spaces of Active Citizenship: The Story of Western Cape Anti-Eviction Campaign in South Africa," *Journal of Planning Education and Research* 25, no. 2 (2005): 200–217, https://doi.org/10.1177/0739456X05282182.

13. Keeanga-Yamahtta Taylor, *Race for Profit* (University of North Carolina Press, 2019).

Interlude: An Interview with Tarson Núñez

1. Carew Boulding and Brian Wampler, "Voice, Votes, and Resources: Evaluating the Effect of Participatory Democracy on Well-Being," *World Development* 38, no. 1 (2010): 125–35; Gianpaolo Baiocchi, *Militants and Citizens: The Politics of Participatory Democracy in Porto Alegre* (Stanford University Press, 2005); Rebecca Abers, "Learning Democratic Practice: Distributing Government Resources through Popular Participation in Porto Alegre, Brazil," in *The Challenge of Urban Government: Policies and Practices*, ed. Mila Freire and Richard Stren (World Bank Institute, 2001).

2. Brian Wampler and Mike Touchton, "Brazil Let Its Citizens Make Decisions about City Budgets. Here's What Happened," *Washington Post*, January 22, 2014; Michael Ryan Touchton, Brian Wampler, and Tiago Carneiro Peixoto, "Of Democratic Governance and Revenue: Participatory Institutions and Tax Generation in Brazil," *Governance* 34, no. 4 (2020): 1193–212; Brian Wampler, Stephanie McNulty, and Michael Touchton, *Participatory Budgeting in Global Perspective* (Oxford University Press, 2021); Brian Wampler and Michael Touchton, "Designing Institutions to Improve Well-being: Participation, Deliberation and Institutionalisation," *European Journal of Political Research* 58, no. 3 (2019): 915–37; Brian Wampler, *Activating Democracy in Brazil: Popular Participation, Social Justice, and Interlocking Institutions* (University of Notre Dame Press, 2015).

250 NOTES TO CHAPTER 7

3. "Participatory Budgeting World Atlas," accessed December 2, 2024, https://oidp.net/en/publication.php?id=1636; Jamie Peck and Nik Theodore, *Fast Policy* (University of Minnesota Press, 2015); Gianpaolo Baiocchi and Ernesto Ganuza, *Popular Democracy: The Paradox of Participation* (Stanford University Press, 2016); Ernesto Ganuza and Gianpaolo Baiocchi, "The Power of Ambiguity: How Participatory Budgeting Travels the Globe," *Journal of Deliberative Democracy* 8, no. 2 (2012), https://delibdemjournal.org/article/id/414/.

4. "Why Did PB Decline in Brazil and Will Lula Revive It?," People Powered, November 7, 2022, https://www.peoplepowered.org/news-content/participatory-budgeting-in-brazil.

5. Paulo Freire, *Pedagogy of the Oppressed* (Continuum, 1968).

6. This comment made me think of town hall meetings or community forums in which participants could let off steam, but had no influence on decision-making, or congressional testimonies, where participants were heard, but only elected representatives made decisions.

7. For more information on these conferences, see "National Public Policy Conferences (Brazil)," Participedia, n.d., https://participedia.net/method/5450.

8. Here Núñez is referring to Angelo Panebianco, *Political Parties: Organization and Power* (Cambridge University Press, 1988).

9. The original sentence is, "I'm a pessimist because of intelligence, but an optimist because of will." Antonio Gramsci, *Letters from Prison: Volume 1*, ed. Frank Rosengarten, trans. Raymond Rosenthal (Columbia University Press, 2011), 299.

Chapter 7: An Invitation to Participatory Budgeting

1. Yves Cabannes, *Another City Is Possible with Participatory Budgeting* (Black Rose Books, 2017).

2. Megan Clement, "Pissoirs and Public Votes: How Paris Embraced the Participatory Budget," *Guardian*, October 3, 2019, sec. Cities, https://www.theguardian.com/cities/2019/oct/03/pissoirs-and-public-votes-how-paris-embraced-the-participatory-budget.

3. Michael Touchton and Brian Wampler, "Improving Social Well-Being through New Democratic Institutions," *Comparative Political Studies* 47, no. 10 (2014): 1442–69.

4. Roberto Pires, "Aspectos regulamentação da participação no OP em Belo Horizonte: Eficiência distributiva aliada ao planejamento urbano," in *Democracia participativa e redistribuição: Análise de experiências de orçamento participativo*, ed. Adalmir Marquetti, Geraldo Adriano de Campos, and Roberto Pires (Xamã, 2008), 55–76; Brian Wampler, *Activating Democracy in Brazil: Popular Participation, Social Justice, and Interlocking Institutions* (University of Notre Dame Press, 2015), https://muse.jhu.edu/pub/200/monograph/book/39937; Sounman Hong and B. Shine Cho, "Citizen Participation and the Redistribution of Public Goods," *Public Administration* 96, no. 3 (September 2018): 481–96, https://doi.org/10.1111/padm.12521; B. Shine Cho, Won No, and Yaerin Park, "Diffusing Participatory Budgeting Knowledge: Lessons from Korean-Language Research," *Asia Pacific Journal of Public Administration* 42, no. 3 (July 2, 2020): 188–206, https://doi.org/10.1080/23276665.2020.1789481.

5. Michael Ryan Touchton, Brian Wampler, and Tiago Carneiro Peixoto, "Of Governance and Revenue: Participatory Institutions and Tax Compliance in Brazil," *Governance* 34, no. 4 (2020): 1193–212; Michael Touchton and Brian Wampler, "Public Engagement for Public

NOTES TO CHAPTER 8   251

Health: Participatory Budgeting, Targeted Social Programmes, and Infant Mortality in Brazil," *Development in Practice* 30, no. 5 (July 3, 2020): 681–86, https://doi.org/10.1080/09614524.2020.1742662.

6. Sónia Gonçalves, "The Effects of Participatory Budgeting on Municipal Expenditures and Infant Mortality in Brazil," *World Development* 53 (2014): 94–110; Touchton and Wampler, "Improving Social Well-Being through New Democratic Institutions."

7. Andrea Cornwall and Vera Schattan P. Coelho, "Spaces for Change? The Politics of Participation in New Democratic Arenas," in *Spaces for Change?* (Zed Books, 2007).

8. These are reported numbers for 2019. "East Harlem Neighborhood Indicators," NYU Furman Center, 2019, https://furmancenter.org/neighborhoods/view/east-harlem.

9. Alexa Kasdan, Erin Markman, and Pat Covey, *A People's Budget: A Report on the Participatory Budgeting in New York City in 2013–2014* (Community Development Project at the Urban Justice Center, 2014), 19.

10. Kasdan, Markman, and Covey, *A People's Budget*, 21–25.

11. Alexa Kasdan and Erin Markman, *A People's Budget: Cycle 4: Key Research Findings* (Community Development Project at the Urban Justice Center, 2015).

12. See, for example, Ron Hayduk, Kristen Hackett, and Diana Tamashiro Folla, "Immigrant Engagement in Participatory Budgeting in New York City," *New Political Science* 39, no. 1 (2017): 76–94, https://doi.org/10.1080/07393148.2017.1278855.

13. For two books that are quite helpful in thinking through this oxymoron and attending dilemmas, see Caroline W. Lee, *Do-It-Yourself Democracy: The Rise of the Public Engagement Industry* (Oxford University Press, 2014); Stephanie L. McNulty, *Democracy from Above?* (Stanford University Press, 2020).

14. Isaac Jabola-Carolus, "Growing Grassroots Democracy: Dynamic Outcomes in Building New York City's Participatory Budgeting Program," *New Political Science* 39, no. 1 (2017): 118, https://doi.org/10.1080/07393148.2017.1278857.

Chapter 8: Terms of Deliberation

1. Brett Stoudt, Michelle Fine, and Madeline Fox, "Growing up Policed in the Age of Aggressive Policing Policies," *New York Law School Law Review* 56 (2011): 1331–70; Jennifer Jee-Lyn García and Mienah Zulfacar Sharif, "Black Lives Matter: A Commentary on Racism and Public Health," *American Journal of Public Health* 105, no. 8 (2015): e27–e30.

2. Teju Cole, "Death in the Browser Tab," *New York Times Magazine*, 2015, MM18.

3. Aren Aizura, "Trans Feminine Value, Racialized Others and the Limits of Necropolitics," *Queer Necropolitics* (2014): 129.

4. See, for instance, Sam Roberts, "Gap between Manhattan's Rich and Poor Is Greatest in U.S., Census Finds," *New York Times*, September 18, 2014.

5. Stuart Hall, "Race, Articulation, and Societies Structured in Dominance," in *Black British Cultural Studies*, ed. Houston A. Baker Jr., Manthia Diawara, and Ruth H. Lindeborg (University of Chicago Press, 1996), 55.

6. Gaston Alonso, Noel S. Anderson, Celina Su, and Jeanne Theoharis, *Our Schools Suck: Students Talk Back to a Segregated Nation on the Failures of Urban Education* (NYU Press, 2009).

252 NOTES TO CHAPTER 9

7. Kate Driscoll Derickson, "Urban Geography 2: Urban Geography in the Age of Ferguson," *Progress in Human Geography* (2016): 1–15.

8. Kimberle Crenshaw, "Demarginalizing the Intersection of Race and Sex: A Black Feminist Critique of Antidiscrimination Doctrine, Feminist Theory and Antiracist Politics," *University of Chicago Legal Forum* 1989, no. 1 (1989), http://chicagounbound.uchicago.edu/uclf/vol1989/iss1/8.

9. Patricia Hill Collins, "The Difference That Power Makes: Intersectionality and Participatory Democracy," *Investigaciones Feministas* 8, no. 1 (2017): 21, https://doi.org/10.5209/INFE.54888. Here I also draw inspiration from Combahee River Collective, "A Black Feminist Statement," in *Feminist Manifestos*, ed. Penny A. Weiss (NYU Press, 2020), 269–77, https://doi.org/10.18574/nyu/9781479805419.003.0063.

10. john a. powell, "Post-Racialism or Targeted Universalism," *Denver University Law Review* 86 (2008): 785–806.

11. Maurice Mitchell, "Building Resilient Organizations: Toward Joy and Durable Power in a Time of Crisis," *Nonprofit Quarterly*, 2022, https://nonprofitquarterly.org/building-resilient-organizations-toward-joy-and-durable-power-in-a-time-of-crisis/.

12. David Leonhardt, "New York Still Has More Gay Residents Than Anywhere Else in U.S.," *New York Times*, March 23, 2023, https://www.nytimes.com/2015/03/24/upshot/new-york-still-has-more-gay-residents-than-anywhere-else-in-us.html; Matthew Morton, *A Youth Homelessness System Assessment for New York City* (Chapin Hill at the University of Chicago, 2019), https://www.nyc.gov/assets/opportunity/pdf/evidence/youth-homelessness-system-assessment-rpt-2019.pdf.

13. Clara Irazábal and Claudia Huerta, "Intersectionality and Planning at the Margins: LGBTQ Youth of Color in New York," *Gender, Place and Culture* 23, no. 5 (2016): 714–32, https://doi.org/10.1080/0966369X.2015.1058755.

14. Nana Gyamfi and Ronald Claude, "Black Alliance for Just Immigration," United Nations Human Rights, 2023, https://www.ohchr.org/sites/default/files/documents/hrbodies/hrcouncil/forums/forum-african-descent/sessions/session1/statements/2023-01-05/Black-Alliance-for-Just-Immigration.pdf.

15. Kea Wilson, "What Is a Feminist City?," *Streetsblog USA*, April 8, 2020, https://usa.streetsblog.org/2020/08/04/what-is-a-feminist-city.

16. Rod Dacombe and Phil Parvin, "Participatory Democracy in an Age of Inequality," *Journal of Representative Democracy* 57, no. 2 (2021): 145–57, https://doi:10.1080/00344893.2021.1933151; Bent Flyvbjerg, "Habermas and Foucault: Thinkers for Civil Society?," *British Journal of Sociology* 49, no. 2 (1998): 210–33.

17. Richard Delgado and Jean Stefancic, *Critical Race Theory: An Introduction* (NYU Press, 2001); Derrick Bell, "Brown v. Board of Education and the Interest-Convergence Dilemma," *Harvard Law Review* 93 (1979): 518.

Chapter 9: Actionable Knowledges

1. Henri Lefebvre, *The Right to the City* [*Le Droit à ville*] (1968; repr., Anarchist Library, 1996), https://theanarchistlibrary.org/library/henri-lefebvre-right-to-the-city; Henri Lefebvre, *Writing on Cities*, trans. Eleonore Kofman and Elizabeth Lebas (Blackwell, 1996).

NOTES TO CHAPTER 9   253

2. Lefebvre, *The Right to the City*.

3. Manuel Delgado Ruiz, "El Urbanismo Contra Lo Urbano. La Ciudad y La Vida Urbana En Henri Lefebvre," *REVISTARQUIS* 7, no. 1 (2018): 65–71.

4. Manuel Delgado, "Elogio y rescate de Henri Lefebvre," *El País*, March 19, 2018, sec. Seres Urbanos, https://elpais.com/elpais/2018/03/16/seres_urbanos/1521194122_492095.html.

5. Elizabeth Anderson, "Epistemic Justice as a Virtue of Social Institutions," *Social Epistemology* 26, no. 2 (n.d.): 163–73; Michael Ryan Touchton, Brian Wampler, and Tiago Carneiro Peixoto, "Of Governance and Revenue: Participatory Institutions and Tax Compliance in Brazil," *Governance* 34, no. 4 (2020): 1193–212; Michael Touchton and Brian Wampler, "Public Engagement for Public Health: Participatory Budgeting, Targeted Social Programmes, and Infant Mortality in Brazil," *Development in Practice* 30, no. 5 (July 3, 2020): 681–86, https://doi.org/10.1080/09614524.2020 .1742662; Miranda Fricker, *Epistemic Injustice: Power and the Ethics of Knowing* (Oxford University Press, 2007); Carolin Hagelskamp, Celina Su, Karla Valverde Viesca, and Tarson Núñez, "Organizing a Transnational Solidarity for Social Change through Participatory Practices: The Case of People Powered–Global Hub for Participatory Democracy," *American Journal of Community Psychology* 69, no. 3–4 (March 15, 2022): 294–305, https://doi.org/10.1002/ajcp.12593.

6. Epistemic justice might not be a popular term, but it should not be difficult to grasp notions of epistemic *injustice*—when someone's argument is dismissed not because of its substance but instead because of who made it. Epistemic injustice is perhaps starkest in courts of law, where judges explicitly dictate who is seen as a credible witness and whose evidence is admissible. In what philosopher Miranda Fricker calls *testimonial* injustice, someone is not taken seriously as a producer of knowledge because of some aspect of their identity. Because testimonial injustice often falls along racial lines—in which Black witnesses and defendants are seen as less credible than White ones—it is perhaps unsurprising that cross-racial mistaken identification is most common when eyewitnesses are White and the alleged perpetrators are Black, and that such cases constitute over a third of wrongful convictions overturned by DNA analysis. James M. Doyle, "Discounting the Error Costs: Cross-Racial False Alarms in the Culture of Contemporary Criminal Justice," *Psychology, Public Policy, and Law* 7, no. 1 (2001): 253–62, https:// doi.org/10.1037/1076-8971.7.1.253. In what Fricker calls *hermeneutical* injustice, someone's interpretations of their experiences are dismissed because these experiences do not fit well-known concepts. In cases of sexual harassment, for example, women's interpretations of hostile work environments can be dismissed as hysterical reactions or taking joking acts of intimidation too seriously, especially when male colleagues interpret their work environments differently. In the realm of budget justice, epistemic justice demands that policymakers take seriously different citizens' interpretations of their experiences in the city—for instance, of overpolicing or having trouble learning in schools. It also demands that policymakers take seriously citizens' ideas for new policies. See Miranda Fricker, *Epistemic Injustice: Power and the Ethics of Knowing* (Clarendon Press, 2007).

7. Quoted in Joe Soss and Vesla Weaver, "Police Are Our Government: Politics, Political Science, and the Policing of Race–Class Subjugated Communities," *Annual Review of Political Science* 20 (2017): 575, https://doi.org/10.1146/annurev-polisci-060415-093825.

8. Jane Perlez, "Answering an Appeal by Mao Led Tu Youyou, a Chinese Scientist, to a Nobel Prize," *New York Times*, June 10, 2015, https://www.nytimes.com/2015/10/07/world/asia/tu -youyou-chinese-scientist-nobel-prize.html; "Tu Youyou: Nobel Prize in Physiology or

254 NOTES TO CHAPTER 10

Medicine in 2015," Nobel Prize, 2015, https://www.nobelprize.org/womenwhochangedscience/stories/tu-youyou.

9. Robin Wall Kimmerer, *Braiding Sweetgrass* (Milkweed Editions, 2013).

10. John M. Bryson, Kathryn S. Quick, Carissa Schively Slotterback, and Barbara C. Crosby, "Designing Public Participation Processes," *Public Administration Review* 73, no. 1 (2013): 23–34; Helen Ingram and Steven Smith, *Public Policy for Democracy* (Brookings Institution Press, 2011).

11. Lester Salamon, *The Tools of Government: A Guide to the New Governance* (Oxford University Press, 2002).

12. John Thomas, "Citizen, Customer, Partner: Rethinking the Place of the Public in Public Management," *Public Administration Review* 73, no. 6 (2013): 788.

13. Adam Dahl and Joe Soss, "Neoliberalism for the Common Good? Public Value Governance and the Downsizing of Democracy," *Public Administration Review* 74, no. 4 (2014): 496–97; Robert Durant and Susannah Ali, "Repositioning American Public Administration? Citizen Estrangement, Administrative Reform, and the Disarticulated State," *Public Administration Review* 73, no. 2 (2013): 278–89.

14. John Bryson, Barbara Crosby, and Laura Bloomberg, "Public Value Governance: Moving beyond Traditional Public Administration and the New Public Management," *Public Administration Review* 74, no. 4 (2014): 447.

15. Kesi Foster, "How to Build Multiracial Democracy at the Local Level," *Nonprofit Quarterly*, April 26, 2023.

16. Terry Cooper, Thomas Bryer, and Jack Meek, "Citizen-Centered Collaborative Public Management," *Public Administration Review* 66, no. s1 (2006): 76–88.

17. Boaventura de Sousa Santos, "Participatory Budgeting in Porto Alegre: Toward a Redistributive Democracy," *Politics & Society* 26, no. 4 (December 1, 1998): 462, https://doi.org/10.1177/0032329298026004003.

18. Alissa Quart, *Monetized* (Miami University Press, 2015), 62.

19. Thomas Bryer, "Public Participation in Regulatory Decision-Making: Cases from Regulations," *Public Performance & Management Review* 37, no. 2 (2013): 263.

20. James C. Scott, *Seeing Like a State: How Certain Schemes to Improve the Human Condition Have Failed* (Yale University Press, 1998).

21. Bryer, "Public Participation in Regulatory Decision-Making," 264.

22. As discussed by Themba in the interview with her earlier in the book.

Chapter 10: No Algorithms, No Shortcuts

1. Caroline W. Lee, *Do-It-Yourself Democracy: The Rise of the Public Engagement Industry* (Oxford University Press, 2014), 226.

2. For more information on the process, see https://www.participate.nyc.gov/. Another major difference between the People's Money and PBNYC is that budget delegates follow a citizens' assembly model; over one hundred volunteers are chosen by sortition (lottery) to serve on borough-wide assembly committees.

3. Ernesto Ganuza and Gianpaolo Baiocchi, "The Power of Ambiguity: How Participatory Budgeting Travels the Globe," *Journal of Public Deliberation* 8, no. 2 (2012): article 8; Gianpaolo

NOTES TO CHAPTER 10 255

Baiocchi and Ernesto Ganuza, *Popular Democracy: The Paradox of Participation* (Stanford University Press, 2016).

4. Rebecca Abers, Robin King, Daniel Votto, and Igor Brandão, *Porto Alegre: Participatory Budgeting and the Challenge of Sustaining Transformative Change* (World Resources Institute, 2018), https://www.wri.org/research/porto-alegre-participatory-budgeting-and-challenge-sustaining-transformative-change.

5. "Why Did PB Decline in Brazil and Will Lula Revive It?," People Powered, November 7, 2022, https://www.peoplepowered.org/news-content/participatory-budgeting-in-brazil.

6. Olúfẹ́mi O. Táíwò, *Elite Capture* (Haymarket Books, 2022).

7. Jamie Peck and Nik Theodore, *Fast Policy* (University of Minnesota Press, 2015), 177.

8. Henri Lefebvre, *The Right to the City* [*Le Droit à ville*] (1968; repr., Anarchist Library, 1996), 150, https://theanarchistlibrary.org/library/henri-lefebvre-right-to-the-city; Mark Purcell, "Possible Worlds: Henri Lefebvre and the Right to the City," *Journal of Urban Affairs* 36, no. 1 (2013): 150, https://doi.org/10.1111/juaf.12034.

9. Francesca Polletta, "How Participatory Democracy Became White: Culture and Organizational Choice," *Mobilization: An International Quarterly* 10, no. 2 (2005): 271–88.

10. Julia Paley, *Marketing Democracy: Power and Social Movements in Post-Dictatorship Chile* (University of California Press, 2001); Baiocchi and Ganuza, *Popular Democracy*.

11. Jerusalem Demsas, "Community Input Is Bad, Actually," *Atlantic*, April 22, 2022, https://www.theatlantic.com/ideas/archive/2022/04/local-government-community-input-housing-public-transportation/629625/.

12. Boaventura de Sousa Santos, *Democratizing Democracy: Beyond the Liberal Democratic Canon* (Verso Books, 2005).

13. Bill Cooke and Uma Kothari, *Participation: The New Tyranny?* (Zed Books, 2001); Incite!, *The Revolution Will Not Be Funded: Beyond the Non-Profit Industrial Complex* (South End Press, 2007).

14. Lee, *Do-It-Yourself Democracy*, 220.

15. Stuart Hall, "The 'Little Caesars' of Social Democracy," *Marxism Today* 25, no. 4 (April 1981): 11–15.

16. "A Progressive, Responsible, Transparent Budget for New York City," New York City Comptroller Brad Lander, June 26, 2014, http://bradlander.nyc/blog/2014/06/26/a-progressive-responsible-transparent-budget-for-nyc.

17. "Capital Projects Tracker," New York City, 2023, https://app.powerbigov.us/view?r=eyJrIjoiMTkwYWMyNGEtMDNiZC00OTY4LTk4YjEtYzI0MzhlOTA3MzllIiwidCI6IjM1YzgyODE2LTZjNTYtNDQzYi1iYWY2LTgzMTIxNjNjYWRjMSJ9.

18. Jocelyn Simonson, *Radical Acts of Justice* (New Press, 2023), 135.

19. "Metro Nashville Community Budgeting (PB Nashville)," Facebook discussion, n.d., https://www.facebook.com/groups/PBNashville/.

20. Yihyun Jeong, "Public Sends Resounding Message in Marathon Nashville Council Hearing: Defund Police," *Tennessean*, March 6, 2020, https://www.tennessean.com/story/news/politics/2020/06/03/nashville-council-hears-defunding-police-message-marathon-meeting/3129715001/.

21. "2020 Campaign," Nashville People's Budget Coalition, n.d., https://nashvillepeoplesbudget.org/2020-campaign/.

256   NOTES TO CHAPTER 11

22. "Participatory Budgeting | Radical Proposal Writing Party," Nashville People's Budget Coalition, May 22, 2023, https://nashvillepeoplesbudget.org/2023/05/22/participatory -budgeting-radical-proposal-writing-party/.

23. "About," Black Nashville Assembly (BNA), n.d., https://www.blacknashvilleassembly .org/about-4 (emphasis added).

24. Seattle Department of Neighborhoods, "City Begins Participatory Budgeting Initiative 'Youth Voice, Youth Choice' with Public Idea Assemblies," Front Porch, January 21, 2016, https://frontporch.seattle.gov/2016/01/21/city-begins-participatory-budgeting-initiative -youth-voice-youth-choice-with-public-idea-assemblies/.

25. "Towards a Solidarity Budget: A Statement of Joint Principles for the 2021 Seattle City Budget Process," n.d., https://docs.google.com/document/d/1cmi91IQ78xqjUVWsEA8DQ Wdjtpi2DLkE9uP8aNIq48c/edit?usp=sharing.

26. "Solidarity Budget Wins Elimination of 80 'Ghost Cops' from City Budget, Protects Investments in Community Well-Being," November 30, 2022, https://docs.google.com /document/d/1fQ6EgLVC1h3bApvnpr-M1ISxvx_UJR5QYa70f8kH1y0/edit.

27. Henri Lefebvre, *Writing on Cities*, trans. Eleonore Kofman and Elizabeth Lebas (Blackwell, 1996), 145.

28. Josh Lerner, *Making Democracy Fun: How Game Design Can Empower Citizens and Transform Politics* (MIT Press, 2014).

29. Michael Ryan Touchton, Brian Wampler, and Tiago Carneiro Peixoto, "Of Governance and Revenue Participatory Institutions and Tax Compliance in Brazil," *Governance* 34, no. 4 (2020): 1193–212.

30. Theda Skocpol, *Boomerang: Health Care Reform and the Turn against Government* (W. W. Norton, 1997), 139.

Chapter 11: Neighborly Citizenship

1. Chana Joffe-Walt, "Nice White Parents," *This American Life*, n.d., https://www .thisamericanlife.org/712/transcript (emphasis added).

2. "Reimagining 'Citizen' as a Verb and Reclaiming Our Collective Power," *How to Citizen*, 2023, https://www.howtocitizen.com/.

3. See Michael Howell-Moroney, "The Tiebout Hypothesis 50 Years Later: Lessons and Lingering Challenges for Metropolitan Governance in the 21st Century," *Public Administration Review* 68, no. 1 (July 1, 2008), https://doi.org/10.1111/j.1540-6210.2007.00840.x.

4. Heather McGhee, *The Sum of Us: What Racism Costs Everyone and How We Can Prosper Together* (Random House, 2021), 23, 179.

5. Wendy Brown, *Undoing the Demos: Neoliberalism's Stealth Revolution* (Zone Books, 2017).

6. Lizabeth Cohen, *A Consumers' Republic: The Politics of Mass Consumption in Postwar America* (Penguin Random House, 2003).

7. Frank Fischer, "Participatory Governance as Deliberative Empowerment: The Cultural Politics of Discursive Space," *American Review of Public Administration* 36, no. 1 (2006): 19–40; Soo Ah Kwon, *Uncivil Youth: Race, Activism, and Affirmative Governmentality* (Duke University Press, 2013); Nikolas Rose, *Powers of Freedom: Reframing Political Thought* (Cambridge University Press, 2009).

NOTES TO CHAPTER 12   257

8. Ashley Dawson, *Extreme Cities: The Peril and Promise of Urban Life in the Age of Climate Change* (Verso Books, 2017).

9. Here, I use statistics reported by the websites of the Centers for Disease Control and Prevention at https://covid.cdc.gov/covid-data-tracker/#trends_totaldeaths_select_00 and the Johns Hopkins University & Medicine Coronavirus Resource Center at https://coronavirus .jhu.edu/map.html.

10. Allison Goldberg, "Mutual Aid during COVID-19 in Brooklyn, New York: A Cross-Class, Interracial Collective Mobilization during Rising Inequality and Ongoing Crises" (master's thesis, University of Washington, 2021).

11. Laura Frances Landau, "Communities of Care: Civic Response, Mutual Aid, and the COVID-19 Pandemic" (PhD diss., Rutgers University, 2024), https://www.proquest.com /docview/3060976465/abstract/A36E1242EFFF4A60PQ/1.

12. Goldberg, "Mutual Aid during COVID-19 in Brooklyn," 42.

13. Kimiko de Freytas-Tamura, "How Neighborhood Groups Are Stepping in Where the Government Didn't," *New York Times*, March 3, 2021, https://www.nytimes.com/2021/03/03 /nyregion/covid-19-mutual-aid-nyc.html.

14. Landau, "Communities of Care," 101.

15. Jia Tolentino, "What Mutual Aid Can Do during a Pandemic," *New Yorker*, November 5, 2020, https://www.newyorker.com/magazine/2020/05/18/what-mutual-aid-can-do-during-a -pandemic.

16. Marshall Ganz, "Public Narrative, Collective Action, and Power," in *Accountability through Public Opinion: From Inertia to Public Action*, ed. Sina Odugbemi and Taeku Lee (World Bank Publications, 2011), 273–89.

17. John Parkinson and Jane Mansbridge, *Deliberative Systems: Deliberative Democracy at the Large Scale* (Cambridge University Press, 2012), 3.

18. Josh Lerner, "From Waves to Ecosystems: The Next Stage of Democratic Innovation," University of Delaware, Stavros Niarchos Foundation Initiative, 2024, https://udspace.udel.edu /items/95bf3dbb-9990-483c-9040-197f42060df1.

19. Anna Lowenhaupt Tsing, *The Mushroom at the End of the World: On the Possibility of Life in Capitalist Ruins* (Princeton University Press, 2021).

20. I am not the only one using this analogy, especially regarding a solidarity economy. See Maliha Safri, Marianna Pavlovskaya, Stephen Healy, and Craig Borowiak, *Solidarity Cities: Confronting Racial Capitalism, Mapping Transformation* (University of Minnesota Press, 2025).

21. See "Mind-Set" at "Raphael Rubinstein and Mónica de La Torre," Dia, October 14, 2014, https://www.diaart.org/program/past-programs/raphael-rubinstein-and-monica-de-la-torre -poetry-reading-2014-10-14/year/2014.

22. Robin D. G. Kelley, *Freedom Dreams* (Penguin Random House, 2002), xii.

Chapter 12: Inventive Solidarities

1. Andrea Cornwall and Vera Schattan P. Coelho, "Spaces for Change? The Politics of Participation in New Democratic Arenas," in *Spaces for Change? The Politics of Citizen Participation in New Democratic Arenas*, ed. Andrea Cornwall and Vera Schatten Coelho (Zed Books, 2007),

258 NOTES TO CHAPTER 12

https://assets.publishing.service.gov.uk/media/57a08c03ed915d622c00107d/Cornwall-intro.pdf.

2. Rod Dacombe and Phil Parvin, "Participatory Democracy in an Age of Inequality," *Representation: Journal of Representative Democracy* 57, no. 2 (2021): 155, https://doi:10.1080/00344893.2021.1933151.

3. J. K. Gibson-Graham, *A Postcapitalist Politics* (University of Minnesota Press, 2006), xxiv.

4. Grace Lee Boggs, *Living for Change: An Autobiography* (University of Minnesota Press, 2016); adrienne maree brown, *Emergent Strategy* (AK Press, 2017).

5. Faranak Miraftab, "Invited and Invented Spaces of Participation: Neoliberal Citizenship and Feminists' Expanded Notion of Politics," *Wagadu: A Journal of Transnational Women's & Gender Studies* 1, no. 1 (2004): article 3.

6. Aldon Morris and Naomi Braine, "Social Movements and Oppositional Consciousness," in *Oppositional Consciousness: The Subjective Roots of Social Protest*, ed. Jane J. Mansbridge and Aldon Morris (University of Chicago Press, 2001), 20–37.

7. Nancy Fraser, "Rethinking the Public Sphere: A Contribution to the Critique of Actually Existing Democracy," *Social Text* 25–26 (1990): 56–80.

8. A wide array of invented spaces are integral to democratic renewal; here I focus foremost on a small selection of those flourishing in cities, with immediate implications for public budgets. And while much of my past research has revolved around the galvanizing work of community organizing groups making specific policy demands, this chapter concentrates on invented spaces in which residents practice citizen-neighbor subjectivities in new ways.

9. Quoted in Allison Goldberg, "Mutual Aid during COVID-19 in Brooklyn, New York: A Cross-Class, Interracial Collective Mobilization during Rising Inequality and Ongoing Crises" (master's thesis, University of Washington, 2021), 35.

10. Jia Tolentino, "What Mutual Aid Can Do during a Pandemic," *New Yorker*, November 5, 2020, https://www.newyorker.com/magazine/2020/05/18/what-mutual-aid-can-do-during-a-pandemic.

11. @safewalksnyc, "Everytime major incidents like these happen . . . ," Instagram, September 26, 2022, https://www.instagram.com/safewalksnyc/reel/Ciz-R8VvTd-/.

12. Dean Spade, *Mutual Aid: Building Solidarity during This Crisis (and the Next)* (Verso Books, 2020).

13. "Mutual Aid Kitchen at La Morada," *Ecologies of Migrant Care* (blog), 2020, https://ecologiesofmigrantcare.org/la-moradas-mutual-aid-kitchen/.

14. "At Long Last, Prominent Immigrant Rights Activist Marco Saavedra Has Won Political Asylum," Center for the Humanities, February 25, 2021, https://centerforthehumanities.org/at-long-last-prominent-immigrant-rights-activist-marco-saavedra-has-won-political-asylum/.

15. "Our Story," Heart of Dinner, accessed October 9, 2024, https://www.heartofdinner.org/.

16. Bureau of Contract Administration, *Annual Report on M/WBE Procurement: FY22 Findings and Recommendations* (New York City Comptroller Brad Lander, 2023), https://comptroller.nyc.gov/reports/annual-report-on-mwbe-procurement/.

17. As Maliha Safri and colleagues write, "The network is global, but the work of defining the solidarity economy has largely fallen to practitioners organizing at national, regional, or local scales." Among others, related terms and concepts include *l'economie sociale et solidaire* in France and francophone Africa, *community economic development* in Canada, the *people's economy* in

NOTES TO CHAPTER 12   259

Southeast Asia and East Africa, and *buen vivir* among Indigenous communities in Ecuador and Bolivia. Maliha Safri, Marianna Pavlovskaya, Stephen Healy, and Craig Borowiak, *Solidarity Cities: Confronting Racial Capitalism, Mapping Transformation* (University of Minnesota Press, 2025), 19.

18. J. K. Gibson-Graham, "Rethinking the Economy with Thick Description and Weak Theory," *Current Anthropology* 55, no. S9 (2014): S147–53, https://doi.org/10.1086/676646.

19. Bernard E. Harcourt, *Cooperation: A Political, Economic, and Social Theory* (Columbia University Press, 2023), https://doi.org/10.7312/harc20954; Stacey Sutton, "Seeding Solidarity Economies: What's Behind the Emerging Ecosystems," *Non Profit News | Nonprofit Quarterly* (blog), December 6, 2023, https://nonprofitquarterly.org/seeding-solidarity-economies-whats -behind-the-emerging-ecosystems/; Safri et al., *Solidarity Cities*; Stacey A. Sutton, "Cooperative Cities: Municipal Support for Worker Cooperatives in the United States," *Journal of Urban Affairs* 41, no. 8 (November 17, 2019): 1081–102, https://doi.org/10.1080/07352166.2019.1584531.

20. Lauren Hudson, "New York City: Struggles over the Narrative of the Solidarity Economy," *Geoforum* 127 (2021): 326–34.

21. Nick Romeo, "How Mondragon Became the World's Largest Co-Op," *New Yorker*, August 27, 2022, https://www.newyorker.com/business/currency/how-mondragon-became-the -worlds-largest-co-op.

22. Sutton, "Seeding Solidarity Economies"; "Community Land Trusts," PolicyLink, accessed October 9, 2024, https://www.policylink.org/resources-tools/tools/all-in-cities /housing-anti-displacement/community-land-trusts.

23. Safri et al., *Solidarity Cities*.

24. Jessica Gordon-Nembhard, *Collective Courage: A History of African American Cooperative Economic Thought and Practice* (Penn State University Press, 2015), 33, https://doi.org/10.1515 /9780271064260.P.

25. Leah Hunt-Hendrix and Astra Taylor, *Solidarity: The Past, Present, and Future of a World-Changing Idea* (Pantheon, 2024).

26. Allison Goldberg, "Reciprocity of Redistribution: Mutual Aid as a Moralized Market in Gentrifying Brooklyn," *Mobilization: An International Quarterly* 29, no. 3 (2024): 353–74.

27. Rinku Sen, "Why Today's Social Revolutions Include Kale, Medical Care, and Help with Rent," *Zócalo*, January 7, 2020, https://www.zocalopublicsquare.org/2020/07/01/mutual-aid -societies-self-determination-pandemic-community-organizing/ideas/essay/.

28. Lauren Hudson, "Building Where We Are: The Solidarity-Economy Response to Crisis," special issue, *Rethinking Marxism: A Journal of Economics, Culture & Society* (2020): 172–80; Hudson, "New York City"; Alexa Kasdan, Erin Markman, and Pat Covey, *A People's Budget: A Report on the Participatory Budgeting in New York City in 2013–2014* (Urban Justice Center Community Development Project, 2014).

29. Benjamin Holtzman, *The Long Crisis: New York City and the Path to Neoliberalism* (Oxford University Press, 2021), 16.

30. "#blackhistory: On January 20, 1969, the First Free Breakfast for School Children Program Is Launched by the Black Panther Party," California African American Museum, January 20, 2020, https://caamuseum.org/learn/600state/blackhistory-on-january-20-1969-the -first-free-breakfast-for-school-children-program-is-launched-by-the-black-panther-party-at-st -augustine-s-episcopal-church-in-oakland.

NOTES TO CHAPTER 13

31. Nik Heynen, "Bending the Bars of Empire from Every Ghetto for Survival: The Black Panther Party's Radical Antihunger Politics of Social Reproduction and Scale," *Annals of the Association of American Geographers* 99, no. 2 (2009): 406–22, https://doi.org/10.1080/00045600802683767.

32. Suzanne Cope, "The Black Panthers Fed More Hungry Kids than the State of California," *Aeon Essays* (blog), May 10, 2022, https://aeon.co/essays/the-black-panthers-fed-more-hungry-kids-than-the-state-of-california; Joshua Bloom and Waldo E. Martin, *Black against Empire: The History and Politics of the Black Panther Party* (University of California Press, 2016).

33. Susan Levine, *School Lunch Politics: The Surprising History of America's Favorite Welfare Program* (Princeton University Press, 2008), https://doi.org/10.1515/9781400841486.

34. Alondra Nelson, "'Genuine Struggle and Care': An Interview with Cleo Silvers," *American Journal of Public Health* 106, no. 10 (October 2016): 1744–48, https://doi.org/10.2105/AJPH.2016.303407.

35. Maddie Crowley, "Disability History: The 1977 504 Sit-In," Disability Rights Florida, accessed October 9, 2024, https://disabilityrightsflorida.org/blog/entry/504-sit-in-history.

36. See, for example, @brooklynevictiondefense, "So You Want to Come to Stoop Watch," Instagram, n.d., https://www.instagram.com/p/CaH2IRvu4-x/?img_index=1.

37. I am grateful to Tarson Núñez for this phrasing.

38. John Keene, *Punks* (The Song Cave, 2021), 17 (emphasis added).

39. Astra Taylor, *Democracy May Not Exist but We'll Miss It When It's Gone* (Verso Books, 2019), 13.

Chapter 13: Budget Lines of Desire

1. Deborah Stone, *Policy Paradox: The Art of Political Decision Making* (W. W. Norton, 1997).

2. Robert Durant, "Sharpening a Knife Cleverly: Organizational Change, Policy Paradox, and the 'Weaponizing' of Administrative Reforms," *Public Administration Review* 68, no. 2 (2008): 282–94.

3. Albert O. Hirschman, *Exit, Voice, and Loyalty: Responses to Decline in Firms, Organizations, and States* (Harvard University Press, 1970); Michel Foucault, "Governmentality," in *The Foucault Effect: Studies in Governmentality*, ed. Graham Burchell, Colin Gordon, and Peter Miller (University of Chicago Press, 1991), 87–104; Samuel Hickey and Giles Mohan, *Participation—from Tyranny to Transformation?* (Zed Books, 2004).

4. In other words, macrobudgeting questions are put aside in favor of microbudgeting. See Allen Schick, "Micro-Budgetary Adaptations to Fiscal Stress in Industrialized Democracies," *Public Administration Review* (1988): 523–33.

5. "Endale Arch Restoration," Prospect Park Alliance, n.d., https://www.prospectpark.org/learn-more/what-we-do/advancing-the-park/endale-arch-restoration/.

6. Jose Fermoso, "Broadway Traffic Endangers Oakland Tech Students, so Activists Added a Pop-up Crosswalk," *Oaklandside*, May 18, 2023, http://oaklandside.org/2023/05/18/broadway-traffic-endangers-oakland-tech-students-activists-added-crosswalk/.

7. James C. Scott, *Domination and the Arts of Resistance: Hidden Transcripts* (Yale University Press, 1990). Here my thinking is also greatly informed by Robin D. G. Kelley's analyses of working-class resistance, especially in his book *Race Rebels: Culture, Politics, and the Black Working Class* (Free Press, 1996).

NOTES TO CHAPTER 13   261

8. Cathy J. Cohen, "Deviance as Resistance: A New Research Agenda for the Study of Black Politics," *Du Bois Review: Social Science Research on Race* 1, no. 1 (2004): 38, 40, https://doi.org/10.1017/S1742058X04040044 (emphasis added).

9. I discuss these interviews with coauthors in Carolin Hagelskamp, Celina Su, and David Schleifer, "When Participatory Budgeting (PB) Funds Schools, Who Benefits? An Equity Analysis of PB-Associated Investments in NYC Public Schools," *Local Development & Society* 5, no. 3 (June 27, 2023): 514–38, https://doi.org/10.1080/26883597.2023.2224950.

10. "Bans on Transgender People Using Bathrooms and Facilities According to Their Gender Identity," Movement Advancement Project, accessed October 9, 2024, https://www.lgbtmap.org/equality-maps/nondiscrimination/bathroom_bans.

11. Kirstyn Brendlen, "Long-Awaited Elevators Open at Park Slope's 7th Avenue Stop," *Brooklyn Paper*, November 27, 2023, https://www.brooklynpaper.com/long-time-coming-elevators-7th-avenue/.

12. This description comes from New York City's list of city council members' expense projects funded in fiscal year 2023, available at https://www.nyc.gov/html/citycouncil/downloads/excel/funded_disclosure_FY2023.xlsx.

13. While this project description comes from a PB voting week project flyer that was publicly available in 2022, more information about the project continues to be available at https://www.carrollgardensassociation.com/current-campaigns/care-forward.

14. Urvashi Uberoy and Keith Collins, "New Yorkers Got Broken Promises. Developers Got 20 Million Sq. Ft.," *New York Times*, July 21, 2023, https://www.nytimes.com/interactive/2023/07/21/nyregion/nyc-developers-private-owned-public-spaces.html.

15. Cited in Uberoy and Collins, "New Yorkers Got Broken Promises." See also "Privately Owned Public Spaces (POPS)," NYC Planning, n.d., https://www.nyc.gov/site/planning/data-maps/open-data/dwn-pops.page.

16. Mary On, "John Jay Outdoor Plaza Hopes for Your Participatory Budgeting Votes," *Park Slope Stoop* (blog), n.d., https://parkslopestoop.com/blog/politics/john-jay-outdoor-plaza-hopes-for-your-participatory-budgeting-votes.html.

17. Hagelskamp, Su, and Schleifer, "When Participatory Budgeting (PB) Funds Schools, Who Benefits?"

18. Stefano Harney and Fred Moten, *The Undercommons: Fugitive Planning & Black Study* (Automedia, 2013).

Interlude: An Interview with Marc Serra Solé

1. "About," Fearless Cities, March 18, 2018, https://fearlesscities.com/en/about.

2. Meaghan Beatley, "Barcelona's Mayor Is on a Quest to 'Feminize' Politics amid Independence Debate," *World*, October 25, 2017, https://theworld.org/stories/2017/10/25/barcelona-s-mayor-quest-feminize-politics-amid-independence-debate.

3. Mark Engler and Paul Engler, "Lessons from Barcelona's 8-Year Experiment in Radical Governance," *Waging Nonviolence*, May 9, 2023, https://wagingnonviolence.org/2023/05/lessons-barcelona-en-comu-ada-colau/.

4. Erik Forman, Elia Gran, and Sixtine van Outryve, "The Municipalist Moment," *Dissent*, 2020, https://www.dissentmagazine.org/article/the-municipalist-moment/; Alfonso L.

262 NOTES TO CHAPTER 14

Congostrina, "Les prostitutes de Barcelona elogien Colau per deixar de multar-les," *El País*, June 2, 2017, sec. Quadern, https://elpais.com/cat/2017/06/02/catalunya/1496420330 _982296.html; Ayuntamiento de Barcelona, "Concilia: Nuevo servicio de canguro municipal para facilitar la conciliación laboral, personal y familiar," *Info Barcelona*, October 20, 2023, https://www.barcelona.cat/infobarcelona/es/tema/servicios-sociales/concilia-nuevo-servicio -de-canguro-municipal-para-facilitar-la-conciliacion-laboral-personal-y-familiar_999089.html.

5. Barcelona en Comú, "How to Win Back the City en Comú: Guide to Building a Citizen Municipal Platform," Barcelona en Comú, 2016, 4, https://www.shareable.net/wp-content /uploads/2016/08/win-the-city-guide.pdf.

6. Cameron Quintana and Mariona Soler, "From Factory to Civic Powerhouse: Rebuilding Local Democracy in Barcelona," *Nonprofit Quarterly*, March 13, 2024, https://nonprofitquarterly .org/from-factory-to-civic-powerhouse-rebuilding-local-democracy-in-barcelona/.

Chapter 14: Insurgent Budgeting

1. Claire Cahen, Jakob Schneider, and Susan Saegert, "Victories from Insurgency: Re-Negotiating Housing, Community Control, and Citizenship at the Margins," *Antipode: A Radical Journal of Geography* 51, no. 5 (January 8, 2019): 1416–35, https://doi.org/10.1111/anti.12558.

2. Adrian Bua and Sonia Bussu, *Reclaiming Participatory Governance: Social Movements and the Reinvention of Democratic Innovation* (Taylor and Francis, 2023), 6.

3. See, for example, Alexa Kasdan, Erin Markman, and Pat Covey, *A People's Budget: A Report on the Participatory Budgeting in New York City in 2013–2014* (Community Development Project at the Urban Justice Center, 2014). See also the discussion in part II of this book.

4. Carolina Johnson, H. Jacob Carlson, and Sonya Reynolds, "Testing the Participation Hypothesis: Evidence from Participatory Budgeting," *Political Behavior* (2021): 1–30.

5. See the discussion of spillover effects earlier in this book. See also Carolin Hagelskamp, Celina Su, and David Schleifer, "When Participatory Budgeting (PB) Funds Schools, Who Benefits? An Equity Analysis of PB-Associated Investments in NYC Public Schools," *Local Development & Society* 5, no. 3 (June 27, 2023): 514–38, https://doi.org/10.1080/26883597.2023.2224950.

6. André Gorz, *Strategy for Labor: A Radical Proposal*, trans. Martin A. Nicolaus and Victoria Ortiz (Beacon Press, 1967), 7.

7. Sanford Schram, *After Welfare: The Culture of Postindustrial Social Policy* (NYU Press, 2000), 184.

8. Ruth Wilson Gilmore, "Making Abolition Geography in California's Central Valley," *Funambulist*, 2018, https://thefunambulist.net/magazine/21-space-activism/interview-making -abolition-geography-california-central-valley-ruth-wilson-gilmore.

9. For one example of the argument that police reforms consistently fail to protect Black lives, see Decriminalize Seattle, n.d., https://decriminalizeseattle.com.

10. For a rich conversation on reformist reforms that further legitimize police violence, and what more helpful strategies and policies might look like, see "Abolition on the Ground: Reporting from the Movement to #DefundThePolice," YouTube, March 1, 2022, https://www.youtube .com/watch?v=H8qz2bcFANc.

11. Dean Spade, "Solidarity Not Charity: Mutual Aid for Mobilization and Survival," *Social Text* 38, no. 1 (2020): 131–51.

NOTES TO EPILOGUE 263

12. For one examination of this dynamic among mutual aid groups since the pandemic, see Laura Frances Landau, "Communities of Care: Civic Response, Mutual Aid, and the COVID-19 Pandemic" (PhD diss., Rutgers University, 2024), https://www.proquest.com/docview/3060976465/abstract/A36E1242EFFF4A60PQ/1.

13. Spade, "Solidarity Not Charity."

14. See, for example, "Non-Reformist Reform," Wikipedia, n.d., https://en.wikipedia.org/wiki/Non-reformist_reform.

15. Ruth Wilson Gilmore, *Golden Gulag: Prisons, Surplus, Crisis, and Opposition in Globalizing California* (University of California Press, 2007), 242, https://www.ucpress.edu/book/9780520242012/golden-gulag.

16. Garrett Felber, "The Struggle to Abolish the Police Is Not New," *Boston Review*, June 9, 2020, https://www.bostonreview.net/articles/garrett-felber-police-abolition-not-new/.

17. "NYPD Overspending on Overtime Grew Dramatically in Recent Years," New York City Comptroller Brad Lander, March 20, 2023, https://comptroller.nyc.gov/newsroom/nypd-overspending-on-overtime-grew-dramatically-in-recent-years/.

18. Deepa Shivaram, "Mental Health Response Teams Yield Better Outcomes Than Police in NYC, Data Shows," NPR, July 23, 2021, sec. Mental Health, https://www.npr.org/2021/07/23/1019704823/police-mental-health-crisis-calls-new-york-city.

19. Doris Fuller, H. Richard Lamb, Michael Biasotti, and John Snook, *Overlooked in the Undercounted: The Role of Mental Illness in Fatal Law Enforcement Encounters* (Treatment Advocacy Center, 2015), https://www.tac.org/wp-content/uploads/2023/11/Overlooked-in-the-Undercounted.pdf.

20. "Re-imagining New York City's Mental Health Emergency Response: Data Overview," NYC Mayor's Office of Community Mental Health, accessed December 11, 2024, https://mentalhealth.cityofnewyork.us/bheard-data.

21. Caroline Lewis, "More 911 Mental Health Calls Are Going to an NYPD Alternative, but Police Still Handle Most," *Gothamist*, September 23, 2024, https://gothamist.com/news/more-911-mental-health-calls-are-going-to-an-nypd-alternative-but-police-still-handle-most.

22. "CCIT-NYC Proposal to Transform Mental Health Crisis Responses in New York City Compared with ThriveNYC's 'B-HEARD' Proposal and City Council Proposal," New York Lawyers for the Public Interest, n.d., https://www.nylpi.org/wp-content/uploads/2021/08/CCITNYC-Proposal-Comparisons4.pdf.

23. "NYC Budget Justice," Communities United for Police Reform, accessed October 9, 2024, https://www.changethenypd.org/nycbudgetjustice.

Epilogue

1. Post in Hi Neighbor! Prospect Heights, Brooklyn Facebook group, April 9, 2024, https://www.facebook.com/photo/?fbid=10161228437536718.

2. Ben Kabak (@2AvSagas), "This isn't a 'fun' way for citizens to decide how to spend $1 million . . . ," Twitter, April 9, 2024, https://x.com/2AvSagas/status/1777848706441593140.

3. Leah Hunt-Hendrix and Astra Taylor, *Solidarity: The Past, Present, and Future of a World-Changing Idea* (Pantheon, 2024), 33.

4. Éireann Lorsung, *Pink Theory!* (Milkweed Editions, forthcoming), 16, 26.

NOTES TO EPILOGUE

5. "About Us," People's Plan NYC, accessed October 10, 2024, https://peoplesplan.nyc/about-us/.

6. William Edward Burghardt Du Bois, *Black Reconstruction in America: Toward a History of the Part Which Black Folk Played in the Attempt to Reconstruct Democracy in America, 1860–1880* (Free Press, 1998), 13, https://www.taylorfrancis.com/books/mono/10.4324/9781315147413/black-reconstruction-america-du-bois.

7. Bernard E. Harcourt, *Cooperation: A Political, Economic, and Social Theory* (Columbia University Press, 2023), 186.

8. Du Bois, *Black Reconstruction in America*, 728.

9. Jaime Jover, "A Global Right-to-Housing Movement versus Financialization," *Metropolitics*, 2021, https://metropolitics.org/A-Global-Right-to-Housing-Movement-Versus-Financialization.html.

10. "Who We Are," Women for Genuine Security, accessed October 9, 2024, http://www.genuinesecurity.org/index.html.

11. George Lipsitz, "Abolition Democracy and Global Justice," *Comparative American Studies: An International Journal* 2, no. 3 (August 2004): 275, https://doi.org/10.1177/1477570004047906.

12. Hunt-Hendrix and Taylor, *Solidarity*.

13. "About Us," Solidarity Research Center, accessed October 9, 2024, https://solidarityresearch.org/about/.

14. Adrian Bua and Sonia Bussu, *Reclaiming Participatory Governance: Social Movements and the Reinvention of Democratic Innovation* (Taylor and Francis, 2023), 7.

15. John Donne, *Devotions upon Emergent Occasions: Together with Death's Duel* (Project Gutenberg, 2007), 108, https://www.gutenberg.org/cache/epub/23772/pg23772-images.html.

INDEX

Page numbers in *italics* refer to illustrations.

Abbott, Greg, 89

abolition democracy, 13, 222–23

abolition of prisons, 171, 212

abortion, 91–92

Adams, Eric, 54, 145

agglomeration in cities, 70

Airbnb, 57, 190

Amazon, 62–63, 201

American Medical Association, xvi

American Recovery and Reinvestment Act
 (2009), 2

American Rescue Plan Act (2021), 73

Americans with Disabilities Act (1990), 140

Anyon, Jean, xii

Apple, Michael, 60

Arab Spring, 68, 226

Arendt, Hannah, 68

Armantrout, Rae, 49

Asian Americans, 8, 47, 125; exclusionary
 laws against, xvi; in New York City, 190;
 in participatory budgeting 113; political
 subjectivities and, viii; poverty among,
 173; violence against, 12, 127, 172

Asians Fighting Injustice, xvi

assemblies, in Barcelona, 194, 198; citizen's
 assemblies, 91, 92; in France, 92; in
 Ireland, 91; in Jackson, MS, 72, 74–80;
 movement assemblies, 68, 152, 194, 198;
 in participatory budgeting, 8, 109–13;
 people's assemblies, 72, 74–80

"astroturf" politics, 154

Athens, 67

Atlantic Yards (Brooklyn, NY), 55

austerity, 12, 48, 119, 128, 134, 144, 161, 209;
 beneficiaries of, 51–55, 61, 85; as default
 policy, xviii, 22, 36, 50; distrust of
 government linked to, 106; ineffective-
 ness of, 22–23, 25, 51–53, 60–61, 63, 65,
 148; in New York City, 3, 17, 22, 51, 69, 133,
 181; opacity linked to, 47, 58, 63, 65, 72, 85,
 90, 106, 154, 175, 212, 218; performative,
 49; pervasiveness of, 21, 22, 181; public
 goods imperiled by, 47, 185; punitivity of,
 6, 10, 24, 34, 39, 52; resistance to, 152, 154,
 175, 178, 182, 183, 187–88, 218; respectability politics reified by, 142; unintended
 strengthening of, 211; vulnerable targets
 of, 22, 24, 25, 47

Baird, Kate Shea, 195

Baker, Ella, 142

balanced budgets, 44

Baltimore, 61

Barber, William, II, 73

Barcelona, 194–206, 225

Barcelona en Comú (BComú), 194–95, 197,
 198, 202, 204, 205

Barclays Center (Brooklyn, NY), 54

Beame, Abraham, 45, 50

Behavioral Health Emergency Assistance
 Response Division (B-HEARD), 215, 216

Berger, John, 36

Betts, Reginald Dwayne, 53

Beveridge, Andrew, 2

bicycling, 127, 132, 185, 200, 205

Biden, Joseph, xvi

265

266   INDEX

Black Americans: austerity and, 47;
disinvestment and, 2; as entrepreneurs,
174; life expectancy of, 125; migration by,
2, 43, 127; in Mississippi, 72–82, 87; in
Nashville, 152; policing of, 7, 26–27,
43–44; pauperization of, 37, 53, 92; as
slaves, 90; voter turnout among, 9; in
workplace, 124, 125
Black Lives Matter, xiv, 1, 33, 67, 121, 151
Black Panthers, 177–78
Black Reconstruction in America (Du Bois),
13, 222
Blackstone Inc., 223
Bland, Sandra, 27
Blinder, Alan, ix
Bloomberg, Michael, 26, 54, 55, 88
Boggs, Grace Lee, 78, 169
Boggs, James, 66
Bolsonaro, Jair, 95, 100, 103
bond-anticipation notes (BANs), 45
book bans, 88
Borowiak, Craig, 175
Bouazizi, Tarek el-Tayeb Mohamed, 68
Bradbury, J. C., 54
Brazil, 78, 94–105, 107, 145
Brenner, Neil, 59
broadband access, 6, 70
Brookings Institution, ix, xii
Brooklyn Eviction Defense, 178
brown, adrienne maree, 169–70
Brown, Michael, 27, 53
Brown, Wendy, 161
Bua, Adrian, 207
Build Back Better plan, 179
bureaucracy, 10, 22, 101, 119, 134–35,
138–39, 209
Bush, George H. W., 211
Bushwick Inlet Park, 55
Bussu, Sonia, 207

Cahen, Claire, 207
Cairo, 67, 68
Califano, Joseph, 178

Can Batlló (Barcelona cooperative center),
201
capital expenses, 34, 192
Caracas, 67
carcerality, 8, 44, 52, 61, 62, 77, 122, 175,
188, 212
Carlson, H. Jacob, 9
CCRs (citizen-centric reports), 40
Central Única dos Trabalhadores (CUT), 96
Centro de Internamiento de Extranjeros
(CIE), 196
charter schools, 59, 159
Chauvin, Derek, 1
Chavez, Cesar, 161
Checkbook NYC (online spending report),
40
Chicago, 20; policing in, 44
childcare, 3, 176, 190, 195
Chinese Exclusion Act (1882), xvi
ciclovias, 185
Citizen (phone app), 160–61
citizenship, 4, 90, 110, 113, 132, 159–62;
substantive and urban, 67–68
citizen subjectivities, 160
City University of New York (CUNY), 50,
52, 61
Civic Engagement Commission, 117
civil rights movement, 142
class, 10, 123, 147, 176
Clean Water Act (1972, 1977), 73
climate change, 92, 128
Clinton, Bill, 134
Cohen, Cathy, 186–87
Cohen, Lizabeth, 161
Colau, Ada, 194–95, 197, 205
Collins, Patricia Hill, 124
colonialism, 38, 224
The Color of Law (Rothstein), 37
Columbia University, 61
Communities United for Police Reform, 216
Community Coalition, 79
Community Development Block Grants, 145
community gardens, 174, 175

INDEX 267

community land trusts, 174
community organizing, 13, 108, 142, 174, 176
Congressional Black Caucus, 77
consumer cooperatives, 174
cooperatives, 210; in Brazil, 94, 103;
consumer, 174; food, 74, 162, 221; of
migrants and refugees, 195; producer, 174;
residential, 104, 174, 175; in Spain, 200,
201; types of, 174; worker, 62, 68, 72, 94,
104, 174, 188, 215, 223, 228
Continental Congress, 91
Cornwall, Andrea, 108, 164
Correct Crisis Intervention Today-NYC
(CCIT-NYC), 215–16
counterpublics, 171, 193, 210
COVID-19 Hate Crimes Act (2021), xvi
COVID-19, xiv–xvi, 2, 37, 70, 117, 126, 145,
162–63, 199, 226; federal funding during,
3, 19, 179; mutual aid during, 11, 142, 179,
188
credit unions, 174
Crip Camp (documentary film), 178
critical race theory, 129
Critical Resistance, 211–12
crowdfunding, 180, 210
curb cuts, curb extensions, 10, 109, 115,
126, 182

Dacombe, Rod, 169
Dakota Access oil pipeline, 70
de Blasio, Bill, 6, 56, 85, 145
debt: municipal, 45, 73; personal, 35, 37–38,
53
decentralization, 149
Decidim (digital platform), 199
deindustrialization, 46
de la Torre, Mónica, 167
deliberative democracy, 128–29, 142, 149
Del Toral, Miguel, 47
democracy. *See* abolition democracy;
deliberative democracy; do-it-yourself
democracy; economic democracy;
ecosystems of participation; elections;

liberal representative democracy;
participatory democracy
Derenoncourt, Ellora, 43
deservingness, xiii, 22, 125, 172, 210, 217
disabilities, 87, 125–26, 140, 178, 184
*Dobbs v. Jackson Women's Health
Organization* (2022), 92
Doctrine of Discovery, 38
do-it-yourself democracy, 149
Domain Awareness System, 33
domestic workers, 189
Donne, John, 225
Du Bois, W.E.B., 13, 132, 222–23

East Palestine, Ohio, 70
ecology of citizenship, 11, 165, 182, 213; lines
of desire and, 183–86, 192, 193
economic democracy, 92–93
economic development, 54–56, 62–63, 148,
174, 203
ecosystems of participation, 7, 104, 169, 180,
213, 218, 221, 224, 227; ecology of
citizenship linked to, 11, 14, 193; mutual
aid linked to, 179; participatory
budgeting linked to, 11, 108, 164, 165, 226
education. *See* public schools
18 Million Rising (Asian American group),
xvi
elections, 86, 90, 104, 132, 194, 224; in Brazil,
94, 95; eligibility for, 8; in Los Angeles,
27; in Spain, 195–99, 205; turnout in, 9,
85, 112–13; voter suppression in, 87
Emancipation Proclamation (1863), 222
Emergency Financial Control Board, 45, 46
eminent domain, 24, 54
employee ownership, 174
EMPowerSF (payroll system), 48–49
Endale Arch, 182
Environmental Protection Agency (EPA), 72
environmental racism, 47
epistemic justice, 10, 131–33, 139, 142, 186,
190, 212
Equal Exchange foods, 174

268 INDEX

Erie County, NY, 54
Erin Brockovich (film), 70
Ethiopia, 51
European Union (EU), 194
Every Student Succeeds Act (2015), 58
evictions, 178, 202, 227

Fair Student Funding (NYC schools
 funding source), 19
Fearless Cities, 194, 225
federalism, 39, 42, 44, 46, 58–60, 72–73, 88,
 91, 99, 203
Felber, Garrett, 212
feminism, 13, 66, 127, 171, 195, 200, 206, 224
Ferguson, MO, 53, 70
Financial Emergency Act of the City of
 New York (1975), 45
Fine, Michelle, 58
fiscal crisis (1970s), 28, 45–46, 49–50, 55, 177
fiscal fundamentalism, 51, 59
Flint, MI, 47
Floyd, Brooke, 80
Floyd, George, xiv, 1, 27, 149, 226
food cooperatives, 74, 162, 221
food delivery, 132, 163
food security, 103, 104, 162–63, 171, 172–73,
 177
Ford, Gerald, 46
foreclosure, 37–38, 92
Forest City Ratner, 55
forum shopping, 146
Foster, Kesi, 134
Foucault, Michel, 36
France, 92
Franklin, Benjamin, 91
Fraser, Nancy, 171
Frediani, Alexandre Apsan, 71
Free African Society of Philadelphia, 175
Freire, Paulo, 97
Fresno, CA, 20

Galloway, Scott, 63
Garner, Eric, 25, 27

gender, 127–28, 191, 195; bathroom bans and,
 187. *See also* feminism
General Motors, 47
generative conflict, 140, 229
gentrification, 13, 24, 65
Gibson-Graham, J. K., 169, 174
Gilens, Martin, 86
Gilmore, Ruth Wilson, xv, 43, 53, 209, 212
Giuliani, Rudolph, 54
Glissant, Édouard, 217
Godfrey, Erin, 8
Goldberg, Allison, 171
Goldman, Emma, 87
Gordon-Nembhard, Jessica, 175
Gorz, André, 208
Gramsci, Antonio, 105
Great Migration, 46
Great Recession, 37, 62, 67
greenlining, 37
Grossman, David, 50

Hagelscamp, Carolin, 8, 192
Hall, Stuart, 10, 123, 149
Hamer, Fannie Lou, 142
Harcourt, Bernard, 222–23
Harney, Stefano, 193
Harvey, David, 67
Haudenosaunee Confederacy (Iroquois),
 91
health care, 109–10
Healy, Stephen, 175
Heart of Dinner, 173
heat waves, 37
Highlander Research and Education
 Center, 78
highway construction, 44
Hinton, Elizabeth, 43
Hitzig, Zoë, 25
Holston, James, 66
Holtzman, Benjamin, 55–56, 177
homelessness, 139, 186
Hong Kong, 67
Hoover, J. Edgar, 177

housing, 29, 43, 54, 55, 147; cooperative, 104, 174, 175; cost of, 3, 56, 62, 64, 85; luxury, 56, 126–27; public, 6, 8, 9, 34, 121, 173
Hudson Yards (New York City), 55
huis (Chinese savings clubs), 175
Hunt-Hendrix, Leah, 176, 220–21
Hurricane Ida (2021), 29, 34
Hurricane Sandy (2012), 29, 162

identity politics, 125
Illinois, 70
immigrants, immigration, 8, 33, 46, 65–66, 113, 127, 173, 223, 224
incarceration, 8, 44, 52, 61, 62, 77, 122, 175, 188, 212
income taxes, 58
Indigenous people, xiv, 4, 13, 38, 92, 133, 175
Indignados (15M movement), 194, 197
inequality, 1, 10, 11, 54, 66, 67, 70, 201, 214; austerity linked to, 22; averages' obscuring of, 41; economic, 3, 37, 111–12, 176; educational, 58, 60, 89, 124; of power, 119, 123, 129, 148; racial, 7, 10, 37, 149, 176, 185; residential, 85, 89; social, 37, 105, 124; structural, 121, 123; widening of, 134
infrapolitics, 186
insurgent budgeting, 12, 207–18
Internal Revenue Service (IRS), 35–36
International Monetary Fund (IMF), 51, 59, 148
intersectionality, 123; as method, 124–26, 130, 142, 217
invented spaces, 11, 12, 169, 170–71, 174, 180
invited spaces, 11, 105, 164, 166; limitations of, 12, 169, 170
Iowa, 70
Ireland, 91
Iroquois (Haudenosaunee Confederacy), 91
Istanbul, 68

Jabola-Carolus, Isaac, 116
Jackson, MS, 72–82

Jackson People's Assembly, 77
Japan, 35
Jenkins, Destin, 43
Joffe-Walt, Chana, 159
Johnson, Carolina, 9
Johnson, Lyndon B., 43
Jordan, June, 90

Kaba, Mariame, 171
Kabak, Ben, 219
Keene, John, 180
Kelley, Robin D. G., 168
Kern, Leslie, 127
Kerre, Peter, 172
Kim, Claire Jean, xiii
Kimmerer, Robin Wall, 133
King, Martin Luther, Jr., 142
King Arthur Baking, 174
Koch, Ed, 55–56

labor unions, 91, 200, 226
La Morada (soup kitchen), 172–73
Landau, Laura, 171
Lander, Brad, 2, 18, 19, 23, 41, 150
Latine Americans, 2, 8, 47, 113, 132
Lee, Caroline, 144, 149
Lefebvre, Henri, 63, 66, 71, 131, 147, 153
Lerner, Josh, 165
Levine, Peter, 90
LGBTQ community, 113, 114, 126–127, 176, 187, 195, 224
liberal representative democracy, 86, 90–91, 132, 201
Liberty Mutual Insurance, 174
libraries, 115, 182
Lincoln Institute, 43
Lindsay, John, 45
lines of desire, 183–86, 192, 193
Lipietz, Barbara, 71
Lipsitz, George, 224
literacy tests, 90
Lorsung, Éireann, 221
Los Angeles, 41, 56, 151

270 INDEX

Lowe, Lisa, xiii

Lula (Luiz Inácio Lula da Silva), 95, 99, 100, 102

Lumumba, Chokwe (father), 72, 74–75, 80

Lumumba, Chokwe Antar (son), 72, 73, 75

Lumumba, Rakia, 80

luxury housing, 56, 126–27

Machado, Antonio, 183

Macron, Emmanuel, 92

Madrid, 67, 68

Making Policy, Making Change (Themba), 79

malaria, 133

managed participation, 133, 136, 181, 182, 191

Mansbridge, Jane, 164

Mapping Police Violence (database), 43–44

Marcuse, Peter, 44

market failure, 157

Maslow, Abraham, 50

McGhee, Heather, 160

Mejia, Kenneth, 27, 28

merit, xiii, xvii, 179

Miami, 56

Michaels, Erin, 59

minimum wage, 225

Miraftab, Faranak, 170

Mitchell, Maurice, 125

Mitsubishi Corporation, xi

Montgomery bus boycott (1955–56), 161

Montseny, Frederica, 200

Moral Mondays, 77

Moten, Fred, 193

Movimento dos Trabalhadores Rurais Sem Terra (MST), 78, 103, 104

Mukhayer, Harum, 229

Municipal Assistance Corporation (MAC), 50

municipal bonds, 24, 47, 50, 62, 73, 88

municipalism, 194, 224–25

Murakawa, Naomi, 52

mushrooms, 165–66, 225

mutual aid, xvii, 108, 163–64, 171–76, 182, 189, 208, 210–11, 218, 226–27; during

COVID-19 pandemic, 11, 142, 179, 188; growth of, 163, 174

mutual insurance companies, 174

MXGM (Malcolm X Grassroots Movement), 74

Nashville, 54, 151–52

Native Americans, 38

Navajos (Diné), xv

neoliberalism, 22, 51, 59, 101, 123, 161, 177

New Haven, Conn., 61

New Orleans, 159

New York City, ix, 20, 151; absentee apartment owners in, 57; affordable housing in, 85; antitax fervor and austerity in, 3, 17, 22, 181; City Council of, 115–16; community engagement councils in, 88; COVID-19 pandemic in, xv, 2, 19; emergency management in, 29, 30, 32; financial reports of, 30, 31, 32, 40, 41; fiscal crisis in, 45–46, 49–50, 51, 55, 69, 177; flooding in, 21; immigrants in, 70; insurgent budgeting in, 209, 213–16; luxury real estate in, 56, 126–27; mental health in, 47, 215, 216; participatory budgeting in (PBNYC), 8, 10, 11, 108–30, 133, 135–42, 145, 150, 169, 171, 179, 181–92, 207, 213, 223, 225–26; policing in, 5–6, 29, 33, 41, 52, 120–21, 214, 216; protests in, 67–68; public reporting in, 27; public schools in, 17–18, 52, 88–89, 115, 182; public spaces privatized in, 189–90; public transit in, 70, 115, 126, 141, 172, 188–89; racialized practices in, 133; tourism in, 55

New York University (NYU), 61

Nixon, Rob, xv

No Child Left Behind Act (2001), 58

nonprofit industrial complex, 148–49

nonreformist reforms, 208–14, 216, 218

North Dakota, 62, 70

not-in-my-backyard (NIMBY) politics, 147, 212

Núñez, Tarson, 96–105
NYC Funds Tracker, 40–41

Oakland, CA, 185
Ocean Spray, 174
Occupy City Hall, 6
Occupy Sandy, 162
Occupy Wall Street, 26, 67–68, 112, 162
Okinawan Women Act Against Military Violence, 223
opacity, of budgets, 7, 19–20; austerity linked to, 47, 58, 63, 65, 72, 85, 90, 106, 118, 154, 175, 212, 218; racism linked to, 47; status quo linked to, 6, 58
Olufemi, Halima, 80

PAFRs (Popular Annual Financial Reports), 40
Page, Benjamin I., 86
Page, Joshua, 53
Page Act (1875), xvi
Panebianco, Angelo, 101
Panel for Education Policy, 18, 88
Pantaleo, Daniel, 25
parent-teacher associations (PTAs), 89
Paris, 67, 106
Park, K-Sue, 38
Parkinson, John, 164
parks, 8, 37, 111, 127, 162
Parks, Rosa, 78, 142, 161
participation industrial complex, 149
participatory budgeting (PB), 7–10, 75–76; abuses of, 133–39; in Barcelona, 194–206; benefits of, 107, 109–10, 123; criticism of, 219; grassroots action linked to, 164; growing use of, 106, 147, 227; as invited space, 11, 12, 164, 170; in Nashville, 151–52; in New York City (PBNYC), 8, 10, 11, 108–30, 133, 135–42, 145, 150, 169, 171, 179, 181–92, 207, 213, 223, 225–26; in Porto Alegre, Brazil, 94–105, 134, 145; proposals for, 144–54; spillover effects from, 11, 150, 225–26

participatory democracy, 85–93, 115
Parvin, Phil, 169
Pathways to Reform, Reconciliation, and Reconciliation, 2
Patient's Bill of Rights, 178
Pavlovskaya, Marianna, 175
payments in lieu of taxes (PILOTs), 61
Peck, Jamie, 22
Pedagogy of the Oppressed (Freire), 97
People Powered, 95
people's budgets, 151–53, 221, 226
People's Plan NYC, 221
personal finance, 35
Philadelphia, 151
Phillips-Fein, Kim, 23–24, 50, 55, 69
Plataforma de Afectadospor la Hipoteca, 194, 196
playgrounds, 126, 182
policing, 6, 12–13, 171; growing budgets for, 39, 43; in New York City, 5–6, 29, 33, 41, 52, 120–21, 214, 216; in schools, 60
Polletta, Francesca, 147
poll taxes, 90
Poor People's Campaign, 77
Portland, OR, 37
Porto Alegre, Brazil, 94–105, 134, 145, 146, 226–27
powell, john a., 125
predatory lending, 92
prefigurative politics, 13, 171, 189
price elasticity, 158
privatization, 22, 67, 159, 166, 189–90
procedural justice, 90
producer cooperatives, 174
Program to Eliminate the Gap (PEG), 28
property taxes, 47
Prospect Park, Brooklyn, 183, 184
protests, 5–6, 67–68, 77, 132, 151, 176, 178, 226
Providence, RI, 61
public banks, 62–63
public goods, 134, 139, 163–64, 228; austerity vs., 47, 185; indivisibility of, 157–58; marketizing and privatizing of, 159, 166;

272 INDEX

public goods (*continued*)
in Porto Alegre, 94; racism and, 160; resistance to privatization and, 189–90, 199, 202
public housing, 6, 8, 9, 34, 121, 173
Public Oversight of Surveillance Technology Act (2020), 33
public safety, 120–22, 171
public schools, 58–60, 150; in Barcelona, 202; in New York City, 17–18, 52, 88–89, 115, 182
public transit, 63; in Barcelona, 202; in New York City, 70, 115, 126, 141, 172, 188–89
Pulido, Laura, 47

Quart, Alissa, 135

racial achievement gap, 124
racial capitalism, 37–38
racial justice, 2, 149, 151
racism, 7, 90; in budgeting, 58; citizen-consumer mentality linked to, 160; in Deep South, 72; environmental, 47; in facially neutral criteria, 129; institutionalized, 2; in managed participation, 133; medical, 189; municipal disempowerment linked to, 43; in policing, 33, 60; in real estate, 92; in schools, 124, 159
Raleigh, NC, 151
Reagan, Ronald, 46, 53, 134
real estate. *See* housing
redlining, 37
Reeves, Tate, 73
REI, 174
rent seeking, 139–40
Republic of New Africa, 74
respectability politics, 142, 186, 217
revenue-anticipation notes (RANs), 45
Reykjavík, 67
Reynolds, Sonya, 9
Right to the City (coalition of community-based groups), 65
right-to-the-city movement, 66–67, 70
Rivlin, Alice, ix

Rothstein, Richard, 37
Ruglis, Jessica, 58
Ruiz, Manuel Delgado, 131

Saavedra, Marco, 173
Saegert, Susan, 207
SafeWalks, 172, 215
Safri, Maliha, 175
St. Louis, 71
sales taxes, 58, 144
sanctuary cities, 65–66, 224
San Francisco, 48–49
Santiago, 67
Santos, Boaventura de Sousa, 134
São Paulo, 67
savings clubs, 175
Scarry, Richard, 64
Schleifer, David, 8, 192
Schneider, Jakob, 207
school boards, 88
"school choice," 59, 157–59
Schwartz, Claire, 38
Scott, James C., 186
Seattle, 151, 152–53
segregation, 37, 53, 89, 146, 160
Sen, Rinku, 176
Serra Solé, Marc, 194–206
sewerage, 34
sex work, xvi, 195
sharing economy, 190
Siemens AG, 72
Silliman, Rebecca, 8
Simonson, Jocelyn, 151
slavery, 90, 175
Smith, Michele, 20
social movements, 78, 95, 99, 101–3, 161, 164, 198, 200–201, 207, 224
social reproduction, 177
solidarity, 12, 167, 190, 208, 211, 223, 227; between cities, 185; during COVID-19 pandemic, 162–63; intergroup cooperation as, 178; transformative, 176, 220
solidarity budgets, 151, 152

solidarity cities, 65

solidarity economy, 12, 72, 102, 174–79, 188, 193, 195, 211, 222

Solidarity Research Center, 225

Solnit, Rebecca, 163

Soss, Joe, 53, 132

soup kitchens, 172–73, 188

sou-sous (savings clubs), 175

South Dakota, 70

Spade, Dean, 210–11

Spain, 194–206

Spence, Lester, 66

sports subsidies, 54

State and Local Fiscal Assistance Act (1972), 46

State Farm Insurance, 174

Stein, Sam, 56

Stiglitz, Joseph, 51

Stone, Deborah, 181

stop-and-frisk policing, 26, 120, 127

Strong Towns (nonprofit), 20

student loan debt, 35

suburbanization, 44, 46

superblocks, 202

surveillance cameras, 120–22, 170, 173, 182, 188, 210, 215

Susaneck, Paul, 37

tactical urbanisms, 185–87

targeted universalism, 125–26, 130, 217

tax-anticipation notes (TANs), 45

taxes, 35, 182; from affluent taxpayers, 58–59; corporate, 153; depreciation allowances and, 44; environmental, 92; federal vs. state and local, 46–47; income, 58; payment in lieu of (PILOTs), 61; property, 47; public opinion of, 3, 17, 22, 27, 47, 49, 107, 154, 181; sales, 58, 144

tax-exempt organizations, 148

tax incentives, 22, 55–56

tax increment financing, 63

Taylor, Astra, 176, 180, 220–21

Taylor, Keeanga-Yamahtta, 7, 92

technocracy, 134, 139, 147

technodemocracy, 134–35, 184, 225

Themba, Makani, 73–82, 151

Theodore, Nik, 59

three-fifths clause, 90

Thurston, Baratunde, 159–60

Tionól Saoránach (Irish citizen's assemblies), 91

tourism, 55, 57, 127, 203

transformative solidarity, 176, 220

transparency, 10, 39, 95, 106; budget increases linked to, 49; insufficiency of, 27, 36, 63, 65; mismanagement revealed by, 48; neutrality conflated with, 5; online, 41; of participatory budgeting, 107; of public banks, 62; public reporting and, 27; surveillance linked to, 217

Trump, Donald, xvi, 56, 179

Trump Tower, 56

Tsing, Anna Lowenhaupt, 165

Tunis, 67

Tu Youyou, 133

Uber, 190, 201

undercommons, 193

unemployment, 46

unfunded mandates, 44

United Nations, 65

urban citizenship, 68

urban homesteading, 177

Vallejo, CA, 144

Venezuela, 89

Vexcel (Microsoft subsidiary), 33

voter suppression, 87

voting. *See* elections

vouchers, for schools, 59

Walia, Harsha, 13

Walker, Julian, 71

walk scores, 42

Wang, Jackie, 53, 85

274 INDEX

Washington Consensus, 148

water supply, 34, 47, 67, 72–73, 77

We Are the Ones We Were Waiting For Levine), 90

Weaver, Vesla, 132

WeGov (civic technology initiative), 34

What Do People Do All Day? (Scarry), 64

White Americans, 129; income of, 10, 123; not-in-my-backyard views of, 147; police violence against, 44; in public schools, 60, 118–19, 159; voter suppression and, 87; in workplace, 124

White flight, 46, 53

Willems, Mo, 184

Wilson, Darren, 53

Women for Genuine Security, 223

worker cooperatives, 62, 68, 72, 94, 104, 174, 188, 215, 223, 228

Workers' Party (Brazil), 94–103

workplace discrimination, 124

World Bank, 148

Yang, Andrew, xiii, 179

Yankee Stadium, 54, 55

Young, Iris Marion, 69

Young Lords, 178

Youth Organizing for Menstrual Equity. Period, 189

zoning, 56, 189

A NOTE ON THE TYPE

This book has been composed in Arno, an Old-style serif typeface in the classic Venetian tradition, designed by Robert Slimbach at Adobe.